MIDLOTHIAN
PUBLIC LIBRARY

Take Me Out to the Cubs Game

ALSO BY JOHN C. SKIPPER

*A Biographical Dictionary
of the Baseball Hall of Fame*
(McFarland, 1999)

*Umpires: Classic Baseball Stories
from the Men Who Made the Calls*
(McFarland, 1997)

*Inside Pitch: A Closer Look
at Classic Baseball Moments*
(McFarland, 1996)

Take Me Out to the Cubs Game

35 Former Ballplayers Speak of Losing at Wrigley

by JOHN C. SKIPPER

McFarland & Company, Inc., Publishers
Jefferson, North Carolina, and London

On the cover: *The Dugout*, by Norman Rockwell. Printed by permission of the Norman Rockwell Family Trust. ©1948

Library of Congress Cataloguing-in-Publication Data

Skipper, John C., 1945–
        Take me out to the Cubs game : 35 former ballplayers speak
of losing at Wrigley / by John C. Skipper.
                p.   cm.
        Includes bibliographical references (p.   ) and index.
        ISBN 0-7864-0810-3 (softcover : 50# alkaline paper) ∞
        1. Chicago Cubs (Baseball team)—History.   2. Baseball
players—Illinois—Chicago—Biography.   I. Title.
GV875.C6 S55 2000
796.357'64'0977311—dc21   00-42379

British Library cataloguing data are available

Manufactured in the United States of America

McFarland & Company, Inc., Publishers
    Box 611, Jefferson, North Carolina 28640
    www.mcfarlandpub.com

For Andrew Kinley Clark

Contents

Contents

Preface

It was the summer of 1954. Dwight D. Eisenhower was president. A family could buy a week's worth of groceries for $25. The Supreme Court was considering a case known as *Brown v. Board of Education* and would ultimately decide that schools in America should not be segregated. In Ohio, Dr. Sam Sheppard, an orthopedic surgeon was arrested on suspicion of killing his wife in their suburban Cleveland home in a case that drew nationwide attention; his conviction was later overturned by the Supreme Court because of pre-trial publicity. Less than an hour's drive from the Sheppard home, the Cleveland Indians played 77 home games and won most of them on their way to winning the American League pennant with 111 wins and just 43 losses. In Washington, D.C., Congress was considering legislation that would change America's travel habits; it was in the process of developing the interstate highway system.

As a nine-year-old boy in Oak Park, Illinois, I was oblivious to most of this, concentrating more on organizing Whiffle Ball games in my backyard and dealing with an unusual "first" in my life: a stirring inside that told me I actually liked Kathy Richards, a little girl who lived down the street.

It was in July or August of 1954 that another sensation hit me as I walked through the living room of our family's home. My father sat where he always sat, in his easy chair in the corner of the living room, watching television on our 16-inch, black-and-white Philco console set. The Chicago Cubs were playing and Hank Sauer was up to bat. I glanced at the set just as Sauer swung and hit the ball out toward left field. The Cubs announcer, Jack Brickhouse, said, "Back, back, back ... it's a home run," and Sauer trotted around the bases as the crowd cheered.

Hank Sauer was my idol in the 1950s and sent me this postcard in 1957. It arrived on September 21, my 12th birthday.

In that moment, I was transfixed. More than that, I was hooked.

It has been said that certain animals bond with whatever they first come in contact with after their birth. So, for example, if a baby chick was placed next to a tennis ball immediately after hatching, it would feel a bond with that tennis ball.

It is precisely that type of love-at-first-sight relationship that a boy experiences when he discovers baseball. It is like a hatching, a new life for the boy, and he develops an affection for the first ballplayer who emerges for him in his new life. For me, the chicken-hatching experience occurred on that summer day in 1954 when I bonded with Hank Sauer of the Cubs. It was enough to make me almost forget Kathy Richards.

I soon developed an interest in baseball cards, baseball autographs and baseball statistics. The Whiffle Ball games in our backyard became more sophisticated. I would play against my brothers. Each of us would represent a major league team. There were no fielders, just a pitcher and a hitter. I was always the Cubs. When I was pitching, I would be Bob Rush or Warren Hacker. When I was hitting, I would be the entire Cubs starting lineup, and I would try to imitate the batting stances of each player. It was great fun, and, playing with my two older brothers, I was much like the real-life Cubs because I almost always lost.

As an adult, my love for baseball has taken on new dimensions, just as the game itself has. I don't play baseball anymore. I watch it and I study it. With all the changes that have taken place over the years — the designated hitter, long-term contracts, free agency, labor strikes, domed stadiums, expansion, inter-league play — it still takes three strikes to strike out, four balls to walk, three outs to complete an inning, and (at least) nine innings to complete a game. That makes baseball essentially the same game it was 100 years ago.

It is the only team sport in which the opponent cannot run out the clock. There is always a last at-bat. Games are still decided by runs, hits, errors, walks and strikeouts.

And for the last 54 years, the Cubs have played thousands of games and have made millions of runs, hits and errors. But they have not won a championship. Why not?

That is not only a great coffee shop question but one that commands the attention of a serious researcher. Seeking the answer, or answers, can even become the subject of a book.

I will always be indebted to my late parents, James and Dorothy Skipper, for teaching me, guiding me, challenging me, encouraging me and having confidence in me, and to my brothers Jim ("Skip") and Tom for their support.

Dale Lancaster, the late, great sports editor of the *Aurora Beacon-News* in Aurora, Illinois, taught me more about writing than any school ever did; and years later, an author named Martin Yoseloff instilled in me the desire to write my first book.

I am grateful to Andy Alexander — baseball fan, friend, and director of the public library in Mason City, Iowa — for posing the question that prompted the start of this book: "What's wrong with the Cubs?" He deserves credit, also, for suggesting the means to the end — talking to former ballplayers who played for the Cubs to see if they could shed some light on why the Cubs always seem to come up short.

Thanks also to Bruce Markusen, the research specialist at the Baseball Hall of Fame Library, who is great at providing answers to fill those annoying little gaps that always seem to pop up in research projects.

A special thanks to a supportive family: my daughters Stephanie, Suzanne and Jennifer, and especially my wife, Sandi, who not only understands the passion I have for my work but also puts up with it.

The ballplayers who took part in this project, every one of them, made the work enjoyable because of their enthusiasm and cooperation. Only three requests for interviews were turned down — two by men in their eighties who said their memories were faltering too much to be of any help, the third by a player not quite that old who said politely that he simply did not care to take part.

One of the special joys of this project was my contact with Hank Sauer, my boyhood hero, who at age 82 was gracious, helpful and kind. Like Sauer, I'm not a kid anymore. My Whiffle Ball games these days are with my grandson, Andrew. But talking with Sauer — having him relive some of the moments that he experienced and that I remember from so long ago — gave me that stirring inside again, that feeling of excitement.

This time, as an adult, a researcher, and a writer, the excitement is a feeling of motivation, of something I must do. I have stories I must tell.

John C. Skipper
Mason City, Iowa
Spring 2000

Introduction

When the Chicago Cubs opened the 1997 baseball season by losing their first 14 games, they achieved a new dimension in the futility that had followed them for more than 50 years: They were out of the race for the championship before it even began.

The Cubs opened the 1998 season with a loss but won their second game. Catcher Scott Servais was amazed at the celebration in the clubhouse. "I've never seen so much excitement about winning the second game of the season. I guess it's all a part of being a Cub," he said.

Indeed, there is a certain "Cubness" about such excitement. Cubness is hard to define but easy to spot.

It is the fan who, on Opening Day of the 1980 season, unfurled a banner that proclaimed, "Wait Til Next Year."

It is Rick Sutcliffe who, given the starting pitching assignment for the Cubs' first night game on August 8, 1988, responded to the historic moment by throwing a home run ball on the first pitch of the ballgame to Juan Samuel of the Philadelphia Phillies.

It is the distinction of having not one but two 1940s infielders, Lenny Merullo and Lou Stringer, holding the record for most errors in a game (four).

And it is Leo Durocher, taking over as Cubs manager in 1966 and declaring, "This is not an eighth place team"— and discovering he was right. The Cubs finished tenth that year.

Theodore Roosevelt was president the last time the Chicago Cubs won a World Series (1908). Franklin Roosevelt was president during the last year the Cubs played in a World Series, though FDR died in April of that pennant winning season (1945).

If the Cubs have been consistent in anything over the last half-century, it has been in losing — 54 years without a World Series appearance as of the end of 1999. They won division championships in 1984 and 1989 but lost to the San Diego Padres and San Francisco Giants respectively in the divisional playoffs. In 1998, they won the National League wild card playoff slot — a position they seemingly had a lock on until they lost six of their last eight games. In one of them, the Milwaukee Brewers were down by two runs with two out in the ninth inning but had the bases loaded. When Cubs outfielder Brant Brown dropped a routine fly ball that would have ended the game, all three Brewer runners scored and the Cubs lost. Cubness had struck again.

Five days later, Chicago beat the Giants in a one-game playoff to win the wild card rites. Then they lost to the Braves in three straight games and went home for the winter — again.

In 1969, the Cubs led the National League for most of the season but started to fade in late August. In September, the Cubs lost eight in a row at just about the time the New York Mets were winning 10 straight. That combination was fatal — the Cubs finished second, 8½ games out.

In 1973, the National League East had a fierce race between six mediocre teams. The Mets won the division with an 82-79 record. Though the Cubs finished fifth, they were only five games out. Other than their division winning years in 1984 and 1989, the wild card year of 1998 and their come-close years, 1969–1973, they've rarely been in the same zip code as the pennant winners.

So the team that represents the oldest franchise in baseball (organized in 1870 as the Chicago White Stockings) has the longest drought between championships. The recent history is bleak. The overall history is glorious.

In 1876, the first year of the National League, Cap Anson's White Stockings brought the Chicago franchise its first championship and the Cubs were champions again in 1880. They won again in 1881, 1882, 1885 and 1886.

As Anson and his teammates aged, the once-dominating Chicago ballclub slid back in the standings and did not return to the top until Frank Chance, a hard-hitting first baseman, became player-manager in 1905.

Chance's Cubs, led by the pitching of Mordecai Centennial Peter "Three Fingers" Brown, won the championship in 1906, earning the right to play in their first World Series against the champions of the five-year-old American League.

The Cubs, winners of 116 games, lost to the "Hitless Wonders" Chicago White Sox. They won again in 1907 and swept the Detroit Tigers, who were led by Ty Cobb, in the World Series.

The 1908 pennant race produced one of the most famous misplays in baseball history. The Cubs were battling the New York Giants for the championship. On September 23, the Giants appeared to have beaten the Cubs in a game at the Polo Grounds when a base hit brought a run home in the bottom of the ninth inning. Fred Merkle, a Giant rookie who was on first base, saw the winning run score as he headed for second. He turned and ran off the field. Johnny Evers, the Cubs second baseman, saw what Merkle had done, called for the ball and touched second. The umpire ruled it a forceout, the third out of the inning — so the run didn't count.

The game was called because of darkness, ending in a tie. When the two teams finished the regular season in a dead heat, the tie game had to be replayed — and the Cubs won. It was an exciting end to an exciting season, and the Cubs beat the Tigers again in the World Series — the last World Series the Cubs have won.

The Cubs of that era had many stars, but perhaps the most famous were Chance, Evers and shortstop Joe Tinker. Chance was the best ballplayer of the three, but all received equal billing in the Franklin P. Adams poem "Tinker to Evers to Chance." As if by poetic license, they were inducted into the Hall of Fame together. Chance was a legitimate contender for the Hall. He was a great manager and a good ballplayer who had a .297 lifetime batting average. Tinker and Evers, who did not like each other and who did not speak to each other for years, benefited from the poem that made them famous. Evers had a lifetime batting average of .270 while Tinker hit .263 for his career.

The Cubs won the National League championship again in 1910 but fell to the Philadelphia A's in the World Series. When the Cubs won again in 1918, one of their leading hitters was Merkle, the man whose blunder set the stage for their pennant drive 10 years earlier. They lost to the Red Sox in the World Series.

In 1921, chewing gum executive William Wrigley purchased the ballclub. The Wrigley family retained ownership for the next 60 years. In 1926, Wrigley hired Joe McCarthy as manager and made a series of deals that brought KiKi Cuyler, Hack Wilson and Rogers Hornsby to the ballclub. They won the pennant in 1929 but lost to a great Philadelphia A's team — Lefty Grove, Jimmy Foxx, Mickey Cochrane and Company — four games to one in the World Series.

They won again in 1932 but were stopped by the Yankees in a World Series best remembered for the game in which Babe Ruth "called his shot" — or didn't, depending on who tells the story. Three years later, the Cubs put on a fabulous late-season surge, winning 20 of 21 games at one point to win the National League championship once again. This time, Detroit — managed by Cochrane — bested them in the World Series in six games.

The Cubs finished second the next two years and then rose to the top once again, in 1938, again with a late-season hot streak. They won nine games in a row in late September, highlighted by Gabby Hartnett's homer in the gloamin' on September 28 — a game winning wallop that was difficult to see because of the fast approaching darkness in Wrigley Field. They suffered their sixth straight World Series loss when they were swept by a great Yankee team led by youngster Joe DiMaggio.

The Cubs finished in the second division for the next four years. In 1945, Charlie Grimm, in his second stint as Cubs manager, put together a collection of veteran ballplayers too old or too banged up for the armed services who filled in for younger players who were off at war.

Grimm, with tongue firmly in cheek, often told the story of the young ballplayer who approached him one day and said he was available because he was 4-F (the military's term for someone unfit to serve, usually because of physical impairment).

"I can hit like Ruth, run like Cobb and field like DiMaggio," the young man told Grimm.

"If you think you can do all that, you must be nuts," said Grimm.

"That's why I'm 4-F," said the young man.

Veteran first baseman Phil Cavarretta won the batting title that year. Pitcher Claude Passeau won his first nine games on his way to a 17-win season. Hank Wyse won 22 and Hank Borowy, a mid-season acquisition from the Yankees, went 11–2 in August and September. When it was over, the Cubs, with another late-season surge — this one including a stretch when they won 26 and lost 4 — brought home their 16th and last National League pennant. They lost a gallantly fought World Series, four games to three to the Detroit Tigers.

Since 1945, the pennant drought is statistically startling. Of the 53 National League championships between 1946 and 1999 (with none in 1994 because of the strike-shortened season), three teams that didn't even exist in 1945 have been in the World Series a total of six times (the Mets three times, San Diego twice and Florida once); the Braves have moved twice and have won it as the Boston Braves once, the Milwaukee Braves twice and the Atlanta Braves five times; the Dodgers won it six times in Brooklyn and nine times in Los Angeles; and the Giants also won the flag representing two different cities, in New York twice and San Francisco twice.

The breakdown of the 53 winners is:

Dodgers	15	(Brooklyn 6, Los Angeles 9)
Braves	8	(Boston 1, Milwaukee 2, Atlanta 5)
St. Louis	7	
Cincinnati	6	
Giants	4	(New York 2, San Francisco 2)
Philadelphia	4	
Pittsburgh	3	
NY Mets	3	
San Diego	2	
Florida	1	

Chicago has produced some great ballplayers over the past half-century, including three Hall of Famers — Ernie Banks, Ferguson Jenkins and Billy Williams — and league MVPs Hank Sauer, Banks, Ryne Sandberg, Andre Dawson and Sammy Sosa.

At times, Cubs management has been innovative. In 1961, they developed a novel idea for managing the team. Why not have rotating coaches instead of a manager? The coaches would go from one Cubs farm club to another where each would work with young players on a particular phase of the game. There could be a hitting coach, a fielding coach, an infield coach, a bullpen coach.

Cubs owner Phil Wrigley liked the idea so much that he instituted the rotating coach plan at the major league level. For the next two years, the Cubs were led by a "head coach" who would be with them for a while and then would rotate back to the minors and be replaced by another "head coach." In 1961, the Cubs had four head coaches — Vedie Himsl, Harry Craft, Lou Klein and Elvin Tappe — and finished in seventh place, winning 64, losing 90. In 1962, with Tappe, Klein and Charlie Metro, the Cubs finished ninth with a 59–103 record. The idea was dropped at the end of the 1962 season.

The Cubs' propensity for letting talent get away from them is legendary. In 1964, they executed what is generally considered to be one of the worst trades in baseball history. The main players in the trade were Lou Brock, a young Cubs outfielder who had good speed but was just an average hitter, and Ernie Broglio, who had won 20 and 18 games in two past seasons with the St. Louis Cardinals.

Brock went on to help lead the Cardinals to the World Series in 1964, 1967 and 1968, set records for stolen bases and finished his career with more than 3,000 hits, retiring after the 1979 season. Broglio won seven games in three years for the Cubs, lost 19 and was out of baseball after the 1966 season.

The Brock-for-Broglio trade is infamous, but is only one of many examples in which the success of ex–Cubs has haunted Chicago fans. They saw Ken Holtzman, who threw two no-hitters in his years with the Cubs, win four games for the Oakland A's in the 1972, 1973 and 1974 World Series. Twenty years later, they saw the dramatic end to the 1993 World Series when ex–Cub Joe Carter hit the game winning homer for Toronto in the seventh game against Philadelphia. The man who gave up the homer was ex-Cub Mitch Williams. More recently, relief pitcher Paul Assenmacher pitched in the World Series for Cleveland after leaving the Cubs, and catcher Joe Girardi made it with the Yankees.

Perhaps the most infamous recent corporate decision, however, was allowing Greg Maddux to become a free agent after winning the Cy Young Award with the Cubs. Maddux signed with Atlanta, where he has won three more Cy Youngs and has led the Braves to four World Series appearances.

Through all of the bleak years, Cubs fan support has never waned. During the Durocher era, 1966–1972, when the Cubs grew into contenders, attendance at Wrigley Field began a steady climb. Today, the club draws more than two million into Wrigley Field every year — and millions more follow the team on the cable superstation WGN.

Anyone looking for a simple answer to the Cubs' futility over the years may find what they need in a response from Tom Trebelhorn, who managed the club for only one year — the strike-shortened 1994 season.

When he was told the Cubs hadn't won a World Series since 1908, Trebelhorn replied, "Hey, anybody can have a bad century." Cubness, to be sure.

My quest in the following pages is to gain insight into why one major league team would experience so much more of a championship drought than any other team.

The question, boiled down to its simplest form, becomes: What's wrong with the Cubs? Who better to ask than those who have played for the club, managed it or been associated with it in some other way over the past 54 years.

The journey to find the answer was a fascinating one, stretching from Connecticut to California, from North Dakota to Texas, and from the 1940s to the 1990s — recording the memories of former Cubs players, ranging in age from 28 to 89, scattered all over the country. Most played for other teams as well as the Cubs, providing them with some means of comparing the Cubs with their competition.

They tell some remarkable stories that have nothing to do with the Cubs but are rich in baseball lore — how Dizzy Dean's wife tried to control his spending, how Charlie Finley spent millions on the stock market with Moe Drabowsky as his broker, how Hank Sauer got traded because Stan Musial had a sub-par year.

But they also offer an assortment of possible answers for why the Cubs have not made it to the top: playing so many day games; playing half their games in windy Wrigley Field; having an inferior farm system for years; bad trades; holding on to mediocre players too long; and a disinterested ownership for too many years.

The completed work is more than just assorted musings about the Cubs. It is a self-portrait of the ballclub, painted by the recollections of 35 players, managers and coaches who have helped shape the team's history.

It is a portrait of a team that, despite the fact it loses more often than it wins ... despite the fact that for years it played its games at a time most working people couldn't see them in person ... despite the fact it plays in a ballpark that has the second-lowest seating capacity in all of baseball ... despite having the longest championship drought in all of professional sports ... despite all of this, the Cubs come closer to being "America's Team" than others who have laid claim to that title.

And ironically, said some of the players, that immense popularity — Cubs fans' love affair with their team — may also be part of the problem.

The book begins with several players recalling the Cubs' last hurrah, the 1945 World Series — and a dandy one it was, with the Tigers winning in seven games. Lenny Merullo still bears a scar on his arm from that series. Pitcher Claude Passeau reflects on his one-hitter, the greatest World Series game ever pitched up until that time. Don Johnson recalls the freak injury to Passeau in the sixth game that he thinks made the difference.

And Hank Borowy, who started three games and pitched four innings in relief in another, offers a lament 54 years later that is a hollow echo in the history of the Chicago Cubs in the second half of the twentieth century:

"We shoulda took 'em."

Part I. The 1940s

Year	W–L	Pct.	Finished	Games Out	Manager
1945	98-56	.636	1st	—	Grimm
1946	82-71	.536	3rd	14.5	Grimm
1947	69-85	.448	6th	25	Grimm
1948	64-90	.416	8th	27.5	Grimm
1949	61-93	.396	8th	36	Grimm/Frisch

CLAUDE PASSEAU

Cubs Pitcher, 1939–1947

"Scouting can be tough. It's hit and miss. But we've made some really bad decisions."

LUCEDALE, Miss. — In the sixth game of the 1945 World Series, veteran Chicago Cubs right-hander Claude Passeau was sailing along with a 5–1 lead. Passeau, 36, had thrown a one-hitter in the third game and seemed destined to pitch the Cubs to victory and into a seventh and decisive game.

With two out, Detroit outfielder Jimmy Outlaw laced a line drive up the middle.

"It hit me straight on, on my ring finger of my pitching hand. And that was it for me," said Passeau, 89, whose voice quickens when the subject is the Cubs. Fifty-one years after he last wore a Cubs uniform, he still says "we" when he talks about the ballclub.

His injury caused Cubs manager Charlie Grimm to have to make a fateful decision concerning a pitching staff that was getting weary.

Grimm called on Hank Wyse, normally a starter, who hadn't worked since a 4–2 loss in Game 2. The Tigers got two in the seventh but the Cubs countered with two of their own in the bottom of the seventh. The roof caved in on Wyse in the eighth as the Tigers scored four to tie it. Starter Ray Prim put out the fire.

Grimm, faced with elimination if the Cubs lost, called on Hank Borowy, another starter, whom Chicago had purchased from the Yankees in mid-season. Borowy slammed the door on the Tigers for four innings and Chicago pushed across a run in the 12th to win it 8–7.

"We should have won it long before that," said Passeau, who, 53 years later, still seemed pained that the Cubs squandered the lead they had when he left the game.

Grimm, who had used all of his starters in an effort to salvage the sixth game, took a chance and started Borowy in the seventh game — his fourth appearance in the Series and his third straight game. Borowy threw a complete game in the Series opener and won it, pitched five innings in the fifth game in which he was the starter and loser, and then pitched the four innings of relief in the sixth game to get the win.

When the first three batters singled off him in Game 7, Grimm took him out — but the floodgates had been opened. The Tigers scored five and coasted to a 9–3 victory.

"He pitched because we didn't have anybody else," said Passeau. "He was the kind of pitcher who could pitch five innings pretty well, but after that, he was going to need some help.

"You know, we had a good team that year, but we had to be pretty well ahead after six or seven innings or we were going to lose," he said.

In the third game of that World Series, Passeau narrowly missed baseball history. Rudy York singled in the third inning and was erased in a double play. Bob Swift walked in the sixth. That was the extent of the Tiger offense. Passeau's one-hitter was the greatest World Series game ever pitched at that time, topped today only by Don Larsen's perfect game in the 1956 World Series.

"It was the easiest game I ever pitched — 28 batters," said Passeau. "The oddsmakers had the Tigers at 6–5 favorites or something like that in both the first and second games. In the third game, the odds were 7–5 or 8–5 for the Tigers — because I was pitching.

"Somebody said to me: 'You only won but 17; that's why the odds are the way they are.' I figure — how many in the league won 17? I was just going out there to do my best, that's all. It was just another day. After the game starts, it's just another ball-game. That's the way you have to look at it.

"I threw a one-hitter — and I won. It doesn't always work out that way. I threw four one-hitters in my career and only won but one of them. I was just one of those fellows who couldn't get many runs. If something strange could happen, it always did.

"I don't mean to alibi but I did have things happen to me. I went to six All Star Games. Ted Williams hit a home run off me in one of them but there was an error right before that or I would have been out of the inning. Things like that happen in baseball," he said. (On July 8, 1941, Passeau worked the last three innings of the 1941 All Star Game and was one out away from victory when Ted Williams hit a three-run homer to win the game.)

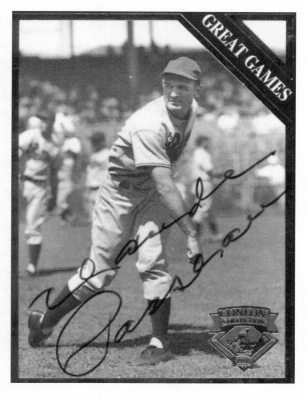

Claude Passeau threw a one-hitter in the third game of the 1945 World Series, but his injury in Game 6 was a turning point in the Series.

He had some great individual achievements with the Cubs. In that stellar 1945 season — the one in which he won "only" 17 — he began the year with nine straight wins. Passeau was also an excellent defensive pitcher. From September 21, 1941, to May 20, 1946, he did not make an error, fielding 273 consecutive chances flawlessly — a National League record.

Passeau still follows baseball closely. On the night we talked, he fretted over the quality of play in the 1998 All Star Game, won by the American League 13–8. "It wasn't a very good game," he said. "I expected better."

He said it's amazing the Cubs haven't been in the World Series since 1945 but dismissed two theories right away. "The fact they play half their games in Wrigley Field — that has nothing to do with it. The fact they play so many day games. That has nothing to do with it. That's just writers' talk. Hey, I preferred day games," he said.

"Our scouting system has been terrible for about the past 20 years. We're not putting out the money we should and our judgment has been just awful. Scouting can be tough. It's hit and miss. But we've made some really bad decisions.

"And it seems like when we pick someone, we stick with him, we keep him whether he's got it or not."

Passeau knows from his own experience the "hit and miss" aspect of picking ballplayers.

He pitched for Millsaps College in Jackson, Mississippi, from 1928 to 1931, and then floundered in the minor leagues for a few years.

"I went from Class A to the major leagues in 1935," he said. "Pittsburgh bought me. I pitched one game, three innings, I think. I had pitched 247-odd innings that year [in the minors] and my arm was shot."

Passeau gave up four runs on seven hits, with two walks and one strikeout in that one outing with the Pirates. His earned run average was 12.00.

"The Pirates gave me that one look and said, 'he isn't going to make it.' I didn't pitch another inning for them."

Between seasons, Passeau was traded to the Philadelphia Phillies. "For some reason, they decided to swap catchers," he said. So on November 21, 1935, the Phillies traded catcher Al Todd to the Pirates for catcher Earl Grace.

"About a week after the deal was made, the Phillies decided they wanted more. So I was traded as part of the same deal. I was really a throw-in," said Passeau.

"Well, the next year, I beat the Pirates about three times. Their manager, Pie Traynor said, 'I believe we made a mistake.'

"You know, it's a funny thing in baseball. There's certain teams you can beat and others give you trouble. It seemed like I could beat Chicago, St. Louis, Pittsburgh and Cincinnati and break even with the rest," said Passeau.

He was 11-15, 14-18 and 11-18 with Phillie teams that finished eighth, seventh and eighth in 1936, 1937 and 1938. On May 29, 1939, the Phillies, in desperate need of help, traded Passeau to the Cubs for three players — Joe Marty, Ray Harrell and Kirby Higbe. He had been 2-4 with the Phillies but put together a 13-9 record for Chicago to finish with a 15–13 season, his first winning season in the majors. The next year, he was 20-13, and he pitched seven more seasons for the Cubs.

For many years after he retired, he participated in old-timers games. "A bunch of us went back to Chicago one time to play in one — and back in those days, you really played. Afterward, we all went in the locker room and talked for a long time. We had a ball.

"And you know what we talked about? Money. All the money ballplayers made compared to when we were playing."

He paused, and then laughed and simply summed it up by saying: "Amazing."

Claude William Passeau
Born April 9, 1909, in Waynesboro, Miss.
6' 3", 190 lbs.; B-right, T-right

Year	Team	W-L	Pct.	ERA	G	IP	H	BB	SO
1935	Pitt	0-1	.000	12.00	1	3	7	2	1
1936	Phil (N)	11-15	.423	3.48	49	217.1	247	55	85
1937	Phil	14-18	.438	4.34	50	292.1	348	79	135
1938	Phil	11-18	.379	4.52	44	239	281	93	100
1939	Phil-Chi	15-13	.536	3.28	42	274.1	269	73	137
1940	Chi (N)	20-13	.606	2.50	46	280.2	259	59	124
1941	Chi	14-14	.500	3.35	34	231	262	52	80
1942	Chi	19-14	.576	2.68	35	278.1	284	74	89
1943	Chi	15-12	.556	2.91	35	257	245	66	93
1944	Chi	15-9	.625	2.89	34	227	234	50	89
1945	Chi	17-9	.654	2.46	34	227	205	59	98
1946	Chi	9-8	.529	3.13	21	129.1	118	42	47
1947	Chi	2-6	.250	6.25	19	63.1	97	24	26
13 years		162-150	.519	3.32	444	2719.2	2856	728	1104

Transactions:

Nov. 21, 1935: Traded with Earl Grace to Philadelphia Phillies for Al Todd.
May 29, 1939: Traded to Chicago Cubs for Joe Marty, Ray Harrell and Kirby Higbe.

WORLD SERIES

Year	Team	W-L	Pct.	ERA	G	IP	H	BB	SO
1945	Chi	1-0	1.000	2.70	3	16.2	7	8	3

LENNY MERULLO
Cubs Shortstop, 1941–1947

"In sports, you gotta have a gambling leadership if you're going to win."

READING, Mass.— Lenny Merullo carries the scars from the 1945 World Series — literally.

"Skeeter Webb spiked me coming in to second base," said the former Cubs shortstop, now 81 years old. "He didn't mean to; it was a close play and, what the heck, it was the World Series and he came in with his spikes a little high. He tore open my left arm.

"I still have the scar because every time it would start to scab over, I'd scratch it off so I'd always have something to remember from playing in that World Series," said Merullo, who still works for the major league scouting bureau.

His injury in the sixth game gave him a bird's-eye view of a decision made after the game that helped shape the outcome of the Series.

"I was in the training room getting stitched up," said Merullo. "We had just won the ballgame in 12 innings, but we had used up our pitchers. Claude Passeau started and Hank Wyse pitched and Hank Borowy pitched the last four innings and did a beautiful job for us." (The Cubs won 8–7 in 12 innings.)

"There was a lot of noise and a lot of confusion in that clubhouse. Charlie Grimm pointed to Paul Derringer and said, 'You're my guy for the seventh game.' A couple of minutes later, Borowy came in and said, 'Hey Skip, I'm feeling pretty good. I'll get a good night's sleep for you.'

"And Grimm said, 'You're my guy for the seventh game.' That's exactly how I remember it happening," said Merullo.

Borowy started the seventh game, pitching in his third straight game and didn't get anybody out as the Tigers scored five runs in the first inning and went on to win 9-3.

"Borowy deserved to pitch that game. He had a great year and he was the reason we got to the World Series in the first place," said Merullo. Borowy had been a mid-season acquisition from the Yankees and won 11 and lost two for the Cubs.

The spike wound and the Cubs loss were not Merullo's only disappointments in the World Series. After playing shortstop in 121 games during the regular season, he only appeared in three World Series games and had no hits in two official at-bats.

"It broke my heart but I understood," he said. "I hadn't been playing very well. I was in kind of a funk and Charlie went with Roy Hughes, who was a veteran, a good ballplayer, and a better hitter than I was." (Hughes started six games, hit .294 and drove in three runs.)

Merullo played two more seasons before a serious injury forced him to retire from playing at the age of 31.

"In 1948, I came up with a very serious sciatica condition

Lenny Merullo is a major league scout who still wakes up every morning and wants to know how the Cubs did.

affecting the nerve in my leg. In spring training, I couldn't play more than one or two games in a row and I'd have to rest. I couldn't stand for very long, I couldn't sit for very long and I couldn't walk for very long. I couldn't even sit in a movie. The Cubs had a kid named Roy Smalley who was ready to come up. He was a good ballplayer and he did very well and that was pretty much it for me," said Merullo.

"I roomed for 10 years with Phil Cavarretta. They used to call us the 'Grand Opera Kids' — two Italian boys, you know. Phil was very competitive and had a fiery personality. I remember one time in Brooklyn, I went into second base hard, trying to break up a double play and Eddie Stanky tagged me in the face with the ball.

"Well, we got into it a little bit and the first thing you know, we're both on the ground and all our teammates are running toward us. Me and

Lenny Merullo remembers Hank Wyse as a good pitcher who took a lot of kidding because he hardly had any hair on his face to shave.

Stanky got thrown out of the game and I wind up with a bruised face.

"That night, Cavarretta's telling me that Pee Wee Reese was in there takin' a swing at me and I shouldn't let him get away with that. Phil was hot.

"Pee Wee was a good ballplayer but he wasn't as 'pee-wee' as a lot of people thought. Phil was so mad about it, he wouldn't let me get to sleep. So the next day, I see Pee Wee in the batting cage and I stepped in front of him and showed him my bruises and asked him about what happened the day before.

"He said, yeah, that in the heat of the moment, he might have done something but at first he was just trying to get between Stanky and me. Well, as I started to walk away, Pee Wee starts yelling at me and walking toward me. Then Dixie Walker hit me from behind and took off.

"Well, I ran after him and tackled him and it took two cops to break us up. I know that was 50 years ago and Dixie isn't around to talk about it, so I'm going to tell you that I won the fight that day. They say Dixie lost a couple of teeth.

"A couple of weeks later, Brooklyn was in Chicago and Dixie was playing right field and the fans in the bleachers threw false teeth at him," said Merullo.

Merullo went to Villanova University where he graduated in 1938 and thought about becoming a teacher. But baseball beckoned, and he signed with the Cubs and was assigned to the Tulsa minor league club.

He was there in 1940 when Dizzy Dean, trying to make a comeback to the major leagues, was on the Tulsa pitching staff.

"When he joined the team, it changed the whole league," said Merullo. "Diz drew crowds wherever he went. We had a good ballclub. Eddie Waitkus was the first baseman, Don Johnson was the second baseman and Hank Wyse was one of our pitchers." (All later played for the Cubs. Wyse, Johnson and Merullo were on the 1945 pennant winner.)

"There were teams in that league from Shreveport and Houston and places like that and it was always very, very hot. They used to have troughs in the dugout. No kidding. You'd come in and just put your spikes in the trough to cool off.

"Diz was something else. He had a home in Galan, Texas, between Dallas and Fort Worth and sometimes he'd invite us over. He had one room in that house that I swear was nothing but newspaper clippings. There was a table in that room that had clippings stacked eight inches high."

Merullo said he once went along for the ride when Dean took his station wagon back to a dealership because the radio didn't work. "Back in those days, when you bought a car, you could get either a radio or a heater. In Texas, you got a radio.

"Well, Diz needed a new radio so I went with him. While he was talking to the fellow, I looked at a black Chevy Coupe in the showroom. Pretty soon, I got in it and sat down. When Diz saw me, he asked if I liked it and, of course, I said I did.

"Diz gave the dealer a $100 down payment and said to me, 'We can work it out.' I made arrangements to buy the car at a much lower price than it was selling for, and when I tried to pay Diz back, he wouldn't let me. I gave him a check and he sent it back to me at Christmastime unsigned. That was Dizzy Dean."

Merullo came up with the Cubs in 1941, played seven years, and finished with a lifetime batting average of .240.

He said Grimm had all the right qualities for a manager. "He was just outstanding. He was great with the players, he could handle the press and he was a crowd-pleaser. You can't beat that," he said.

Not long after his playing days were over, Cavarretta, his old roommate, became manager of the Cubs. "And the first thing you know, I'm coverin' the New England area for the Cubs," said Merullo. He scouted for the Cubs until 1973 when the major leagues started a scouting bureau. Merullo signed on and still works for the scouting bureau.

"I worked for the Cubs for many, many years and I still wake up to the Cubs score every day," he said.

Merullo said the Cubs' failure to come up with another winner can be traced to the team's front office being unable to make big decisions when they counted most.

"Mr. Wrigley owned the ballclub. Philip Wrigley, I'm talking about, a nice guy who treated the players well. But he put the ballclub in the hands of his general managers and let them run the show," he said.

"We had general managers like Jim Gallagher and Wid Mathews and John Holland. I can't say too much about Gallagher because he got us a pennant. But Mathews and Holland wouldn't take the bull by the horns.

"Whenever anything came up, they'd have to go ask Mr. Wrigley. Well Mr. Wrigley didn't know anything. That's why he hired them. We had the chance to sign some good ballplayers but we lost them because we couldn't make a decision.

"In sports, you gotta have a gambling leadership if you're going to win. And if you look, over the years we just haven't had what it took to go out and bring a winner in," said Merullo.

The old Cubs shortstop is in the record book for a dubious distinction — most errors in an inning — four, on September 13, 1942. He said he doesn't mind talking about it.

"I thought for a long time that I had the record all by myself but now they tell me I'm tied with Ray Chapman." (Chapman, the Cleveland Indians shortshop, committed four errors in the same inning on June 14, 1914. It occurred one other time, on August 17, 1888, when Shorty Fuller of Washington was the victim.)

Merullo may have the others topped in one respect: "Three of those errors happened on the same play. I made a wild throw, then booted a relay throw from Bill Nicholson and then threw it over the catcher's head," he said.

"You know, my oldest son was born that day — and to this day, they still call him 'Boots.'"

Leonard Richard Merullo
Born May 5, 1917, in Boston, Mass.
5' 11", 166 lbs.; B-right, T-right

Year	Team	G	AB	R	H	D	T	HR	RBI	Ave.
1941	Chi (N)	7	17	3	6	1	0	0	1	.353
1942	Chi	143	515	53	132	23	3	2	37	.256
1943	Chi	129	453	37	115	18	3	1	25	.254
1944	Chi	66	193	20	41	8	1	1	16	.212
1945	Chi	121	394	40	94	18	0	2	37	.239
1946	Chi	65	126	14	19	8	0	0	7	.151
1947	Chi	108	373	24	90	16	1	0	29	.241
7 years		639	2071	191	497	92	8	6	152	.240

WORLD SERIES

Year	Team	G	AB	R	H	D	T	HR	RBI	Ave.
1945	Chi (N)	3	2	0	0	0	0	0	0	.000

JOHNNY SCHMITZ
Cubs Pitcher, 1941–1942, 1946–1951

"It hurts the Cubs and other teams, too. Starters
don't even go seven innings anymore."

WAUSAU, Wis.— Johnny Schmitz came close to playing in a World Series.

Oh, so close. So many times.

The Cubs left-hander, who won 18 games for Chicago in 1948, was stationed at nearby Great Lakes Naval Training Station, in Glenview, Illinois, a Chicago suburb, trying to get out of the service to rejoin his old ballclub, when the Cubs won the pennant in 1945.

"I was due to get out, but they worked it on some kind of point system. I didn't understand it then and I don't understand it now," said Schmitz, 77, who listened to the World Series on the radio that year.

"But that's not the closest I ever came to getting into a World Series. The closest I ever came was 1951 when I was with the Dodgers. We're in the third game of the playoffs with the Giants, and Thomson hits the home run, a three-run homer in the bottom of the ninth to beat us. One out to go. That's how close I came.

"I'll tell you something about that home run. It's a can of corn in most any other ballpark. But not the Polo Grounds. I was sitting in the bullpen down the left field line and you just knew it was gone when he hit it. It was heartbreaking," said Schmitz.

"I wasn't lucky like some of the other guys were. I was with both the Dodgers and the Yankees in '52 but finished the season at Cincinnati. Both the Dodgers and Yankees wind up in the World Series and I wind up in Cincinnati.

"Then I was back with the Yankees in 1953 before they sent me to Washington. And the Yankees won again in '53 and went to the World Series. I won 11 games for the Senators in 1954 and it was like I was with the Cubs — we finished seventh," he said.

(His two short tenures with the Yankees were part of a Yankees pattern in the early 1950s in which general manager George Weiss was a master of the waiver wire, picking up aging National League ballplayers who might be able to fill in here and there for a few games to round out those great Yankees teams. So players like Schmitz, Johnny Mize, Johnny Sain,

Ewell Blackwell and Enos Slaughter each had stints with the Bronx Bombers.)

Schmitz, who won 93 games in his 13-year career, said it is amazing how sometimes pitchers seem to have a mastery over certain teams. For him, it was the Dodgers and the Cardinals. "I saw a newspaper headline one time that said 'Schmitz — The Dodger Killer' and it was true," he said.

The highlight of his major league career, though, involved a game against the Cardinals.

"It was the last day of the season in 1946, the year after the Cubs won it, and the Dodgers and Cardinals were tied for first place. The Braves beat the Dodgers in the afternoon. We played at night and I beat the Cardinals 8–3. I think Harry Brecheen was the losing pitcher in that game. When you're not in the pennant race yourself, a win like that is really satisfying," said Schmitz. (Schmitz's win over the Cardinals forced them into a playoff series in which they beat the Dodgers, two games to none, to win the pennant.)

He was involved in several big trades in his career. On June 15, 1951, the trading deadline, the Cubs sent Schmitz, catcher Rube Walker, outfielder Andy Pafko and infielder Wayne Terwilliger to the Dodgers for catcher Bruce Edwards, and infielders Joe Hatten, Eddie Miksis and Gene Hermanski.

Schmitz remained with the Dodgers through their fateful pennant race and into the next season. He was released on August 1, 1952 and picked up by the New York Yankees on waivers. Twenty-seven days later, the Yankees traded Schmitz, outfielder Jim Greengrass, pitcher Ernie Nevel and outfielder Bob Marquis along with $35,000 in cash to Cincinnati for veteran pitcher Ewell Blackwell. (Blackwell won a game in September and pitched in one game in the World Series for the Yankees.)

On February 17, 1953, Cincinnati sold Schmitz back to the Yankees, who held on to him for less than three months before selling him to the Washington Senators. He pitched for the Senators for parts of three seasons before packing his bags again.

On November 8, 1955, he was traded with veteran first baseman Mickey Vernon, pitcher Bob Porterfield and outfielder Tommy Umphlett to the Boston Red Sox for outfielder Karl Olson, pitchers Dick Brodowski, Truman Clevenger and Al Curtis, as well as outfielder Neil Chrisley.

His last stop was Baltimore. He was sold by Boston to the Orioles on May 14, 1956.

"They used to give us travel money when we got traded. I made more money getting shipped around than I did playing," said Schmitz, who couldn't help but laugh at his travel adventures. "The most I ever made in the big leagues was $21,000."

He broke in with Hopkinsville, Kentucky, in 1938 and then went to Bloomington, Illinois, in the 3-I League in 1939. He spent 1940 with Madison, Wisconsin, and 1941 with the old Milwaukee Brewers and was drafted by the Cubs after that season. "The Cubs got the first pick and they took me. Dave Koslo then went to the Giants," said Schmitz.

His first major league win came in 1942 against the Dodgers. He replayed it verbally as if no time had passed. "I came in in the ninth inning with the bases loaded. Cookie Lavagetto was up. He hit into a double play—I think it was on the third pitch—and then Bill Nicholson homered for us and that was that. My first win," he said.

Schmitz said pitchers aren't handled the way they used to be and that has particularly hurt the Cubs over the years.

"In my day, if you were a starter, you were expected to finish what you started and sometimes that meant going 11 or 12 innings. Now, they take 'em out too quick because they got relievers who specialize in coming in and closing a game.

"The trouble is, a lot of the relievers don't even belong in the major leagues. The only reason they're up there is because of expansion. And it hurts the Cubs and other teams, too. Starters don't even go seven innings anymore.

"I say—make 'em go nine innings; that's what they're getting paid for. And they're getting paid millions. They get paid for everything today—for standing up, sitting down, for looking out the window. And none of them can go seven innings any more. And they make millions. How many of 'em are worth it?"

Schmitz retired from baseball after the 1956 season, at age 35, and returned to his hometown of Wausau where he worked as a greenskeeper at a golf course for 33 years.

"I made just about as much money as I did playing ball," said the man who came so close—oh, so close—to playing in a World Series.

John Albert Schmitz
Born Nov. 27, 1920, in Wausau, Wis.
6', 170 lbs.; B-right, T-left

Year	Team	W-L	Pct.	ERA	G	IP	H	BB	SO
1941	Chi (N)	2-0	1.000	1.31	5	20.2	12	9	11
1942	Chi	3-7	.300	3.43	23	86.2	70	45	51
1946	Chi	11-11	.500	2.61	41	224.1	184	94	135
1947	Chi	13-18	.419	3.22	38	207	209	80	97
1948	Chi	18-13	.581	2.64	34	242	186	97	100

Year	Team	W-L	Pct.	ERA	G	IP	H	BB	SO
1949	Chi	11-13	.458	4.35	36	207	227	92	75
1950	Chi	10-16	.385	4.99	39	193	217	91	75
1951	Chi-Bk	2-6	.250	5.99	24	73.2	77	43	26
1952	Bk-NY-Cin	3-2	.600	3.71	18	53.1	47	30	17
1953	NY-Wash	2-7	.222	3.62	27	112	120	40	39
1954	Wash	11-8	.579	2.91	29	185.1	176	64	56
1955	Wash	7-10	.412	3.71	32	165	187	54	49
1956	Bos-Bal	0-3	.000	3.59	20	42.2	54	18	15
13 years		93-114	.449	3.55	366	1812.2	1766	757	746

Transactions:

June 15, 1951: Traded with Rube Walker, Andy Pafko and Wayne Terwilliger to Brooklyn for Bruce Edwards, Joe Hatten, Eddie Miksis and Gene Hermanski.

Aug. 1, 1952: Sold to New York Yankees for waiver price.

Aug. 28, 1952: Traded with Jim Greengrass, Ernie Nevell, Bob Marquis and $35,000 to Cincinnati for Ewell Blackwell.

Feb. 17, 1953: Sold to New York Yankees.

May 13, 1953: Sold to Washington Senators for waiver price.

Nov. 8, 1955: Traded with Bob Porterfield, Mickey Vernon and Tommy Umphlett to Boston for Karl Olson, Dick Brodowski, Truman Clevenger, Neil Chrisley and Al Curtis.

May 14, 1956: Sold to Baltimore Orioles.

LOU STRINGER

Cubs Second Baseman, 1941–1942, 1946

"Some guys can win, some can't...The Cubs over the years just haven't been able to get those 'winning' players."

LAKE FOREST, Calif.— Lou Stringer was a hard-luck ballplayer whose career milestones are a series of bad breaks.

Yet Stringer, 81, has no regrets. "Baseball was very, very good to me," he said.

Maybe so, but...

• In his debut with the Cubs, he made four errors.

• After establishing himself as a starter, he entered the armed services in World War II — and missed playing in a World Series.

• When he returned from the service, he not only didn't have a job, but he soon didn't have a team. The Cubs sent him to the minor leagues.

Stringer played second base for Ponca City, Oklahoma, in 1937 and 1938 and for the Cubs farm team in Los Angeles in 1939 and 1940 before being brought up by the Cubs at the start of the 1941 season.

"Jimmie Wilson was the Cubs manager. Billy Herman had been the second baseman for about 10 years — so Wilson started me at shortstop. I had never played shortstop before. But he started me there in my first big league game and I made three errors... Was it four?... My gosh... But I got a couple of hits and we won the game," he said.

(On April 15, 1941, Stringer made four errors in his major league debut but the Cubs got clutch pitching from Claude Passeau and a big home run by Bill Nicholson to beat Pittsburgh 7–4.)

"Passeau really gave me hell when that game was over but he was really a nice guy, a real gentleman. But I heard it from him pretty good after that game," said Stringer. His futility record for an Opening Day was tied by Pokey Reese of Cincinnati who made four errors on Opening Day of 1998.

Less than a month into the 1941 season, Herman was sent to Brooklyn and Stringer moved over to the much more comfortable confines of second base where he played in 145 games. The following season, he was once again the regular second baseman, appearing in 121 games.

But World War II beckoned and Stringer spent the next three years in the military. It cost him his only chance to be in a World Series because the Cubs won the National League pennant in 1945. When Stringer returned for the 1946 season, he was 29 years old and Don Johnson was the regular second baseman. And the Cubs had a different manager, Charlie Grimm, an old warhorse and former Cubs player and manager. Grimm took over after the Cubs had a dismal start in 1944 and led them to the pennant the following year.

"Grimm was okay but I was just a mediocre ballplayer and he never really gave me a chance," said Stringer. "Besides, he was crazy about Don Johnson. So there I was."

Stringer appeared in only 80 games in 1946 and then suffered an indignity at the hands of Grimm the following year.

"He sold me to Hollywood in the Pacific Coast League because they offered more money for me than any major league team did. So I found myself in the minor leagues. Mel Ott, the Giants manager, drafted me for $10,000, but pretty soon I was back in Hollywood," he said. "Then the Red Sox picked me up and I stayed with them for three years but I didn't play very much. They had Bobby Doerr, Vern Stephens and Johnny Pesky. How are you going to break into a lineup like that?"

Stringer didn't break into it, playing in only four games in 1948, 35 games in 1949 and 24 games in 1950. "Those were great Red Sox teams back then. We finished one game out of first place in two of those years and I think we were four games back in the other year," said Stringer. (Boston tied with Cleveland in 1948 and lost a one-game playoff. In 1949, the Red Sox finished one game behind the champion New York Yankees. In 1950, Boston was third, four games back of New York and one game behind the second place Detroit Tigers.)

"I've got no complaints. I got to play major league baseball and I got a decent pension out of it, of course nothing like they have today. After I retired, I sold cars for 21 years and made more money at that than I did playing baseball.

Stringer said he thinks the missing link for the Cubs over the years has been the inability to get what he calls winning ballplayers.

"Some guys can win, some can't. I wish I could put my finger on it, whatever it is that makes the difference. But sometimes, a team can have a lot of good players and never win," he said. "On the other hand, there are guys who jump from club to club and win no matter where they go. Baylor, for example."

Former Colorado Rockies manager Don Baylor played for six teams in his 19-year career and appeared in the World Series with three different teams in the last three years of his career: Boston in 1986, Minnesota in 1987 and Oakland in 1988. In addition, he made it to the League Championship Series with Baltimore in 1973 and 1974, California in 1979 and 1982 and with Boston, Minnesota and Oakland in 1986, 1987 and 1988.

"The Cubs over the years just haven't been able to get those 'winning' players," said Stringer.

He still keeps up with baseball but has cut back on watching games. "I'm getting old," he said. "I only watch the last two or three innings of games now. But I try to keep up with what's going on — and I like that McGwire!"

Louis Bernard Stringer
Born May 13, 1917, in Grand Rapids, Mich.
5' 11", 173 lbs.; B–right, T–right

Year	Team	G	AB	R	H	D	T	HR	RBI	Ave.
1941	Chi (N)	145	512	59	126	31	4	5	53	.246
1942	Chi	121	406	45	96	10	5	9	41	.236

Year	Team	G	AB	R	H	D	T	HR	RBI	Ave.
1946	Chi	80	209	26	51	3	1	3	19	.244
1948	Bos (A)	4	11	1	1	0	0	1	1	.091
1949	Bos	35	41	10	11	4	0	1	6	.268
1950	Bos	24	17	7	5	1	0	0	2	.294
6 years		409	1196	148	290	49	10	19	122	.242

HANK WYSE

Cubs Pitcher, 1942–1947

"They didn't spend any money on players."

PRYOR, Okla. — "It was Grimm's fault."

Fifty-three years after the Chicago Cubs' last appearance in a World Series, their 22-game winner in 1945 summed up why he thought the Cubs lost the seventh game.

"I thought I was going to pitch," said 80-year-old Hank Wyse, who might have won the Cy Young Award that year, had there been one.

Wyse paused from watching the Cardinal-Rockie game on the television in his home to reflect on his disappointment about what happened in that one ballgame that occurred so many years ago.

The Cubs and Detroit Tigers had battled to a seventh game, but the Cubs pitching staff had paid the price in Game 6, which went 12 innings. Claude Passeau pitched into the seventh inning for the Cubs and left with a hand injury and a 5–1 lead. Grimm called on Wyse, who hadn't pitched since Game 2 and had trouble containing the Tigers. Another starter, Ray Prim, helped end the Tiger uprising in the eighth inning.

By the ninth inning the score was knotted at 7–7 and Grimm, knowing there was no tomorrow if the Cubs lost, brought in Hank Borowy, a starter whom the Cubs had purchased from the Yankees in June. Borowy went 11–2 for the Cubs the rest of the way and shut out the Tigers 9–0 in the World Series opener. In Game 5, he pitched into the sixth inning but was knocked out when the Tigers got four straight hits en route to an 8–4 victory.

Summoned in the ninth inning of Game 6, Borowy responded by pitching four shutout innings as the Cubs won, 8–7 in 12 innings, setting the stage for the finale at Wrigley Field. And once again, Grimm went with Borowy.

"It was a mistake," said Wyse. "I thought so then and I still do. I should have pitched that seventh game."

Borowy, pitching in his third consecutive game and fourth in the seven-game series, gave up three straight hits in the top of the first inning. Paul Derringer came on in relief, but before the fire was out, the Tigers had scored five runs and went on to win, 9–3.

"Grimm was hung up on Borowy. He'd done a good job for us when he came over from the Yankees and Grimm went with him. I had expected to pitch that game. Grimm didn't say anything to me about it. He just said Borowy was pitching. That was it."

So Wyse, who was 22–10 during the regular season and who led the staff with 278⅓ innings pitched, worked only 7⅓ innings in the World Series. He started Game 2 and lost 4–1 in a game decided by Hank Greenberg's three-run homer. After that, he was relegated to two relief appearances.

The Cubs of 1945 were made up of wily veterans and brash youngsters. Among the team leaders were Wyse, who was 28, as well as 36-year-old pitcher Claude Passeau, 34-year-old second baseman Don Johnson, and 29-year-old first baseman Phil Cavarretta, who was the National League MVP.

"We had a bunch of players from Triple-A, because of the war — guys like Peanuts Lowrey and Andy Pafko— and everyone got hot at the same time. That's how we won it," said Wyse.

Lowrey, an outfielder in his second full major league season, hit .283. Pafko, also an outfielder in his second full season, hit .298 and drove in 110 runs. The club veteran was Cavarretta who had played for 12 years and had been on the 1935 and 1938 pennant winning teams.

Wyse said that by mid-season the Cubs were in the thick of a pennant race with the defending champion St. Louis Cardinals. "The Cubs were looking for another pitcher and thought they could get Borowy," said Wyse.

"But before they got him, they sat us all down and told us we might have to go on two or three days rest. I said, 'I don't know whether I can do that.' Mr. Wrigley said, 'If you do this, I'll take care of you for the rest of your life.' I told him I'd try.

"Well, I did try, and they did get Borowy. But if Mr. Wrigley was going to take care of me for the rest of my life, well, I'm still waiting," said Wyse, chuckling. He said the most money he ever made as a ballplayer was $12,500. He worked 40 years as an electrician after his retirement.

Hank Wyse won 22 games for the Cubs in 1945 and still thinks he should have started the seventh game of the World Series.

He broke in with Tulsa in his native state in 1940 on a team that featured an aging Dizzy Dean trying to make a comeback to the major leagues, as well as future Cubs players Eddie Waitkus, Don Johnson and Lenny Merullo.

"Wyse was a handsome kid who had a rubber arm," said Merullo. "We used to kid him because he had a full head of black hair — and not another hair on his face. We always used to ask him when he was going to start shaving. But boy, he could pitch."

But the pitching attraction on that Tulsa team was Dean, whose best days were behind him but who was valiantly trying to make it on the Cubs. After getting hammered in four of five starts, he volunteered to go down to Tulsa to work on his side-arm delivery. On June 9, 1940, he started and won for Tulsa, drawing 7,000 fans. By August, he was back up with the Cubs — and the Oilers concentrated on developing young pitchers like Wyse.

Wyse stayed with Tulsa until the end of the 1942 season when the Cubs gave him a look. "They brought me up and I got into a couple of games, I think," he said. (Wyse started four games, completed one, and had a 2–1 record.) He then pitched five years for the Cubs with his best year being the 1945 championship season when was 22–10. He won 16 in 1944 and 14 in 1946 before slipping to 6–9 in 1947.

"In 1947, I hurt my arm throwing batting practice. They put it in a cast and sent me home and that was it," said Wyse. He never pitched for the Cubs again.

"I pitched in Shreveport and then in Los Angeles. I pitched the season opener for LA in 1949 and had a 3–0 lead going into the ninth inning. They got the bases loaded on me and the manager comes out and calls in a relief pitcher, some guy named Lee. The manager said to me: If I'm going to lose, I'm going to lose with my best."

That was a stinging humiliation for Wyse, the former major leaguer who four years earlier had led the Cubs to the World Series.

"I don't remember if we won or lost but I remember what that manager said," said Wyse.

He resurfaced in the majors in 1950, winning nine games for Connie Mack's Philadelpia A's team and then retired in 1951 after brief stints with the A's and Washington Senators.

So his careeer lasted eight years in which he won 79 games — more than one-fourth of them in the 1945 season and two-thirds of them in a three-year span with the Cubs, 1945–1947.

Wyse was a Cub when Jackie Robinson broke in with the Brooklyn Dodgers in 1947 — an event that almost led to a strike of major league ballplayers. In a 1997 interview in conjunction with the 50th anniversary of Robinson's debut, Wyse said Cubs captain Cavarretta held a team meeting on Opening Day in which he held up a telegram and said all other teams had voted to strike if Robinson played. He asked the Cubs how they felt about it and, according to Wyse, the ballclub agreed to go along with it.

They waited in their clubhouse for a call from Dixie Walker, the Dodger player organizing the strike. The call never came. A month later, more than 40,000 fans packed Wrigley Field to see Robinson and the Dodgers beat the Cubs. Wyse pitched one-third of an inning in relief but did not get the decision.

A highlight of his pennant winning year came on July 12, 1945, when Wyse held Tommy Holmes hitless, ending the Boston Braves star's hitting streak at 37, a National League record that stood for 33 years until Pete Rose of Cincinnati hit in 44 straight games in 1978.

Wyse has followed the Cubs over the years and it didn't take him long to think of a reason why they haven't been back to the World Series since 1945.

"They didn't spend any money on players," said Wyse, the ballplayer-turned-electrician who is "still waiting" on that promise made to him 53 years ago.

Henry Washington Wyse
Born March 1, 1918, in Lunsford, Ark.
5' 11", 185 lbs.; B-right, T-right

Year	Team	W-L	Pct.	ERA	G	IP	H	BB	SO
1942	Chi (N)	2-1	.667	1.93	4	28	33	6	8
1943	Chi	9-7	.563	2.94	38	156	160	34	45
1944	Chi	16-15	.516	3.15	41	257.1	277	57	86
1945	Chi	22-10	.688	2.68	38	278.1	272	55	77
1946	Chi	14-12	.538	2.68	40	201.1	206	52	52
1947	Chi	6-9	.400	4.31	37	142	158	64	53
1950	Phil (A)	9-14	.391	5.85	41	170.2	192	87	33
1951	Phil-Wash	1-2	.333	8.63	12	24	41	18	8
8 years		79-70	.530	3.52	251	1257.2	1339	373	362

WORLD SERIES

Year	Team	W-L	Pct.	ERA	G	IP	H	BB	SO
1945	Chi (N)	0-1	.000	7.04	3	7.2	8	4	1

Don Johnson
Cubs Second Baseman, 1943–1948

"You don't put a plumber in charge of an airline."

Laguna Beach, Calif.— Don Johnson, the scrappy second baseman on the 1945 pennant winning Cubs, thinks he knows one of the reasons why the team hasn't made it back to the World Series.

"You don't put a plumber in charge of an airline or vice versa," said Johnson, 86, who played six years for the Cubs. "But that's the way the Cubs were run for years. At least, that's my opinion.

"Mr. Wrigley was a nice guy but he didn't care about baseball. He could chew gum all day."

Johnson was referring to Philip K. Wrigley, the Cubs owner, who also owned the Wrigley chewing gum company.

"You gotta have an ownership that will take charge. That's what the winners had — the Cardinals, the Dodgers, the Giants. If you don't have that, you're not going to win," he said.

In Johnson's era, many ballclubs were run by "baseball people" — families whose primary business — and income — came from baseball. Across town on the south side of Chicago, the Comiskeys owned the White Sox. In Philadelphia, Connie Mack owned and managed the A's for 50 years. The Griffith family owned the Washington Senators. The Stonehams ran the New York Giants. The Ebbets family, and later the O'Malleys, operated the Brooklyn Dodger franchise.

But on Chicago's north side, the Cubs had Mr. Wrigley, as everyone called him, who had inherited the chewing gum company and the ballclub from his father. And Mr. Wrigley left the details of running the ballclub to others.

"Jim Gallagher, our general manager in those days, was a great guy, a terrific person. But he was a sportswriter. Did you know that? He was a sportswriter and Mr. Wrigley made him the general manager of the Cubs. What did he know about general managing?

"But I'll say this. He made the deal that got us the pennant when he got Hank Borowy from the Yankees," said Johnson.

Borowy, a veteran right-hander, was 10–5 with the Yankees when the Cubs picked him up on waivers in June. He went 11–2 for Chicago the rest of the way to complete his finest season in the major leagues.

"Nobody could figure out how Gallagher pulled that one off. Everyone figured he had a friend with the Yankees who owed him a favor," he said.

The Cubs played the Detroit Tigers in the World Series. Because of wartime travel restrictions, the first three games were played in Detroit with the final four scheduled for Chicago. The Cubs won two out of three in Detroit with Borowy and Claude Passeau winning the first and third games.

The Tigers won the first two games at Wrigley Field in Chicago. The Cubs sent Passeau to the mound in the sixth game, coming off the greatest game of his life, a one-hitter in Game 3.

He was winning 5–1 going into the seventh inning of Game 6 when disaster struck. Johnson remembers it well."When Passeau got hurt, that was the Series. That was it right there," he said.

Detroit's Jimmy Outlaw lined a ball up the middle that struck Passeau on his pitching hand, forcing him to leave the game. Hank Wyse, the starter and loser in Game 2, came on to pitch for the Cubs, followed by another starter, Ray Prim.

Going into the ninth inning, the score was tied 7–7 and the Cubs called on yet another starter, Borowy, to keep their hopes alive. Borowy pitched shutout ball for four innings and the Cubs won 8–7 in 12 innings. But the damage was done. Manager Charlie Grimm had used four starting pitchers to salvage the win.

"If Passeau hadn't gotten hurt, he'd have probably won that game by himself," said Johnson. "Now, we go into the seventh game and we got nobody fresh. I remember Borowy begged Charlie to start him. Well, he did — and Borowy had nothing.

"I don't have a problem with Borowy starting. The whole staff was tired — and we wouldn't have been in the series if it hadn't been for Borowy."

He was knocked out in the first inning and the Cubs went on to lose, 9–3. "It was a lot to ask of Borowy. He wasn't that big a guy. There wasn't much heft to him and he just didn't have anything left," said Johnson.

"I hit .302 that year for the Cubs. I had a pretty good year but I had a lousy Series. I didn't even know I hit .302 until the Series. They didn't keep track of statistics in those days as quickly as they do now," he said.

Johnson broke in with the Cubs in 1943 at the age of 31. He was named to the National League All-Star team in both 1944 and 1945. His father, Ernie Johnson, was an American League infielder for 10 years who played in the 1923 World Series for the New York Yankees.

"He didn't play much for the Yankees because he was a shortstop and they had a fellow by the name of Everett Scott who was setting a record for consecutive games played," said Johnson.

(Scott played in 1,307 consecutive games for the Boston Red Sox and Yankees between 1916 and 1925, a record later broken by Lou Gehrig in 1939. Gehrig's record was broken by Cal Ripken Jr. in 1997. Ernie Johnson appeared in 64 games for the Yankees in 1924 and 76 games in 1925 and appeared in two games but did not bat in the 1925 World Series.)

Don Johnson broke into professional baseball with Tulsa and was a teammate of Dizzy Dean's in 1940.

"He was trying to make a comeback to the major leagues and the rest of us were just trying to make it," said Johnson. "Ol' Diz was a character. I remember one game where Diz was pitching in Tulsa. It was a real close game in the ninth inning and somebody got a hit — and a runner on second tried to score.

"Diz ran over between third and home and stood in the baseline and began waving his arms up and down, blocking the runner from scoring. He shouted at the runner, 'Hey, nobody here came to see you play.' Well, of course, they called interference and the run was allowed and we lost the ballgame but everybody had a good laugh over it.

"I remember another time we were at the Rice Hotel in Houston. We played a lot of games in Houston and it was always hot. It seems like we went to Houston and didn't leave for a month. Well, we were at the hotel and one of our players, Claire Bertram, says, 'I'm going up to see Diz.' We all knew Diz did a little betting on the horses, so I said, 'I'll go with you.' We went up to his hotel room and I'm telling you, I never saw anything like it.

"Diz had three phones in there, they were all hooked up, and he was talkin' on all of 'em, placing bets. He had a lot of money and he was pretty free with it. The way I heard it, all of his checks had to be co-signed. He couldn't spend a dime out of his checkbook unless his wife signed, too.

"But he treated us well. Here he was, a famous big-leaguer playing with us. Whenever we took the train somewhere, he was always the last one on, and he always had his arms full of sandwiches and drinks for the team.

"Back in those days, we only got about $1.20 a day meal money. Today's ballplayers get more in a day's meal money than I used to make in a month's salary — but it was tight back then."

Johnson played his entire career with the Cubs. At the end of the 1948 season, he became a free agent. "I didn't hold out for $5 million," he said, chuckling. "In fact, I wound up playing for Sacramento in the Pacific Coast League. For the first two weeks, I was hotter than a firecracker. Then the

next two weeks weren't so good. And after that, it got worse." By the end
of the season, he was out of baseball.

"I took a milk route for about four weeks and then I was in retail,
selling pottery and jars and things like that, for about 12 years. Then my
wife and I managed an apartment house for about 15 years until it got to
be a little too much for me — and so did the tenants," he said.

Johnson said he marveled at a Cubs second baseman who came along
40 years after he retired — Ryne Sandberg.

"I couldn't carry that guy's glove," he said. "He made plays I know I
never could have. He had great reflexes. You know, he retired and sat out
a year and then came back. I saw him make two errors one day and I knew
he was through. But in his day, he was the best."

Johnson said two exciting Cubs players on the 1945 pennant winner
were team captain Phil Cavarretta and outfielder Andy Pafko.

"Phil was a competitor who didn't hesitate to chew you out if he
didn't think you were getting the job done. He could really give you hell.
I was lucky. My locker was two or three down from him.

"Pafko was a good ballplayer. He caused a change in the ground rules
in Wrigley Field. Somebody hit a ball over his head and Andy went after
it. The ball went in the vines, which were really thick. Andy practically
got lost in those vines, trying to find the ball and never did. The batter
got an inside-the-park home run.

"Andy really raised cane with the groundskeepers after the game. And
it wasn't too long after that that the ground rules were changed and any
ball lost in the vines was a ground rule double," said Johnson.

In 1984, the Cubs won the National League East division championship and defeated the San Diego Padres in the first two games of the
league championship series. One more win and they would be in the World
Series.

"My wife and I made hotel reservations and started the drive from
our home in California to Chicago for the World Series," said Johnson.
"All the Cubs needed to do was win one out of three in San Diego and they
were in."

But the Cubs lost all three in San Diego and missed out on their best
chance at a World Series since 1945.

"I listened to all three games on the car radio," said Johnson. "In
Albuquerque, we turned around and went back home."

He said the Cubs fans in Wrigley Field are loyal and patient as they
wait for another winner. And when that day finally comes, Johnson says,
it will be because they finally recovered from the days when the plumber
was running the airline.

Donald Spore Johnson
Born Dec. 7, 1911, in Chicago, Ill.
6', 170 lbs.; B-right, T-right

Year	Team	G	AB	R	H	D	T	HR	RBI	Ave.
1943	Chi (N)	10	42	5	8	2	0	0	1	.190
1944	Chi	154	608	50	169	37	1	2	71	.278
1945	Chi	138	557	94	168	23	2	2	58	.302
1946	Chi	83	314	37	76	10	1	1	19	.242
1947	Chi	120	402	33	104	17	2	3	26	.259
1948	Chi	6	12	0	3	0	0	0	0	.250
6 years		511	1935	219	528	89	6	8	175	.273

WORLD SERIES

Year	Team	G	AB	R	H	D	T	HR	RBI	Ave.
1945	Chi (N)	7	29	4	5	2	1	0	0	.172

DEWEY WILLIAMS
Cubs Catcher, 1944–1947

"The Cubs never went out and got the good pitchers."

WILLISTON, N.D. — Dewey Williams was a role player for the Chicago Cubs in the late 1940s — an unusual role for a catcher.

"Any time we got ahead by a run or two from the sixth inning on, I'd put my stuff on. I knew I'd be coming in," said Williams, 82, recalling that he seldom started. "The other catchers couldn't field or throw as good as I could but they could hit a little better."

Williams, like his teammates from the 1945 National League championship team, has bittersweet memories of the World Series and particularly the sixth and seventh games.

The Cubs used four starting pitchers to salvage the sixth game, with Hank Borowy pitching the final four innings in relief to get the win.

Manager Charlie Grimm chose Borowy to start the seventh game, the third straight game in which he pitched, and his fourth appearance of the World Series. The first three batters got hits off him, knocking him out of the box. The Detroit Tigers scored five in the first inning and went on to win 9–3.

"I tried to get 'em not to start Borowy," said Williams, who still talks with pride about his ability to handle pitchers. "I talked my head off. I talked to Grimm, I talked to Cavarretta [team captain Phil Cavarretta], I talked to Merullo [shortstop Len Merullo].

"Vandenberg should have started that game." Harold "Hy" Vandenberg had a 6–3 record during the regular season and had worked just 2⅓ innings in two relief appearances in the World Series.

"But for some reason, Grimm had it in for Vandenberg. Borowy

Dewey Williams was a backup catcher who took pride in his ability to handle a pitching staff.

wanted to start that seventh game and he talked Grimm into it. And I said 'there goes our loot.' I warmed Borowy up that day and I knew he didn't have anything."

Williams started his professional baseball career with Atlanta in 1937 and then played for Toronto and Williamsport before going back for another stint in Atlanta. He made it to the major leagues with the Cubs in 1944.

"I could throw and that was a big deal for a catcher. In 1945, I think only two guys stole second base on me, Pee Wee Reese and Red Schoendienst. And I could handle pitchers. I always could. When I was at Cincinnati after I left the Cubs, Warren Giles paid me to go down to Tulsa to get Joe Nuxhall ready," he said.

(Giles, who would later become president of the National League, was the president of the Reds when he assigned Williams to work with Nux-hall. The left-hander was the youngest person ever to play major league baseball when the Reds used him in a relief appearance in 1944 at the age of 15. He lasted two-thirds of an inning and gave up two hits and five walks. It was his only appearance of the year and it left him with an earned run average of 67.00. He didn't return to the major leagues until 1952. This time he stayed for 16 years and won 135 games.)

"Another guy I helped along the way was Gene Conley who later pitched for the Milwaukee Braves. I helped him get to the majors," said Williams. (Conley had an 11-year career with the Braves, Phillies and Boston Red Sox in which he won 91 and lost 96. He also played pro basketball several years with the Boston Celtics.)

"One of the reasons why the Cubs have had so much trouble winning over the years is they haven't had the pitching. You've got to have that — and you've got to have someone who can teach them. I made a helluva pitcher out of Nuxhall.

"The Cubs never went out and got the good pitchers. They might have one or two but they never had enough. Now this year, they're probably one pitcher away from the World Series," said Williams. (The interview took place in 1998. The Cubs made it to the division playoffs as a wild card entry but lost three straight to Atlanta.)

"The guy who taught me most everything I knew was Paul Richards at Atlanta. He taught me how to catch. There's no one in the big leagues today who can catch like he used to. He was the best."

Richards was a major league catcher for eight years — brief stints with four National League teams in the 1930s and four years with the Detroit Tigers in the 1940s. He later managed the Chicago White Sox and Baltimore Orioles. In the late 1930s, he managed the Atlanta minor league team where Williams was one of his players.

"Sometimes when I was playing, I'd come back in the dugout and there'd be Richards sitting there with his equipment on, like he was just waiting for me to mess up. You learn real fast that way," said Williams.

"I learned from Richards how to work with pitchers, how to handle pitchers. The years I was in the big leagues, I was not only handling them — I was teaching them. And they respected me. In Chicago, I had 'em carrying my bags," he said.

Williams said he had a lot of roommates when he played for the Cubs because he was often roomed with rookie pitchers — part of the Cubs' effort to help bring the pitchers along.

He played in only 193 games in his five-year career and had 464 at-bats, a low total due to his main role as a late-inning defensive replacement. He said his biggest thrill was playing in the World Series. "I threw a guy out at second in the sixth game," he said.

"I hit a home run every once in a while," said Williams, referring to his lifetime total of three. "I remember my first one — it was off Bill Voiselle in the Polo Grounds in New York. You always remember your first home run."

He said the hitter that gave the Cubs the most trouble was Stan Musial of the St. Louis Cardinals. "We just couldn't get him out. And he smiled all the time. I called him 'Smilin' Jack.' We'd pitch him every which way.

"We were playing in St. Louis one night. I never will forget it. When we went over the hitters before the game, we all agreed we were going to knock Musial down. I was behind the plate and the first pitch comes in and floors him. I mean he went down in a heap.

"Well, you know what would happen today if you did that to a player. But it was a different game in those days and we had decided what we wanted to do. So—first pitch, boom, he goes down. We leveled him.

"And he got up and smiled at me. I never will forget it. And then he got a hit. From that point on, I told our pitchers to forget about Musial. Get the other Cardinal hitters out. It didn't matter if you knocked him down, he'd just smile at you and still get a hit," said Williams.

He has a vivid recollection of the tension associated with Jackie Robinson breaking the color line with the Brooklyn Dodgers in 1947. Word had gotten to other teams that a player strike was being planned to protest Robinson's signing.

Williams said Dodger outfielder Dixie Walker was supposed to call the Cubs clubhouse when Robinson took the field; that would be the signal to start the strike, which the Cubs players agreed to do. Walker never called. If he had, the course of baseball history might have been considerably altered.

The old Cubs catcher has lived in North Dakota all his life and coached youngsters in American Legion ball in his hometown after his playing days were over.

"Phil Jackson [Los Angeles Lakers coach, former New York Knicks player and Chicago Bulls coach] pitched on my Legion team," he said. "My advice to him was he better stick to basketball."

One other thing about the 1945 World Series sticks in the craw of Williams, the man who still feels his greatest attribute was working with pitchers.

Paul Richards, his old mentor at Atlanta, was a catcher for Detroit in 1945 and got the big hit in the first inning of the seventh game — a bases-loaded double. Williams watched from the Cubs bench.

His reaction 53 years later: "Richards helped beat us. He wouldn't have if I had been catching."

Dewey Edgar Williams
Born Feb. 5, 1916, in Durham, N.C.
6', 160 lbs.; B-right, T-right

Year	Team	G	AB	R	H	D	T	HR	RBI	Ave.
1944	Chi (N)	79	262	23	63	7	2	0	27	.240
1945	Chi	59	100	16	28	2	2	2	5	.280
1946	Chi	4	5	0	1	0	0	0	0	.200
1947	Chi	3	2	0	0	0	0	0	0	.000
1948	Cin	48	95	9	16	2	0	1	5	.168
5 years		193	464	48	108	11	4	3	37	.233

WORLD SERIES

Year	Team	G	AB	R	H	D	T	HR	RBI	Ave.
1945	Chi (N)	2	2	0	0	0	0	0	0	.000

HANK BOROWY

Cubs Pitcher, 1945–1948

"You've gotta have the horses."

FORT LAUDERDALE, Fla.—It's been long enough ago that 83-year-old Hank Borowy can laugh about it now. He was the starting and losing pitcher for the Chicago Cubs in the seventh game of the 1945 World Series against the Detroit Tigers—the last World Series in which the Cubs have been a participant.

In fact, he was the losing pitcher in the Cubs' last two losses but also has the distinction of being the last Cubs pitcher to win a World Series game. All of that occurred in the fifth, sixth and seventh games of one of baseball's wackiest World Series.

"You gotta have a winner and you gotta have a loser—that's baseball," said Borowy. "But we should have took 'em. We should have took 'em."

The Cubs wouldn't have been in the World Series at all if it hadn't been for Borowy, a mid-season acquisition from the New York Yankees. He was 10–5 with the Yankees when the Cubs got him on July 27, 1945, in a cash waiver deal for $97,000. He went 11–2 for the Cubs to help stop the St. Louis Cardinals from winning a third straight National League championship.

Then he appeared in four of the seven World Series games, winning two and losing two. Manager Charlie Grimm was second-guessed by players and fans alike for using Borowy so much, especially starting him in the seventh game after he'd started Game 5 and worked four innings of relief in Game 6.

The deal that brought Borowy to the Cubs was a bombshell pulled off by Cubs general manager Jim Gallagher, who wasn't a born-and-bred baseball man. He was a former sportswriter hired by Cubs owner Phil Wrigley to run the business side of the ballclub, with no previous experience — and he made the deal of the decade for the Cubs when he acquired the Yankees' right-hander.

With Red Ruffing in the military, Borowy was clearly the ace of the New York staff. Asked why the Yankees would want to get rid of him, Borowy said 54 years later, "Aw, hell, they claim I threw a pitch that a guy hit so hard, it went out of the ballpark and into some railroad boxcar. The next thing you know, I was gone.

"You know how baseball is — you don't have a good seat unless you buy one," he said with a laugh.

Cubs players were astonished by the deal. "People figured the Yankees owed Gallagher a favor for something or other," said second baseman Don Johnson, musing on the Borowy acquisition a half-century later.

Yankees players were astonished, too. Borowy had played college ball at Fordham University (whose most famous baseball alumni was Frankie Frisch, a St. Louis Cardinals star who later managed the Cubs). Borowy came up with the Yankees in 1942. He was an immediate success, winning 15 and losing just 4, leading them to the World Series. He was 14–9 in 1943 as the Yankees won the championship again. In 1944, Borowy was 17–12. At the time he was sold to the Cubs, his lifetime record with the Yankees was 56–30.

Larry MacPhail, who had become part owner and president of the Yankees early in 1945, brushed off criticism about the deal with the Cubs, saying, "This was a good chance to get rid of a pitcher who has never been a winner much in the last month or so of a season."

Borowy did all right in the "last month or so" with the Cubs. He pitched in 15 games, starting 14, winning 11, losing only 2 and getting a save in his one relief appearance. The Yankees finished fourth — and Borowy's 10 wins for them through July 27 were second highest on that staff for the whole season.

Baseball observers were astonished, too, at the Cubs' acquisition of Borowy, for a number of reasons. The deal had been made when Yankees manager Joe McCarthy was home recuperating from a stomach ailment and reportedly was not consulted about the transaction. Borowy had been passed over by 15 other teams in order for the Cubs to land him. Washington Senators' owner Clark Griffth was especially angry that MacPhail had dispatched Borowy to the other league.

As a result of the Borowy deal, Commissioner "Happy" Chandler was severely criticized for not launching an investigation into it — and rules governing waiver deals were tightened so that there could be closer scrutiny over them.

It was 39 years before the Cubs appeared in post-season play again — and a mid-season acquisition from the other league was a key factor again. In June of 1984, Chicago made a six-player trade with Cleveland in which the key figure for the Cubs was right-hander Rick Sutcliffe. He was 4–5 with the Indians but he fashioned a 16–1 mark for the Cubs to lead them to the National League Eastern Division championship.

Borowy had the same kind of impact in 1945. As a Cub, he joined a pitching staff that already boasted of having Hank Wyse, who would win 22 games that year and Claude Passeau, whose 17 wins turned out to be third best because of Borowy's combined record of 21–7.

His eleventh win for the Cubs came on September 29, 1945, when Borowy beat Pittsburgh 4–3 to clinch the National League pennant.

Then it was on to face the Detroit Tigers in the World Series, one of the strangest World Series ever played. World War II had just ended, and in order to get returning troops home as soon as possible, restrictions were put on civilian train travel to make room for soldiers. For that reason, the first three Series games were played in Detroit, with the remaining games to be played in Chicago — a huge advantage for the Tigers.

Both clubs had a mixture of players too young to be in the military, too old to be in the military or having an ailment or injury that kept them out of the military. "I've seen both teams play," said Chicago columnist Warren Brown before the Series began. "I don't think either team can win."

The Series was ugly from the start. On October 3, Grimm handed the ball to Borowy in Game 1 in what was envisioned as a classic pitching duel between Chicago's best pitcher and Hal Newhouser, Detroit's ace, who won 26 games during the regular season.

But Newhouser gave up seven hits and eight runs in the first three innings and the Cubs coasted to a 9–0 win. Borowy had thrown a shutout but it was hardly a gem. He gave up six hits and five walks, and he hit a batter. "I never got loose in that game," Borowy told John Drebinger of the *New York Times* after the game. "I never did stay warm and my arm never was loose."

Detroit came back to win the second game, beating Wyse 4–1, scoring all of their runs in the fifth inning — and three of those on Hank Greenberg's home run. The third game went to Chicago, 3–0, as Passeau threw a one-hitter — the best pitching performance in a World Series game ever, and surpassed since then only by Don Larsen's perfect game 11 years later.

The Tigers were held hitless for 3⅓ innings in Game 4 by Chicago starter Ray Prim. So the American League champions had one hit in their last 12⅓ innings. They scored four in the fourth and won the game 4–1. Still, in 35 innings of World Series play, the Tigers had scored in only two innings, and yet the teams were tied at two games apiece heading to Chicago.

Borowy and Newhouser hooked up again. This time Borowy got hit hard and the Tigers won, 8–4. Looking back on that game 53 years later, Borowy said, "Sometimes you have the zip, sometimes you don't. That's baseball." Some felt Newhouser could have had a shutout but several balls hit into the gusty Wrigley Field winds dropped between Detroit fielders. Sportswriter Brown said, "Newhouser won a doubleheader today. He beat both the Cubs and his own team."

Passeau started Game 6 and was sailing along with a 5–1 lead in the seventh inning when he was struck on the pitching hand with a line drive. Grimm brought in Wyse, who hadn't pitched since Game 2, to relieve Passeau. The Tigers scored two in the seventh and then four in the eighth off of Wyse and his replacement, Prim, to take a 7–5 lead. The Cubs came back with two in the bottom of the eighth to tie the game.

Grimm did what he had been doing since July — he called on his ace, Borowy, and Borowy responded by pitching four shutout innings. The Cubs and Borowy won 8–7 in 12 innings. Characteristic of the whole series, the winning run scored when Cubs third baseman Stan Hack singled to left but the ball hit a sprinkler head that was imbedded in the outfield ground and bounded over left fielder Greenberg's head.

There was a lot of celebrating in the Cubs clubhouse, of course, but Grimm had a huge decision to make.

In trying to salvage the sixth game — a win for Detroit would have given the Tigers the championship — Grimm had used all four of his starters: Passeau, Wyse, Prim, and Borowy. Who would he start in Game 7?

Lenny Merullo, Cubs shortstop, said Grimm walked around the

clubhouse talking to his pitchers, and everyone was eager. Merullo claims Grimm had settled on starting aging veteran Paul Derringer when Borowy practically begged him to give him the ball.

Borowy remembers it this way. "Charlie was going around the club-house saying, 'Who's ready? Who's ready?' Well, I was dead tired, of course, but you know, sometimes something inside of you takes over."

He said athletes often have a surge of adrenalin before a big game. He compared it to sexual arousal. "Sometimes, you get that feeling. You gotta have that feeling now and then in sports," said Borowy. He told Grimm, "I'm ready, I'm ready."

He might have been ready — but so were the Tigers. Borowy was gone after three batters. Skeeter Webb, Eddie Mayo and Doc Cramer opened the game with three straight singles off the weary pitcher. Down 1–0, reliever Derringer gave up a sacrifice bunt, an intentional walk to load the bases and then an unintentional walk to force in a run. Detroit catcher Paul Richards cleared the bases with a double, giving the Tigers a five-run first inning. They went on to win 9–3.

"With a little luck, I might have made it," said Borowy, reflecting on how hard he tried to come through in Game 7. "The zip just wasn't there."

Borowy pitched three more years with the Cubs but nothing approached his 1945 season. He was 12–10 in 1946. One of those wins, on May 5, was a 13–1 victory over the Phillies, a game in which Borowy hit two doubles and drove in four runs in one inning — an 11-run seventh inning for the Cubs.

He was 8–12 in 1947 and 5–10 in 1948. On December 27, 1948, Borowy was traded with first baseman Eddie Waitkus to the Philadelphia Phillies for pitchers Monk Dubiel and Dutch Leonard.

He was 12–12 for the Phillies in 1949. In 1950, the Phillies, who were on their way to winning the pennant, sold him to the lowly Pittsburgh Pirates. Two months later, Pittsburgh sold him to the Detroit Tigers. In that patchwork season, he was 2–4. He was relegated to the bullpen where he went 2–2 for the Tigers in 26 appearances in 1951, his last season in the major leagues.

His 10-year career had several highlights. In his rookie year with the Yankees, Borowy narrowly missed a no-hitter. On September 2, 1942, he gave up only a single to Harlond Clift of the St. Louis Browns. On April 18, 1944, he shut out the Red Sox in Boston's home opener at Fenway Park — but not many people saw it. Only 8,570 showed up. On July 11, 1944, Borowy was the starting pitcher in the All Star Game. He pitched three scoreless innings and drove in a run — but it was the only run the American League got in a 7–1 loss.

Borowy doesn't have an easy answer for why the Cubs have never made it back to the World Series since he led them to their last appearance in 1945. "You've gotta have the horses," he said with his characteristic laugh. "If you don't have 'em, you gotta go get 'em. And the Cubs just haven't done that."

Clearly, 1945 was Borowy's banner year — the only year he won more than 17 games in a season — and he won huge games — the pennant clincher, the first game of the World Series, and the sixth game — the one the Cubs had to win to stay alive. Game 7 was the big one that got away.

Years later, Derringer, who gave up the two walks and the double in relief of Borowy, ran into his old general manager, Gallagher, at a social event and they reminisced about the 1945 World Series. Recalling the seventh game, Derringer told him, "You know, it's funny. That's the first time in my career I ever walked a guy with the bases loaded." Gallagher's reaction: "What's so funny about that?"

Time heals wounds, and Borowy, who now has a home in Michigan and a winter home in Florida, is able to look back and laugh.

But he still has the ballplayer's competitive instincts. More than 50 years later, he maintains: "We should have took 'em."

Henry Ludwig Borowy
Born May 12, 1916, in Bloomfield, N.J.
6', 175 lbs.; B-right, T-right

Year	Team	W-L	Pct.	ERA	G	IP	H	BB	SO
1942	NY (A)	15-4	.789	2.52	25	178.1	157	66	85
1943	NY	14-9	.609	2.82	29	217.1	195	72	113
1944	NY	17-12	.586	2.64	35	252.2	224	88	107
1945	NY-Chi (N)	21-7	.750	2.65	33	254.2	212	105	82
1946	Chi	12-10	.545	3.76	32	201	220	61	95
1947	Chi	8-12	.400	4.38	40	183	190	63	75
1948	Chi	5-10	.333	4.89	39	127	156	49	50
1949	Phil (N)	12-12	.500	4.19	28	193.1	188	63	43
1950	Phil-Pitt-Det	2-4	.333	4.83	27	63.1	60	29	24
1951	Det	2-2	.500	6.95	26	45.1	58	27	16
10 years		108-82	.568	3.50	314	1716.0	1660	623	690

Transactions:

July 27, 1945: Sold by New York Yankees to Chicago Cubs for waiver price of $97,000.

Dec. 14, 1948: Traded with first baseman Eddie Waitkus to Philadelphia Phillies for pitchers Monk Dubiel and Dutch Leonard.

June 12, 1950: Sold to Pittsburgh Pirates.
Aug. 3, 1950: Sold to Detroit Tigers.

WORLD SERIES

Year	Team	W-L	Pct.	ERA	G	IP	H	BB	SO
1942	NY (A)	0-0	.000	18.00	1	3	6	3	1
1943	NY (A)	1-0	1.000	2.25	1	8	6	3	4
1945	Chi (N)	2-2	.500	4.00	4	18	21	6	8
3 years		3-2	.600	4.97	6	29	33	12	13

DOYLE LADE
Cubs Pitcher 1946–1950

*"The Cubs weren't really into the farm system like
other teams. The Cardinals and Dodgers were
always bringing guys up. The Cubs tried to get players in trades. I think that made a difference."*

GENEVA, Neb.— Doyle Lade said his most memorable game in the
major leagues was his first one.

"We were in Ebbets Field in Brooklyn and I beat the Dodgers and
Ralph Branca, 3–1. How could you ever forget something like that?" said
Lade, 79, who pitched for the Cubs for five years.

World War II robbed him of a chance of playing in a World Series.
He was a 22-year-old Chicago Cubs farmhand when he went into the military in 1943 and remained in the service through 1945, when the Cubs
won the National League pennant.

Lade said one of the reasons Chicago reigned in 1945 was that the
club had some good players who didn't serve in the military, mostly because
of age. "That's really how they won it," said Lade. "They were a good ballclub and they weren't hit with as many guys leaving for the service as other
teams."

The main cogs on that 1945 pitching staff were Hank Borowy, who
was 29; Hank Wyse, who was a "youngster" of 27; and Claude Passeau,
who was 36. Third baseman Don Johnson was 34, shortstop Lenny Merullo

was 28, MVP first baseman Phil Cavarretta was 29, and slugging outfielder Bill Nicholson was 31.

Lade played five years for the Cubs, winning 25 and losing 29 for Chicago teams that got progessively worse. They finished third in 1946 with an 82–71 record, 14½ games out of first; 69–85, good for sixth place in 1947, 25 games out; 64–90, eighth in 1948, 27½ games out; 61–93 in 1949, another eighth place finish and 36 games out; and 64–89 in 1950, moving up to seventh place and 26½ games out.

Lade's best year was 1947 when he was 11–10 but it was

Doyle Lade pitched for the post-war Cubs for two managers with opposite personalities — Charlie Grimm and Frankie Frisch.

also the year that an injury affected his career. "I hurt my arm sliding into second base at the Polo Grounds in New York," he said. "I played the rest of the season but when I came to spring training the next year, I couldn't do nothing. They sent me to Los Angeles and I spent two-and-a-half months there before they brought me back."

Lade never won more than five games after that, going 5–6 in 1948, 4–5 in 1949 and 5–6 in 1950. "I left the Cubs after that but I wasn't done with baseball. I played two more years in the Pacific Coast League and then two more years at Shreveport," he said.

His rise to the major leagues included a stop at Shreveport early in his career after spending a year at Oklahoma City.

"It's kind of unusual, I guess. I never played high school or college ball," said Lade. "They didn't have baseball at my little high school — just football and basketball. But I was playing Legion ball when I was 13 years old and we had a Ban Johnson League in our town for college-age guys. It was an eight-team league and it was competitive.

"A scout for Oklahoma City was at one of our games and he signed me. Oklahoma City was an independent team but was part of the Texas League. That was in 1941. Then I got traded to Shreveport, which was an independent team but they sort of had a working relationship with the White Sox. In fact, I had a pretty good year at Shreveport and the White

Sox bought my contract. But they ran into some money problems and sent me back to Shreveport," said Lade.

"My manager at Oklahoma City was Rogers Hornsby. Now there was a no-nonsense guy. The thing I remember most about Hornsby is that he used to take batting practice with us. He could still get in there and stroke the ball, I'll tell you that. What a hitter." (Hornsby was 45 years old when he managed Oklahoma City in 1941.)

Salty Parker, who later coached with pennant winning New York Giants teams of the 1950s, was his manager at Shreveport. "He was another good baseball man, a good teacher," said Lade.

"It was hot all the time in that Texas League. We always played in Beaumont at 4 o'clock in the afternoon. There might be hotter places but I don't know where. And we played in Tulsa, Dallas, San Antonio. You had to love baseball. You had to eat it, sleep it and live it," he said.

"I don't know that I can point to any one person who particularly helped me get to the big leagues. I got help from a lot of people along the way, but mostly, I worked hard. I can tell you who wanted it the most for me — that was my dad. He was a railroad man all of his life but he was a great baseball fan and my biggest fan."

When Lade arrived with the Cubs in 1946, he played for Charlie Grimm, a man he described as "a true character, but he knew his baseball."

Two incidents in particular show what it was like to play for Grimm, said Lade. "We were in St. Louis and someone hit one and Red Schoendienst, their second baseman, made a helluva stop and threw the guy out. On the very next pitch, their shortstop Marty Marion did the same thing. And Charlie Grimm [coaching at third] threw his arms up in the air and fell flat on his back.

"Another time, we were in Cincinnati and we were getting the daylights beat out of us and Charlie dug a hole in front of the dugout and buried the lineup card in the hole. That was Charlie Grimm. You don't see guys like that anymore," he said.

In 1949, Grimm was fired and was replaced by Frankie Frisch, a great ballplayer in his day but someone who was not universally liked as a manager. Lade was hesitant to talk much about Frisch, except to say that he was much like Hornsby and not as fun-loving as Grimm. "He was a lot tougher. I just tried to stay out of his roads," said Lade.

He said he didn't think the fact that the Cubs played all day games had anything to do with their failure to win a pennant over the next half-century. (Lights were installed in Wrigley Field in 1988.) "You hear that a lot, but I don't think it's a good reason. I preferred day games and I know other guys did, too.

"The Cubs weren't really into the farm system like other teams. The Cardinals and Dodgers were always bringing guys up. The Cubs tried to get players in trades. I think that made a difference.

"Now, I think it boils down to pitching. It always has boiled down to pitching, but now with expansion the way it is, you've got to have the pitching. Look at Atlanta. Why are they always on top? Pitching.

"You've got guys now who probably wouldn't have made the major leagues back when there were only 16 teams — and they're making millions of dollars. The game has really changed," said Lade.

After he left baseball, he ran a package liquor store for 10 years and then operated a Mobil gas and oil distributorship in southwestern Nebraska until he retired in 1980.

His career with the Cubs was not spectacular, and fate prevented him from having his only chance at playing in a World Series.

But Lade is grateful that a kid from Nebraska who never played high school or college ball was able to make it to the major leagues.

"I'll tell you the way I look at it," said Lade. "I wouldn't take a million dollars for my experiences in the big leagues."

Doyle Marion Lade
Born Feb. 17, 1921, in Fairbury, Neb.
5' 10", 183 lbs.; B-right, T-right

Year	Team	W-L	Pct.	ERA	G	IP	H	BB	SO
1946	Chi (N)	0-2	.000	4.11	3	15.1	15	3	8
1947	Chi	11-10	.524	3.94	34	187.1	202	79	62
1948	Chi	5-6	.455	4.02	19	87.1	99	31	29
1949	Chi	4-5	.444	5.00	36	129.2	141	58	43
1950	Chi	5-6	.455	4.74	34	117.2	126	50	36
5 years		25-29	.463	4.39	126	537.1	583	221	178

WARREN HACKER
Cubs Pitcher, 1948–1956

"The other teams had outfielders like Mays and Ashburn and Snider who would climb the walls going after fly balls. Ours let them drop ten feet in front of them."

Warren Hacker wished he had Willie Mays or Richie Ashburn in the outfield behind him when he was pitching.

Lenzburg, Ill.— Warren Hacker was a mainstay in the starting pitcher rotation for the Chicago Cubs for nine years but he says one of his biggest thrills came in relief.

"We were playing the Dodgers and Bob Rush was pitching a good ballgame," said Hacker, 74. "He got the first two guys out in the ninth inning and then he walked a guy and our manager, Stan Hack, brought in Hal Jeffcoat from the bullpen. As Stan was walking back to the dugout, he looked down at me and motioned for me to start warming up.

"I gave him kind of a 'who, me?' look but I did what he told me and started warming up. Well, Jeffcoat goes 2-and-0 on Don Zimmer and all of a sudden Hack is out of the dugout and waving me into the game. And I'm saying to myself, 'Good gracious' because I had only thrown about two warm-up pitches.

"I went to the mound, threw my seven warm-up pitches there and then threw ball three to Zimmer. Then I struck him out on the next three pitches. It's the only time in my baseball career I ever got goose pimples but they were as big as goose bumps," said Hacker.

His thrills were few and far between on Cubs teams that consistently finished near the bottom of the league. Hacker was 15–9 in 1952 and 12–19 in 1953, accounting for more than 40 percent of his 62 wins in a 12-year major league career.

In 1952, he threw a one-hitter against the Boston Braves, surrendering a home run to pinch hitter George Crowe with two out in the ninth inning. "I had been going with fastballs the whole game but I threw Crowe a knuckler and he really creamed it. Harry Chiti, my catcher, told me afterward he wanted me to throw a fastball six to eight inches outside because he said the ump would have given it to me. And I said, 'now you tell me.' [Chiti recalls the incident differently. He says he went out to the mound *before* the fateful pitch to try to convince Hacker to stick with the fastball but to no avail.]

"I think I threw five shutouts that season. That was probably one of the best games I ever pitched, not because it was a one-hitter but because there weren't many balls hit hard. That's what makes a good game for a pitcher. You can throw a shutout where there were five line drives that someone caught to save you.

"I think in that game against the Braves, Aaron hit one that was caught up against the fence but that was about it," said Hacker.

(The record shows that Hacker tossed six shutouts in his career — and five of them were in 1952, just as he said.)

He recalled another game where he also made a mistake, and this time it cost him the ballgame.

"I'll never forget it," said Hacker. We were in New York, playing the Giants, and I had them shut out on two hits. Don Mueller hit two knuckleballs for base hits off me. Now it's the ninth inning. Dusty Rhodes comes up as a pinch hitter and pops up. Then Davey Williams hits a groundball to Randy Jackson at third but Randy's throw pulls Steve Bilko off the bag at first.

"Whitey Lockman's coming up. Walker Cooper, our catcher, walks out to me and says, 'Whatever you do, don't give this guy a ball inside.' So what do I do? I throw it inside, Lockman hits it out, and we lose. I still think about that game," said Hacker.

He thinks the Cubs have been hampered over the years by playing in Wrigley Field.

"The Cubs get used to it but they need to win about 50 games there for it to be an advantage because opposing clubs love to play there. They look forward to it. It's a tough place for pitchers. You hit a fly ball there in June or July and the wind blows it out. Cubs pitchers have to deal with that every day and you get jumpy after a while.

"We had the worst outfield in the league in those days. The other teams had outfielders like Mays and Snider and Ashburn who would climb the walls going after fly balls. Our outfielders let the balls drop 10 feet in front of them. Let me tell you something—a good outfield makes a good pitching staff. Like they always say, you have to be strong up the middle," he said.

"Another thing—when I first broke in, our spring trainings were too long. Frisch used to start us in February. [Frankie Frisch was Cubs manager from 1949 through part of the 1951 season.] That made for a longer season than most other teams had and we were pretty well beat by the time August rolled around.

"Frisch was the worst manager I ever had. He was just plain mean to the players. He ridiculed everybody. I don't know why he did that. Maybe it was because he was such a great ballplayer himself and he didn't know how to handle us, because we were not a very good team.

"I remember in my rookie year I was pitching against the Dodgers. We had gone over all the hitters before the game. We were going to pitch Gil Hodges away. In the middle of the ballgame, I got a ball inside and he hit a little dribbler that got through between third and short for a base hit.

"Frisch comes out and says, 'I thought we were going to pitch him outside—you ought to get beat.' My God, I was a rookie and I made a mistake and he hit a little dribbler. But that's the way Frisch was," said Hacker.

Hacker's career with the Cubs came to an end on November 13, 1956, when he was traded with infielder Don Hoak and outfielder Pete Whisenant to Cincinnati for pitcher Elmer Singleton and infielder Ray Jablonski.

He played a half-season with Cincinnati and then was picked up on waivers by the Philadelphia Phillies. He had a combined record of 7–6 with the Reds and Phillies and appeared in nine games with Philadelphia in 1958 before being released.

He languished in the minor leagues for two years before the Chicago White Sox brought him up, at the age of 36, in 1961. He appeared in 42 games in relief, had a 3–3 record with eight saves.

"I got my name in the record book in '61," said Hacker. "I served up Roger Maris' 40th home run. It was a sinker low and away. Don Larsen, the old Yankees pitcher who was on our team, told me to pitch him that way. I should have known better, the way he was hugging the plate."

(Larsen should have known better, too. Maris homered off Larsen earlier on that same day, July 25, 1961. The Yankees played a doubleheader against Chicago. In the first game he homered off Frank Baumann and Larsen. In the second, he homered off Russ Kemmerer and Hacker.)

"I went to spring training with the White Sox in 1962. They said they were going to send me to Indianapolis for a while but that they would bring me back. But they lied, which was nothing unusual in those days.

"Ed Short was the general manager. He was an alcoholic and I think he just forgot. I saw him on a street corner once after that and he just waved like 'Hi, how are you' as if nothing had happened. I think he just forgot what he told me," said Hacker.

"But I had a great time at Indianapolis, maybe the best days I ever had in baseball. I played for Indianapolis in 1962, 1963, 1964 and 1965. We had good crowds and we were like family. I didn't mind it. In 1963, I had the best year of my life. I think I struck out 108 and walked four. Can you imagine that? Those are major league statistics."

Hacker served as a minor league pitching coach for the Oakland A's from 1967 to 1971 and then spent nine years as the pitching coach for the San Diego Padres.

"I don't do nothing but mow the lawn now," he said.

Hacker played for sub-par teams in the major leagues, never played in a World Series and ended his pitching career in the minor leagues because of broken promises.

But he has no regrets.

"I spent 34 years in baseball and I am well pleased with my career," he said.

Warren Louis Hacker
Born Nov. 21, 1924, in Marissa, Ill.
6' 1", 185 lbs.; B-right, T-right

Year	Team	W-L	Pct.	ERA	G	IP	H	BB	SO
1948	Chi (N)	0-1	.000	21.00	3	3	7	3	0
1949	Chi	5-8	.385	4.23	30	125.2	141	53	40
1950	Chi	0-1	.000	5.28	5	15.1	20	8	5
1951	Chi	0-0	.000	13.50	2	1.1	3	0	2
1952	Chi	15-9	.625	2.58	33	185	144	31	84
1953	Chi	12-19	.387	4.38	39	221.2	225	54	106
1954	Chi	6-13	.316	4.25	39	158.2	157	37	80
1955	Chi	11-15	.423	4.27	35	213	202	43	80
1956	Chi	3-13	.188	4.66	34	168	190	44	65
1957	Cin-Phil	7-6	.538	4.76	35	117.1	122	31	51
1958	Phil	0-1	.000	7.41	9	17	24	8	4
1961	Chi (A)	3-3	.500	3.77	42	57.1	62	8	40
12 years		62-89	.411	4.21	306	1283.1	1297	320	557

Transactions:

Nov. 13, 1956: Traded with infielder Don Hoak and outfielder Pete Whisenant
    to Cincinnati for pitcher Elmer Singleton and infielder Ray Jablonski.
June 26, 1957: Purchased by Philadelphia Phillies on waivers.

BOB RUSH

Cubs Pitcher, 1948–1957

"The Cubs didn't seem to have an organization."

MESA, Ariz.— Bob Rush remembers the best game he ever pitched.

"I lost 3–2 in 16 innings, but I went all the way," said Rush, 72, a soft-spoken man who toiled 10 years for the Cubs in an era when they finished in fifth place once and lower every other year.

"We were playing the Giants in the Polo Grounds and you know they had that short porch in right field," he said. "Willie Mays was on first. I think it was their third baseman, Ray Jablonski, the guy they got from the Cardinals, who hit a ball down the right field line. It went off the wall, bounded back and went right through our right fielder's legs. Mays scored all the way from first and I lost the game."

(His memory of the game helps identify when it took place. Jablonski played eight years in the major leagues, but only one with the New York Giants—1957, Rush's last year with the Cubs.)

During Rush's 10 years with Chicago, the Cubs finished eighth four times (in an eight-team league), seventh four times, sixth once and fifth once. He had a winning percentage higher than his team's percentage in five of six years between 1951 and 1956.

Bob Rush pitched on some bad Cub teams, then got into the World Series with the Milwaukee Braves.

In 1950, his third full season, Rush won 13 and lost 20. Teammate Johnny Klippstein lauded his teammate's effort. "Hey, that was a good year, considering he was playing for the Cubs," said Klippstein. Rush managed to have three winning seasons in his decade with Chicago, his best being 17–13 in 1952.

Another old teammate, Hank Sauer, says Rush was one of the best pitchers in the National League in his day. "He had a good fastball and a fair curveball, but the thing about Bob was, he always had to pitch against the other team's best. The Cubs saved him to pitch against the best. If he had been with most any other team in the major leagues, he would have won 20 games several times," said Sauer.

Rush was the winning pitcher in the 1952 All Star Game, one in which Sauer homered in a 3–2 National League win in a rain-shortened, five-inning game.

On December 5, 1957, he was traded with Eddie Haas and Don Kaiser to the Milwaukee Braves for pitcher Taylor Phillips and catcher Sammy Taylor. Haas and Kaiser dropped out of sight for the Braves, and Phillips and Taylor had average careers for lackluster Cubs teams. For Rush, the trade provided him with the opportunity of a lifetime.

He started the third game of the 1958 World Series for the Braves. "Of course, that was my biggest thrill in baseball. I pitched six innings and got taken out for a pinch hitter. We were losing 2–0 when I left the ballgame and I wound up getting the loss.

"I didn't pitch too badly. I got into a little trouble in the fifth and Bauer dropped a base hit in off me and drove in two runs." (On October 4, 1958, Rush was the starter and loser in that third game of the World Series at Yankee Stadium. He walked the bases loaded in the fifth inning before giving up Hank Bauer's single. Two innings later, Bauer homered off reliever Don McMahon, driving in all the runs in the Yankees 4–0 victory.)

Rush pitched two years with the Braves and then was sold to the Chicago White Sox where he finished out his career in 1960. He had a lifetime record of 127–152.

His experience with the Braves organization gave him insight into the reasons perhaps that the Cubs have failed to win a pennant for more than 50 years.

"The Braves organization had top people in key positions from the president all the way down to the field," he said. "So did the Dodgers. I never played for the Dodgers but their organization was always solid from top to bottom.

"The Cubs didn't seem to have an organization. They'd have a general manager who would be there for a couple of years and then he'd do something else and then he'd come back and be general manager again.

"And the same with the managers. I played for Charlie Grimm, Frankie Frisch, Phil Cavarretta, Stan Hack and Bob Scheffing. That's about one every two years. And that hasn't changed much. How long has Riggleman been there — three years? That could be a record." (In 1999, Jim Riggleman was in his fifth year as Cubs manager — the longest tenure for a Cubs skipper in 30 years, since Leo Durocher was at the helm from 1966 to midway in the 1972 season. Thirty men have managed the Cubs since they won the pennant in 1945. In 1961–1962, they had no manager but were led by rotating coaches — a failed experiment of owner Phil Wrigley.)

"They always had a lot of turnover with ballplayers, too. They never seemed to have an established nucleus that they could build around. All the good teams have that. In my day, the Brooklyn Dodgers had it, the Giants had it, and later, the Braves had it.

"And just look at the Atlanta Braves today. Sure, they have all that pitching but they always have the established nucleus and they build on that every year. The good teams have it and the Cubs never did," said Rush. "When you have constant turnover, it takes time for a team to jell."

Another weakness Rush saw in the Cubs compared to other teams in his era was a lack of executing the fundamentals. "In Brooklyn, the D-league team played the same type of ball that the Dodgers did. They were taught the right way to play from the lowest levels and everybody taught the same thing the same way all the way up.

"By the time those guys got to the big leagues, they already knew how to play the Dodgers kind of baseball. They didn't have to be taught. They could fit right in," he said.

"To me, the Cubs consistently didn't make the routine play over the years, and it's the routine play, the little things, that can make the difference between winning and losing. The good teams make those plays.

"And where that all starts is in the minor leagues. That's the way the Dodgers and other teams did it and they were winners. Why, even today, the Cubs might have lost because they didn't execute," said Rush, referring to Chicago's 8–7 loss to the Giants, a game he watched on television.

"The Cubs are down by a run and Manny Alexander tries to stretch a double into a triple and is out at third base for the third out in the inning. And who's up next? Sammy Sosa. So instead of having the tying run in scoring position with Sosa up, he leads off the next inning with nobody on. And of course he singles.

"Who knows what he would have done the previous inning but the point is that bad baserunning took them out of that inning and they lost the game."

Rush said another possible flaw in the Cubs system in the 1950s was their failure to adequately scout the Negro Leagues. "I don't think it was intentional in terms of not wanting to look at black ballplayers. I just think they had their scouts in other places," he said.

The Cubs' first black ballplayer was Ernie Banks who came up in 1953. By that time, Jackie Robinson, Don Newcombe, Joe Black, Roy Campanella and others had led the Dodgers to three pennants and Willie Mays, Monte Irvin, Hank Thompson and others were leading the Giants to the top of the league.

Despite the long seasons he spent with the Cubs, Rush said he went to spring training every year with high hopes. "We were optimistic every spring," he said. "Everybody starts out the same."

He said the hitter he had the most trouble with over the years was Stan Musial. "If you ask who the toughest one was, I'd say there was a bunch of them. But Musial was the best. He was just a tough out," said Rush.

"I had a good fastball in my day and I could strike out a lot of people. But I could not get the ball by Musial. He knew the strike zone and he knew how to go with the pitch. So if you threw the ball anywhere in the strike zone, he'd hit it. You simply could not get it by him."

One of Rush's fondest memories of his playing days was the appreciation of the fans at Wrigley Field.

"When I was playing, they were the greatest and I think they still are. Even when we were losing, they were the best. I think the reason is that Cubs fans come out to see a ballgame. They appreciate seeing players like Stan Musial and Willie Mays and they appreciate a good ballgame, win or lose," he said.

After retiring from baseball, Rush worked for many years as a customer service representative for the Motorola Corporation and was also the purchasing agent for a swimming pool company. Players in his era not only had to find jobs after they retired in order to support their families, but most also worked in the off-season during their playing days.

Today's minimum salaries in major league baseball are more than five times the amount Rush earned in his best year. In fact, he laughed when he thought about players' salaries today compared to when he played.

"The most I ever made was $22,000 a year," he said. "Today they get more than that in meal money."

Robert Ransom Rush
Born Dec. 21, 1925, in Battle Creek, Mich.
6' 4", 205 lbs.; B-right, T-right

Year	Team	W-L	Pct.	ERA	G	IP	H	BB	SO
1948	Chi (N)	5-11	.313	3.92	36	133.1	153	37	72
1949	Chi	10-18	.357	4.07	35	201	197	79	80
1950	Chi	13-20	.394	3.71	39	254.2	261	93	93
1951	Chi	11-12	.478	3.83	37	211.1	219	68	129
1952	Chi	17-13	.567	2.70	34	250.1	205	81	157
1953	Chi	9-14	.391	4.54	29	166.2	177	66	84
1954	Chi	13-15	.464	3.77	33	236.1	213	103	124
1955	Chi	13-11	.542	3.50	33	234	204	73	130

Year	Team	W-L	Pct.	ERA	G	IP	H	BB	SO
1956	Chi	13-10	.565	3.19	32	239.2	210	59	104
1957	Chi	6-16	.273	4.38	31	205.1	211	66	103
1958	Mil	10-6	.625	3.42	28	147.1	142	31	84
1959	Mil	5-6	.455	2.40	31	101.1	102	23	64
1960	Mil-Chi (A)	2-0	1.000	4.91	19	29.1	40	10	20
13 years		127-152	.455	3.65	417	2410.2	2334	789	1244

Transactions:

Dec. 5, 1957: Traded with Eddie Haas and Don Kaiser to Milwaukee for Taylor Phillips and Sammy Taylor.

June 11, 1960: Sold to Chicago White Sox.

WORLD SERIES

Year	Team	W-L	Pct.	ERA	G	IP	H	BB	SO
1958	Mil	0-1	.000	3.00	1	6	3	5	2

HANK SAUER
Cubs Outfielder, 1949–1956

"Teams used to beat the hell out of us at night. I think all those day games hurt us; at least they did in my day."

MILLBRAE, Calif.— Hank Sauer laughs when he recalls some of the bizarre incidents that marked his 15-year major league career.

In 1948, he set the Cincinnati Reds home run record when he hit 35 in his first full season with the Reds. The next year, he was traded to the Chicago Cubs. Why?

"Because the Reds said they wanted me to hit the ball more to right field," said Sauer, 81, who was a right-handed, dead pull hitter. "I set the record, I go to spring training and they tell me I have to try to hit the ball to right. That kind of hurt me. I said: Let me hit the way I hit. But Bucky Walters was the manager and I did what he told me and I bruised my thumb so bad in the process that it was as big as my bat.

"The next thing you know, I'm in Chicago," he said. "I had about

Hank Sauer was a Cubs slugger who was traded by Cincinnati after he set the team home run record, traded by the Cubs because he didn't trust the general manager and traded by the Cardinals because Stan Musial had an off year.

four home runs at the time. And in Chicago, my manager Frankie Frisch says, 'Hank, you're here because we want you to hit home runs. Pull the ball.' And I hit 27 for the Cubs giving me 31 for the year," he said.

Sauer hit 30 or more home runs in five of the next six years for the Cubs, including 37 in 1952 when he won the National League's Most Valuable Player Award and 41, his career best, in 1954. In 1953, he suffered two broken fingers during the course of the season and hit only 19.

Then, in 1955, coming off his 41–home run year, Sauer had another injury-plagued season and his statistics tailed off. And he had another unusual reaction from management.

"Wid Mathews, the general manager, said to me, 'Hank, we want to send you to Los Angeles in the Pacific Coast League. You play there this year and next year we'll make you the manager.' I told him I couldn't believe it [that he was to be sent to the minor leagues]. I asked him if he remembered that I hit 41 home runs the year before. I asked him what my other choices were.

"He said the Cardinals wanted me. He could trade me to St. Louis. I said, 'Trade me. I don't trust you.' And he did."

On March 30, 1956, Sauer was traded to the Cardinals for little-known outfielder Pete Whisenant. "To tell you the truth, I really felt cheated then," said Sauer. "I thought they should have gotten a lot more for me," he said with a laugh.

(Whisenant played for seven teams in an eight-year career in which his lifetime batting average was .224. He hit .239 for the Cubs in 1956 — his only year with them — with 11 homers and 46 RBIs.)

Sauer's strange experiences with management were not over. "I go to the Cardinals and I room with Stan Musial, one of the nicest kids in the world," he said. "And I'm not doin' too bad for myself either — hittin' .298 or .299." (Sauer hit .298 for the Cardinals in 1956.)

"Stan and I got along well, but I gotta tell you the truth; we weren't rounders or anything like that, but once or twice a week we'd go out and have a couple of toddies. At the end of the year, Frank Lane, the general manager, comes and says to me, 'We're gonna have to let you go.'

"I say: 'Why? I had a good year.' He said because Musial's hitting .315. And I said: 'What's wrong with that?' And he said, 'Musial's a .330 hitter and you're on your way.' And the next year, I'm with the Giants."

He batted cleanup behind Willie Mays, hit 26 home runs, and won the Comeback of the Year Award in the National League.

Sauer pointed out that not long after that, Lane tried to trade Musial to the Phillies for Robin Roberts but the deal fell through. While Sauer was with the Cardinals, Lane did trade Bill Virdon, Rookie of the Year in 1955, to the Pittsburgh Pirates for Bobby Del Greco, a 14-year veteran with a .229 lifetime batting average.

Sauer spent the next 35 years with the Giants — three as a player, the rest as a batting instructor and scout.

His years with the Cubs were his most productive, although the team floundered. Chicago finished fifth in Sauer's MVP year of 1952. The Cubs finished sixth in 1955 and seventh or eighth in all his other years.

He said the fans in Wrigley Field are a special breed, remaining loyal to a team that hasn't won a pennant in over 50 years. "The fans in Chicago, and in New York, too, know the game as well as the ballplayers who are playing it. The thing I noticed about the fans in Wrigley Field is they appreciate it when you go all out.

"They don't like loafers. If you went 0-for-20 but you hustled, they'd be all for you. But if you were hitting .300 and you loafed running down to first base, they'd be all over you. They'll chew your ass out.

"I remember the fans got on our shortstop, Roy Smalley. He was a good ballplayer and a heck of a nice guy but he didn't run out a ground-ball one day and the fans never forgave him. He got booed for a long time and he didn't deserve it."

(Smalley played six years with the Cubs, from 1948 through 1953, in

Hank Sauer used to store chewing tobacco in the outfield vines in Wrigley Field.

which he never hit higher than .249. He had the misfortune of becoming symbolic of the Cubs futility during that era. Forty years after Smalley left the Cubs, author George Will recalled how, as a youngster, he learned the meaning of the word "overdue" and could use it in a sentence: "Roy Smalley is overdue.")

"That's the only guy I ever saw really get it from the fans. The fans in Chicago appreciate good baseball. They were like that in my day and they're like that now. They're great fans," said Sauer.

He was hardly ever seen on a ballfield without a chaw of tobacco bulging in his cheek, but he said he never partook of it off the field. "The fans in the outfield used to throw pouches of tobacco at me. I'd stuff as many as I could in my pocket and the rest I'd store in the outfield vines.

"I'd give a lot of it to Yosh Kawano, our equipment man, who was a bigger chewer than I was. Then when the game was over, I'd run out and get it all out of the vines and give it away. Nobody in Chicago ever had to buy tobacco when I was there," he said.

(Yosh Kawano is still the equipment manager of the Cubs and has the longest tenure of any Cubs employee. He began work as a clubhouse attendant in 1943, two years before the Cubs won their last pennant, and was promoted to equipment manager in 1953.)

Sauer was originally a Yankees farmhand, signed by Paul Krichell, the scout who years earlier had signed Lou Gehrig and Tony Lazzeri and later Vic Raschi and Whitey Ford.

"You know, when they first looked at me after I signed, they wanted me to pull the ball. So I'm hitting the ball like crazy but everything I'm hitting is going foul. I play a couple of years in the Yankees farm system and then Frank Lane gets me for the Reds. It's funny that he got me as a pull hitter and years later he trades me because I'm not hitting the ball enough to right. That's my ole buddy Frank. That's baseball," said Sauer.

He recalled an incident in 1942 that serves as an example of how baseball has changed over the years. In those days, brushback pitches were an accepted part of the game. "I only played about seven games that year, but in the second game of the season against the Cubs, I came up against Claude Passeau, who was a pretty good pitcher and I hit a home run into the center field seats.

"As I'm rounding second base, he yells at me, 'you bush son of a bitch, you're going down next time.' And sure enough. The next time up, down I go. And the next time after that, too. One time after he knocked me down, he looked at me on the ground and said, 'Try hittin' it that way.' That was Claude Passeau," said Sauer.

He played briefly with the Reds in 1941 and 1942, then was in the service in 1943, 1944 and most of the 1945 season. "I had a helluva September in 1945. Then I go to spring training in 1946, and I hardly get a look. They had all of these guys coming back from the war and nobody paid any attention to me.

"In fact, they sent me down to Syracuse. I'm the MVP there in 1947. Just recently, I got elected to the Syracuse Hall of Fame and was named the left fielder on their all time best team. Then I set the home run record for the Reds in '48," he said.

Sauer was 31 years old by then. He finished his career with 288 home runs. Baseball analyst Bill James speculates that Sauer would have been one of baseball's greatest home run hitters had he not played sparingly for the Reds in 1941 and 1942, been in the service from 1943 to 1945 and then curiously be shipped to the minor leagues by the Reds in 1946-1947. In 1947, when he was the minor league MVP, he hit 50 home runs for Syracuse.

On June 14, 1949, Sauer and fellow outfielder Frankie Baumholtz were traded to Chicago for Harry Walker and Peanuts Lowrey. Sauer said he learned about the trade from a teammate, Ewell Blackwell, the veteran

FRANK BAUMHOLTZ

Frankie Baumholtz came to the Cubs along with Hank Sauer in a trade but had trouble gaining favor with feisty manager Frank Frisch.

pitcher. He asked Sauer "How do you want me to pitch to you?" Sauer thought Blackwell had been traded but soon learned otherwise.

Baumholtz, who hit around .300 for most of his career, had as much trouble getting noticed with the Cubs, and his new manager Frankie Frisch, as Sauer had in Cincinnati.

"Baumholtz was a good ballplayer and he and I were good friends until the day he died," said Sauer. "But for some reason, Frisch didn't like him. Frisch was a tough manager. He wanted to win. He didn't care what he said, and if he hurt your feelings, well that was just too bad.

"He was just the opposite of one of my other managers with the Cubs, Stan Hack, the old third baseman, the nicest guy you'd ever want to meet, but quite a contrast in style to Frisch," he said.

Sauer's greatest games came in consecutive appearances against the Phillies' Curt Simmons, though the appearances were years apart. "In 1950, I hit three home runs off of him and he walked me the next time up. Then he went in the service and was out of baseball for a while.

"He came back, and in 1952 I faced him again and hit three homers off him again. So I hit six home runs off him in six official at-bats. Hey, I don't want to take anything away from him. He was a good pitcher. Those things just happen in baseball," said Sauer.

(Sauer is the only man in baseball history to hit three home runs in a game off the same pitcher twice. He first victimized Simmons on August 28, 1950. Sauer's three home runs off of Simmons on June 11, 1952, were all solo shots — and the only runs the Cubs got in a 3–2 victory over the Phillies.)

He said the toughest pitchers he faced in his career were both Dodgers — Don Drysdale and Sandy Koufax, although Koufax had not yet reached his peak during Sauer's era.

"The Dodgers always had great pitching. Drysdale was a tough competitor who thought nothing of knocking you on your ass and you knew that every time you came to bat against him. When I faced Koufax, he didn't have the control that he later learned. But he had a fastball that was out of sight. When he learned to get the curveball over, it was Katie-bar-the-door," said Sauer.

Musial was the best hitter he ever played with — but Ted Williams was the best hitter he ever saw, which was only in All Star Games. Sauer said the difference between the two is that Williams hit every ball hard. His timing never seemed to be off one iota.

Sauer said Musial sprayed the ball all over the field and was a better all-around player while Williams was a pull hitter who hit with more power than Musial.

Sauer's highest salary was $37,500, which was not bad pay for players in those days. But like so many other players, he sometimes had to stand firm in salary demands. After his 41–home run year in 1954, general manager Mathews sent him a contract cutting his pay by $1,500. Sauer said he sent it back, thinking it was a mistake.

It was no mistake. Mathews said Sauer might have had a good year — but the Cubs finished seventh, using the old Branch Rickey logic that they could have finished seventh without him. Sauer held out in spring training and eventually signed for the same money he had received the previous year.

He thinks the Cubs have been at a great disadvantage over the years by the number of day games they play because of the adjustment hitters have to make for night baseball.

Sauer said it's no coincidence that the team that plays the most day games is also the team that hasn't won a pennant in more than 50 years.

"Teams used to beat the hell out of us at night. I think all those day games make a difference — at least they did in my day," he said. "In the daytime, as a hitter, you see three-quarters of the ball as it comes in there. You can pick up the spin sometimes and know what's coming.

"At night, you only see half the ball. That's a fact. And so while other teams were playing most of their games at night, they'd be accustomed to seeing the ball that way. The Cubs always had to make that adjustment. You'd play at home for two weeks and then go on the road and it was tough, and I think it made a difference.

"Then the teams that played mostly at night would come in to Wrigley Field and see the ball real good."

In Sauer's years with the Cubs, Wrigley Field had no lights. The Cubs played all day games at home until 1988 when lights were installed. All other teams had been playing night games at home for almost 50 years.

"Another thing about playing half our games at Wrigley Field. In my day, there were fans in the center field seats and most of them wore white shirts or it sure seemed that way. And it was really tough seeing the ball when you're batting," said Sauer.

His biggest regret in baseball is that he never got to play in a World Series — a trait of most players in the past half-century who spent most of their careers with the Chicago Cubs.

"But I really have no regrets. From the time I was a kid, I always wanted to be in baseball and it turned out to be my life," said the man who thinks the difference between the Cubs' success and lack of it over the years is the difference between night and day.

As a child, I followed Hank Sauer's career the way any youngster tracks his "favorite ballplayer." I knew, for example, that Sauer was born on March 17, 1919, in Pittsburgh, Pennsylvania — because that's what it said in my 1955 edition of *Who's Who in Baseball*.

I was chagrined when I noticed that recent publications listed Sauer's year of birth as 1917, not 1919. I asked my boyhood hero about the discrepancy.

"You caught me," said Sauer, amazed at how a statistic like that would stick in someone's mind for 40 years.

"When I was in the minor leagues, I lied about my age because younger kids had a better chance of moving up. So I cut two years off my age and just kept it that way because it didn't matter. But when I got close to pension time, it did matter. I thought I better correct it — and I did."

Henry John Sauer
Born March 17, 1917, in Pittsburgh, Pa.
6' 2", 198 lbs.; B-right, T-right

Year	Team	G	AB	R	H	D	T	HR	RBI	Ave.
1941	Cin	9	33	4	10	4	0	0	5	.303
1942	Cin	7	20	4	5	0	0	2	4	.250
1945	Cin	31	116	18	34	1	0	5	20	.293
1948	Cin	145	530	78	138	22	1	35	97	.260
1949	Cin-Chi	138	509	81	140	23	1	31	99	.275
1950	Chi	145	540	85	148	32	2	32	103	.274
1951	Chi	141	525	77	138	19	4	30	89	.263
1952	Chi	151	567	89	153	31	3	37	121	.270
1953	Chi	108	395	61	104	16	5	19	60	.263
1954	Chi	142	520	98	150	18	1	41	103	.288
1955	Chi	79	261	29	55	8	1	12	28	.211
1956	StL	75	151	11	45	4	0	5	24	.298
1957	NY (N)	127	378	46	98	14	1	26	76	.259
1958	SF	88	236	27	59	8	0	12	46	.250
1959	SF	13	15	1	1	0	0	1	1	.067
15 years		1399	4796	709	1278	200	19	288	876	.266

Transactions:

June 15, 1949: Traded with Frankie Baumholtz to Chicago Cubs for Harry Walker and Peanuts Lowrey.

March 30, 1956: Traded to St. Louis Cardinals for Pete Whisenant.

Part II. The 1950s

Year	W-L	Pct.	Finished	Games Out	Manager
1950	64-89	.418	7th	26.5	Frisch
1951	62-92	.403	8th	34.5	Frisch/Cavarretta
1952	77-77	.500	5th	19.5	Cavarretta
1953	65-89	.442	7th	40	Cavarretta
1954	64-90	.416	7th	33	Hack
1955	72-81	.471	6th	26	Hack
1956	60-94	.390	8th	33	Hack
1957	62-92	.403	7th (tie)	33	Scheffing
1958	72-82	.468	5th (tie)	20	Scheffing
1959	74-80	.481	5th (tie)	13	Scheffing

HARRY CHITI
Cubs Catcher, 1950–1952, 1955–1956

"There's too much nature in that ballpark."

MEMPHIS, Tenn.— Harry Chiti was the youngest player in the major leagues when he got into three games with the Chicago Cubs in 1950. He was 17.

The following year, he was still the youngest player in the majors

71

Harry Chiti was the youngest player in the National League for two years in a row.

when the Cubs brought him up and used him in nine games. In 1952, he was called up for a third time and stayed long enough to play in 32 games and hit five home runs.

"Those were the days of bonus babies," said Chiti, now 65 years old and a retired sheriff's deputy. "If you were a bonus baby, they had to bring you up to the big leagues within a year. My bonus was $6,000."

Chiti was signed by veteran scout Tony Lucadello out of Northwestern High School in Detroit, the same high school that produced another Cubs catcher, Hobie Landrith. (Lucadello, a scout for 50 years, signed 50 major league players, including two Hall of Famers — Mike Schmidt and Ferguson Jenkins.)

Chiti played a few games for Springfield, Missouri, in the Class D Western League after his high school graduation before being brought up by the Cubs.

After his three brief stints, he was drafted and spent two years in the Army. Chiti returned to play two more years with the Cubs before being traded to the Kansas City A's. He also spent time with Detroit, Cleveland and the New York Mets.

But he said his experience with the Cubs provides insight into what he thinks has been wrong with the organization over the years.

"The good teams like the Dodgers and the Braves had instructors all the way through the system — and they all taught the same thing. When their players got to the big leagues, they all played the same brand of ball — the Dodgers' way or the Braves' way — the way they had been taught to play.

"One of the problems with the Cubs in those days is the same problem you see in baseball today — too many people in the front office who know nothing about baseball. If something comes up, they look it up in a book. They don't do anything based on their gut feeling about the game because they don't have one."

(In Chiti's day, the Cubs were owned by chewing gum magnate Philip K. Wrigley.)

"I learned more in Richmond, Virginia, in 1957 than I did in all my years with the Cubs," said Chiti. "My manager was Eddie Lopat, the old Yankees pitcher. We'd sit and watch a game and he'd show me how to call a game. He knew his pitchers and he knew the hitters who were coming up and he'd say, 'Watch, he's going to bust him inside and he's going to pull it foul' or he'd say, 'This guy's weakness is low breaking stuff; he'll beat it into the dirt.'

"Many people judge a catcher by his batting average, not by how he can call a game. When I was with the Cubs, I was judged by my batting average, which wasn't good, and by my size, which was big.

"They didn't think about: Can he call a good ballgame? Can he work with veteran pitchers? Can he handle young pitchers? Does he know the hitters? That's the catcher's value to a team. It's not just: Can he hit?"

Chiti said one advantage he did have when he came up with the Cubs was his roommate, veteran catcher Clyde McCullough. "He was great for a young guy like me to room with and I'm sure they did it because we were both catchers. Clyde talked to me a lot about how to call a game, the basis for calling the fastball and the curveball — but he also taught me how to act. You act a certain way when you win and you act a certain way when you lose. You know when to go out at night and when to stay in. I looked up to the guy."

(McCullough played 15 years in the major leagues, the first seven with the Cubs, the next four with Pittsburgh, and the last four with the Cubs. He and Chiti were teammates and roommates in 1955 and 1956).

"Back in those days, the Cubs had an old veteran pitcher, Dutch Leonard, who threw nothing but knuckleballs. He was at the end of his career and was used only in relief. His ball went all over the place so whenever Dutch got up to warm up, our manager, Phil Cavarretta, would send me down to warm him up. And whenever Dutch came into a ballgame, Phil would bring me in to be his catcher," said Chiti. Cavarretta didn't want his older, veteran catcher chasing knuckleballs all over the place. That was Chiti's duty, a job for the kid catcher.

Chiti's most memorable game came in Milwaukee when Warren Hacker was pitching for the Cubs. "He was strictly a fastball pitcher and I mean strictly a fastball pitcher. If he had a good one, he would literally throw it all day.

"Well, we're in Milwaukee and he's got a good one. He's just mowing everybody down and he's got a no-hitter going into the ninth inning. He gets the first two guys on that fastball which is still biting and the Braves send up George Crowe to pinch hit.

"Crowe was a good hitter. He had a real slow bat until he popped his wrists, similar to the way Ernie Banks used to bat. Well, I'm calling the game from behind the plate and I do what I've done all night and put one finger down. Hacker blows two fastballs right by him.

"I put my 'number one' down and Warren shakes me off. I do it two more times and he shakes me off both times. So I go out to the mound to talk with him and Cavarretta comes out too. Cavarretta says to me, 'What's going on?' and I say, 'He just threw two fastballs past this sucker and now he's shaking me off.'

"So Phil asks Hacker what's going on and Hacker says, 'I wanna throw my knuckleball.' Phil says to me, 'Harry, it's his game,' so we go with the knuckleball. I'll bet I don't have to tell you what happened. Crowe hit the ball so hard and so far, it's probably still rolling. Hacker gets the next guy out on fastballs and we win 2–1 on a one-hitter," said Chiti.

The only crazier game than that, said Chiti, was the no-hitter thrown by Cubs right-hander "Sad Sam" Jones in 1955. Jones walked the first three Pittsburgh Pirates in the ninth inning — and then struck out the next three batters.

Chiti said he thinks the Cubs have been victimized by playing half their home games in Wrigley Field every year. It has particularly hurt pitchers.

"There's too much nature in that ballpark. You hit a pop-up one day and it's out of the park and hit a screaming mimi the next day and it stays in. That's a tough place to play half your games.

"And there's no advantage to playing half your games during the day. We always had to adjust to playing at night, and other teams didn't. And the other teams used to love to come to Wrigley Field where they could see the ball better," he said.

Chiti said today's game is tilted too far in favor of hitters. "Years ago, they lowered the mound six inches so they don't have the ball barreling down on them like they used to. With each expansion, the pitching becomes more diluted and they're gonna expand again. Also, the new ballparks are getting smaller and smaller.

"Look at the good teams today. Look at what they do. The Yankees. The Braves. They look for good pitching and they sign those guys to long-term contracts. That never used to happen, especially with pitchers. But it's a hitter's game now and there aren't that many good pitchers around.

"So when the Braves get people like Greg Maddux and Tom Glavine and John Smoltz, they sign 'em to long-term contracts — and the Yankees do the same thing. And look at which teams are winning year after year," he said.

When he retired from baseball, Chiti worked for several years as a salesman for Columbia Pictures and eventually became the branch manager for Columbia's Memphis office.

In time, Columbia closed its Memphis office and Chiti found himself looking for work. "My son was dating the sheriff's daughter at the time so I asked the sheriff if he could get me a job," he said. Chiti took the required tests and became a sheriff's deputy working with juvenile offenders, a job he held for 22 years.

His son, Harry D. Chiti, was a pitcher who was a second-round pick of the Atlanta Braves but his career was cut short by arm problems. He now works in the front office of the Cleveland Indians.

After leaving the Cubs in 1956, the elder Chiti signed on with Kansas City and played a year at Richmond where Lopat was the manager. He then played two years with the A's before being sold to the Detroit Tigers on July 26, 1960. He played two years with the Tigers and then was signed by the Baltimore Orioles after the 1961 season but never played for them. The Orioles traded him to Cleveland in November of 1961, setting the stage for one of the most novel deals in baseball history.

On April 26, 1962, Chiti was traded to the New York Mets for a player to be named later. On June 15, he was sent back to Cleveland to complete the trade. The Mets summed it up in a one-sentence press release: "The New York Mets sent Harry Chiti to Cleveland to complete an earlier deal." In effect, Chiti had been traded for himself.

"It gave me an opportunity to be part of a very interesting team," said Chiti, and who could argue?

The Mets, managed by Casey Stengel, won only 40 games and lost 120. Chiti, a 10-year veteran, retired at the end of the season at the ripe old age of 29.

Harry Dominick Chiti
Born Nov. 16, 1932, in Kincaid, Ill.
6' 2", 221 lbs.; B-right, T-right

Year	Team	G	AB	R	H	D	T	HR	RBI	Ave.
1950	Chi (N)	3	6	0	2	0	0	0	0	.333
1951	Chi	9	31	1	11	2	0	0	5	.355
1952	Chi	32	113	14	31	5	0	5	13	.274
1955	Chi	113	338	24	78	6	1	11	41	.231
1956	Chi	72	203	17	43	6	4	4	18	.212
1958	KC	103	295	32	79	11	3	9	44	.268
1959	KC	55	162	20	44	11	1	5	25	.272
1960	KC-Det	95	294	25	59	7	0	7	33	.201

Year	Team	G	AB	R	H	D	T	HR	RBI	Ave.
1961	Det	5	12	0	1	0	0	0	0	.083
1962	NY (N)	15	41	2	8	1	0	0	0	.195
10 years		502	1495	135	356	49	9	41	179	.238

Transactions:

July 26, 1960: Sold to Detroit Tigers.

Nov. 16, 1961: Traded with Ray Barker and Art Kay to Cleveland for Johnny Temple.

April 26, 1962: Traded to New York Mets for a player to be named later and cash.

June 15, 1962: Sent back to Cleveland to complete the deal with the Mets.

MOE DRABOWSKY
Cubs Pitcher, 1956–1960

"Everybody wants to win. What it comes down to is the Cubs have always been a little short in the talent department."

SARASOTA, Fla.—Moe Drabowsky knows the feeling and he wishes everyone could experience it.

"There's nothing like being out there in the October sunshine, looking back over your shoulder at the scoreboard and seeing only two teams are playing today. It's the World Series," said Drabowsky, 63, who had that experience twice as a member of the Baltimore Orioles, in 1966 and 1970.

In a relief appearance in 1966, he struck out 11 Los Angeles Dodgers. That remains a World Series record for a relief pitcher—but Drabowsky will be the first to admit he was lucky even to be there.

He was born in 1935 in Ozanna, Poland. He and his mother came to the United States when he was three and his father joined them a year later. All were in this country when Germany invaded Poland at the start of World War II.

"It's funny how stories get going," said Drabowsky. "After I won that World Series game in 1966, the papers were full of headlines about how my mom and dad fled from war-torn Poland, but it didn't happen that way at all."

Moe Drabowsky was touted as one of the two best players in the country when the Cubs drafted him. Later, he starred with the Baltimore Orioles in the World Series.

The family settled in Hartford, Connecticut, and young Moe, whose real name is Myron, was enrolled in boarding school. "It was a tough environment. There were classes six days a week and you had to wear a coat and tie. That wasn't easy for a kid," he said.

While he was growing up, he learned to throw a baseball pretty hard and later made the starting pitching staff at Trinity College in Hartford.

"My sophomore year, I was 10-1 and my only loss was 1–0. At the end of my junior year, I went to play in Nova Scotia and there were a lot of scouts there. Several teams approached me. In fact, through that experience, I got to work out at Yankee Stadium and at Fenway Park.

"The Cubs flew me into Chicago where I met with their general manager, Wid Mathews. We talked for a few minutes and then he said, 'You're going to be in our starting rotation in 10 days.' I was shocked. I mean, I was dumbfounded. He said the Cubs were after the two best college players in the country — me and Jerry Kindall, and he signed us both. I signed a three-year contract for the minimum salary of $6,000," said Drabowsky.

He joined a pitching staff that was filled with old-timers — Bob Rush, Warren Hacker, Sam Jones, but by the next season would include bright prospects in Dick Drott, Glen Hobbie and Drabowsky.

"When you get to the big leagues, it's imperative that you have immediate success. That's very important not only for your confidence but their confidence in you. In 1957, my first full year, Drott and I tied for second in the league in strikeouts with 170. Only Jack Sanford of the Phillies was ahead of us." (Sanford struck out 188 while posting a 19-9 record and was the National League's Rookie of the Year.)

Drabowsky won 13 and Drott won 15 but no other pitcher won more than six and the Cubs finished in seventh place.

"In 1958, I had a lot of arm problems. It was a real struggle to get through the year. First I hurt my elbow. It actually locked at a right angle. Then I tried to pitch too soon afterward and I hurt it again," he said. He finished the season with a 9-11 record — for a Cubs team that was 72-82 with Hobbie leading the staff with 10 victories.

"Those were interesting days with the Cubs. We weren't very good. We were always finishing close to the bottom of the league. You'd hear guys in the clubhouse after a game saying things like, 'Boy if it hadn't been for those seven runs they got in the seventh inning, we'd have been right in that game.'

"We'd get beat 9–1 and 8–2, day after day, and yet, day after day, Ernie Banks would come in the clubhouse smiling, saying it was a great day for a ballgame and 'let's play two' and all of that. And I sometimes wondered: What's with this guy? We're getting clobbered. And I finally figured it out.

He was making $80,000 a year and I was making $6,000. Perspective means a lot," Drabowsky said with a laugh.

Arm problems continued to plague him for the next two years with the Cubs.

On March 13, 1961, the Cubs traded Drabowsky to the Milwaukee Braves for Andre Rodgers and Daryl Robertson. It was the start of the major league merry-go-round for Drabowsky, who, less than five years earlier, was the best college player in the country. He appeared in only 16 games for the Braves and didn't win any while losing two, still fighting arm problems.

At the start of the 1962 season, he was picked up by the Cincinnati Reds, managed by Fred Hutchinson, an old pitcher who was sharp enough to recognize a young pitcher trying to overcome pain.

"I needed to pitch a half a season to qualify for a pension. It was the most pressure I've ever had in my life. I just kept popping pain pills and counting the days. Hutch would ask me if I was all right and I'd say 'yeah' and I could hardly comb my hair. But I had worked this long and hard, and I wanted that pension.

"We were in LA the day I qualified for a pension. I knew the Dodger clubhouse man real well and I took all my pain pills and said to him, 'Look what I'm going to do.' And I flushed them all down the toilet," said Drabowsky.

He qualified for a pension while with the Reds but he didn't stay with them long enough to have any other distinction. On August 13, 1962, he was sold to the Kansas City A's, a team that was always in need of pitching, so much so that the club was willing to take a chance on a man with a recent history of arm problems.

Drabowsky had two tours of duty with the A's in his career — and it provided him the opportunity to have a business relationship with baseball's maverick owner, Charles O. Finley. He wound up being his stockbroker.

And something else was happening. His arm was getting better. In fact, Drabowsky threw the best regular season game of his life with the A's — a one-hitter against the Washington Senators. "The only hit was a bunt by Don Blasingame," he said.

Drabowsky was well known for his practical jokes — and he could imitate Finley's voice almost to perfection. "One time between seasons, I called our shortstop Wayne Causey down in Louisiana and put on the Finley voice. 'Wayyyyyyne,' I said, 'this is Charlie Finley. I'm sending you a contract for $13,500.'

"And Causey went nuts. He said it was unacceptable and that he would send the contract back unsigned. And I said, 'Well, Wayyyyyyne, take it or leave it,' and I hung up."

When his playing days in Kansas City were over, Drabowsky was hired by Finley to be his broker. "In his first dealing with me, he said, 'Here's $100,000. Do what you want with it.' One time he called me and asked me about a particular stock. I told him I'd have to research it and that I'd get back to him.

"Well, I called him back and told him I didn't like the company and that we don't want to buy. He said, 'Fine. Buy me 10,000 shares.' That's the kind of guy Charlie Finley was. I have three checks framed in my office, all from Finley. One is for $460,000, another for $500,000 and one for $1.3 million, the biggest deal he ever did with me."

Drabowsky said it's hard for him to pinpoint any specific problems with the Cubs over the years that have kept them from the World Series. "I never have thought day games had much to do with it. Day games actually help you because you're on a normal schedule. You work during the day and go home at night. Stan Musial used to say that if he ever got traded from the Cardinals, he wanted to go to the Cubs, and it was because of the day games.

"I don't think attitude really has anything to do with it either. Everybody wants to win. What it comes down to is the Cubs have always been a little short in the talent department."

Drabowsky left the major leagues after the 1972 season and was out of baseball for 14 years. Only a chance meeting with an old Kansas City teammate, Ken "Hawk" Harrelson, brought him back.

"Hawk and Don Drysdale were doing Chicago White Sox broadcasts, and in 1985 Drysdale had to go to Cooperstown for his Hall of Fame induction. Hawk called and asked me to fill in on the broadcast. After the game, we're in the Bard's Room [the Comiskey Park restaurant for the media] having a beer and Hawk says, 'You know what baseball needs — a pitching coach for right-handed pitchers and a pitching coach for left-handers.'

"Well, we talked about it and I told him that with the number of right-handers there are, compared to left-handers, how would the workload be distributed. How could you possibly find enough work for a pitching coach for left-handers? Basically, I told him that was about the dumbest idea I had ever heard.

"But I told him something that might work would be to have a pitching coach for starting pitchers and a pitching coach for relievers because the disciplines of the two were so different. He loved the idea.

"A year later, he calls me up and says, 'Moe, I want you to be my relief pitching coach.' Hawk was now the general manager of the White Sox. He might have liked the idea, but Tony LaRussa, the manager, and Dave Duncan, the pitching coach, didn't. We started the year losing 18 of our first 25 games and I got reassigned to the minor leagues. But I was back in baseball."

He has worked the past four years as pitching coordinator for the Orioles and spent 1999 in A-ball trying to instill the spirit in young pitchers that he had on his greatest day as a major league pitcher — October 5, 1966, in sunny Los Angeles — the first game of the World Series between the Orioles and the Dodgers.

The pitching matchup was Drysdale for Los Angeles and Dave McNally for Baltimore. The Orioles jumped on Drysdale for three runs in the first inning, but the Dodgers pecked away at McNally, scoring runs in the second and third and threatening for more. When McNally walked Lou Johnson, Tommy Davis and Jim Lefebvre in succession, Oriole manager Hank Bauer summoned Drabowsky.

"My only goal was to get my name in a World Series box score," said Drabowsky. "But I did on that day what I try to teach kids to do now. Observe. Plan. Execute. I came in with the bases loaded and one out. You've got to have a plan. Believe me, and I tell the kids this, if you have a plan, it does an awful lot to relieve the pressure."

Drabowsky shut out the Dodgers the rest of the way, not only getting his name in a World Series box score, but getting the win as well, and setting the World Series record for most strikeouts by a relief pitcher, 11, a mark that stands today.

"Observe. Plan. Execute. Have you ever watched Greg Maddux in the dugout? He's always watching something, trying to find something that can help him improve his game. He knows how to observe, plan and execute."

But Drabowsky looks back on that day in the World Series for another reason. "Here we were in Los Angeles. I never expected to be there again. And I saw my old buddy, the clubhouse man — the guy who five years earlier had seen me flush the pain pills down the toilet. On many days, I had been struggling just to raise my arm. Now I'm in the World Series. That's baseball."

Myron Walter Drabowsky
Born July 21, 1935, in Ozanna, Poland
6' 3", 190 lbs.; B-right, T-right

Year	Team	W-L	Pct.	ERA	G	IP	H	BB	SO
1956	Chi (N)	2-4	.333	2.47	9	51	37	39	36
1957	Chi	13-15	.464	3.53	36	239.2	214	94	170

Year	Team	W–L	Pct.	ERA	G	IP	H	BB	SO
1958	Chi	9-11	.450	4.51	22	125.2	118	73	77
1959	Chi	5-10	.333	4.13	31	141.2	138	75	70
1960	Chi	3-1	.750	6.14	32	50.1	71	23	26
1961	Mil	0-2	.000	4.62	16	25.1	26	18	5
1962	Cin-KC	3-7	.300	5.03	33	111	113	41	75
1963	KC	7-13	.350	3.05	26	174.1	135	64	109
1964	KC	5-13	.278	5.29	53	168.1	176	72	119
1965	KC	1-5	.167	4.42	14	38.2	44	18	25
1966	Bal	6-0	1.000	2.81	44	96	62	29	98
1967	Bal	7-5	.583	1.60	43	95.1	66	25	96
1968	Bal	4-4	.500	1.91	45	61.1	35	25	46
1969	KC	11-9	.550	2.94	52	98	68	30	76
1970	KC-Bal	5-4	.556	3.52	45	69	58	27	59
1971	StL	6-1	.857	3.45	51	60	45	33	49
1972	StL-Chi (A)	1-1	.500	2.57	37	35	35	16	26
17 years		88-105	.456	3.71	589	1640.2	1441	702	1162

Transactions:

March 31, 1961: Traded to Milwaukee Braves for infielders Andre Rodgers and
 Daryl Robertson.
Aug. 13, 1962: Sold to Kansas City.
June 15, 1970: Traded to Baltimore for infielder Bobby Floyd.
Nov. 30, 1970: Traded to St. Louis for infielder Jerry Da Vanon.

WORLD SERIES

Year	Team	W–L	Pct.	ERA	G	IP	H	BB	SO
1966	Bal	1-0	1.000	0.00	1	6.2	1	2	11
1970	Bal	0-0	.000	2.70	2	3.1	2	1	1
2 years		1-0	1.000	0.90	3	10.0	3	3	12

FRANK ERNAGA
Cubs Outfielder, 1957

*"They held on to some average ballplayers over the
years, that's for sure."*

SUSANVILLE, Calif.— Frank Ernaga broke in with the Cubs in May of 1957 and hit a home run off Warren Spahn in his first at-bat. The next time up he tripled. The next day he was on the bench. The day after that, he hit a double and a homer off Juan Pizarro. A month after that, he was in the minor leagues.

If the Chicago Cubs are to be faulted for not adequately recognizing and developing young talent over the years — and many former players do criticize them for this — then Frank Ernaga might be the best example.

Ernaga, 68, said he was stunned when he was sent down to the minors after getting off to such a fast start — including a double, a triple and two home runs in his first six at-bats. Not long after that, Clarence "Pants" Rowland, a Cubs vice president, met him in a hotel lobby in Pittsburgh and told him he was being sent down to Fort Worth.

"He said they wanted me to play myself into shape," said Ernaga. "I thought I was in shape. I don't know why they sent me down but I was a small town kid who really didn't know how to stick up for myself.

"There was a lot of politics in baseball — still is — and I should have been more aggressive. I should have jumped up and down with both feet and told them I knew I could do the job.

"I wasn't quick, but I could hit and I had a great arm. I had 29 home runs and 110 runs batted in for Stockton in 1954, 23 homers and 103 runs batted in for Burlington in 1955 and 18 home runs and 90 RBIs for Tulsa in 1956. So I had proven myself. And then when they called me up in '57, I thought I was proving myself.

"After Rowland told me in Pittsburgh I was going down to Fort Worth, Ernie Banks came up to me and asked me what happened. I told him and he shook his head and said, 'That's what you get for showing the regulars up.' I hope he was kidding," said Ernaga.

He came back up in September and faced Spahn again and hit a single and a double off of him. He finished the season with a .314 average in 20 games. Of his 11 hits in 35 at-bats, seven were for extra bases: three doubles, two triples and two home runs.

In spring training of 1958, Ernaga worked out at three positions — catcher, third base and first base. "They tried to make a catcher out of me. That's what they really wanted. I had been an outfielder for my whole career but they had guys in the outfield they liked and I wasn't going to break that up," he said.

It wasn't as if the 1957 Cubs outfield had Willie Mays, Mickey Mantle and Joe DiMaggio. The three regulars were Walt "Moose" Moryn, Chuck Tanner and Lee Walls. Jim Bolger, Bob Will and Bob Speake also got playing time.

Frank Ernaga hit it big early with the Cubs and then disappeared quickly from the major leagues.

Ernaga said it's easy, when you're not playing, to look at who is playing and make some judgments. "Like I said, there's politics involved in who plays and who doesn't and who stays and who doesn't.

"I can't say why the Cubs kept some players and let others go. They held on to some average ballplayers over the years, that's for sure," said Ernaga.

The experiment to make him a catcher ended when he split his finger in spring training. Sammy Taylor and Cal Neeman shared the Cubs catching duties in 1958. On May 20, they traded pitcher Jim Brosnan to St. Louis for Alvin Dark, who was the Cubs regular third baseman for the next two years.

So they had the outfielders they wanted, the catchers they wanted and the third baseman they wanted. Ernaga was the odd man out. After eight dismal pinch-hitting opportunities in 1958 in which he got only one hit, a single, the Cubs dropped him. He was signed by the Washington Senators but never played in the major leagues again.

He says today that his claim to fame in the major leagues was hitting for the cycle against Warren Spahn — a homer and a triple in April and a double and a single in September.

Ernaga was a hard-hitting outfielder on his town baseball team in Susanville, California, when the UCLA baseball team came through on a barnstorming tour to drum up fan interest.

"I played junior college ball for two years and was the quarterback on the football team. When our town team played UCLA, the coach saw me and signed me to go to UCLA. I didn't play football there, just baseball. And Jack Vorneir, who was a great West Coast scout, signed me to my contract with the Cubs," said Ernaga.

His major league career was brief but he has some terrific memories of some of his teammates.

"Hank Sauer suckered me into a bet in spring training," he said. "Hank was a big guy and he didn't run very well. He came up to me on the field one day and said, 'I'll race you to center field for a Coke.' Well, that was a bet I knew I could win. So I said 'okay' and we took off running.

"I ran hard and he just kind of loped behind me. And of course, I won, but he said, 'Okay, I said I'd race you for a Coke and I did. I raced you. So you owe me a Coke.' I don't think I was the only rookie he ever pulled that on.

"Jim Brosnan was a pitcher on that team. A nice guy and probably the smartest ballplayer I ever knew. That guy could work a crossword puzzle in 10 minutes — and what a memory. He could tell you what he had for breakfast 20 years ago," said Ernaga.

After Ernaga's major league career ended so abruptly, he returned to Susanville and started his own construction company which he ran for about 40 years. Most recently, he has been a school inspector.

He still follows baseball. "I bet on the Dodgers but I root for the Cubs," he said. "I'll always be a Cubs fan." He regrets not getting a chance to play more but he's glad he was given the chance to play at all.

"When Jack Vorneir signed me, he said, 'You're going to be the next right fielder for the Chicago Cubs,'" said Ernaga.

"And I was — for about four days," he said with a hearty laugh.

Frank John Ernaga
Born Aug. 22, 1930, in Susanville, Calif.
6' 1", 195 lbs.; B-right, T-right

Year	Team	G	AB	R	H	D	T	HR	RBI	Ave.
1957	Chi (N)	20	35	9	11	3	2	2	7	.314
1958	Chi	9	8	0	1	0	0	0	0	.125
2 years		29	43	9	12	3	2	2	7	.279

GLEN HOBBIE
Cubs Pitcher, 1957–1964

"There's a knack for finding the right players. You've got to have people who not only play well but have the heart to win."

RAMSEY, Ill. — Glen Hobbie remembers the game in 1960 when he was locked in a pitcher's duel with Wilmer "Vinegar Bend" Mizell of the Pittsburgh Pirates.

"It's a 1–1 ballgame and we're up in the bottom of the ninth," said Hobbie, 62, who pitched eight years for the Cubs. "The first two guys up ground out on curveballs on the first pitch.

"Now I come up to bat and I'm thinking that Smokey Burgess is catching and he's gotten two out on two pitches, both curveballs. Ole Smokey

Opposite: Glen Hobbie was part of a promising young Cubs pitching staff until back problems shortened his career.

isn't going to change habits at this stage of the game so I have a pretty good idea of what's coming on the first pitch.

"Curveball — I guessed right. I hit it out and we win, 2–1," said Hobbie, who played on Cubs teams that never got over .500.

He won 16 games in 1959 and again in 1960 and seemed headed for a stellar career as one of the National League's top pitchers until back problems caused him to alter his delivery — and his effectiveness. By the age of 28, he was out of the big leagues.

In 1964, the Cubs traded him to the St. Louis Cardinals for Lew Burdette, the old warhorse who had helped the Milwaukee Braves to the World Series in 1957 and 1958 but was now just finishing out a fine career.

Hobbie only pitched 44⅓ innings for the Cardinals that year but says he pitched in a game that helped propel them to the National League championship.

"We were playing the Dodgers. I can't remember who started for us but Sandy Koufax was pitching for them," said Hobbie. "They jumped on us for about five runs in the first two innings. That's tough when Koufax is pitching.

"I went in and pitched four or five innings and only gave up a run. It was a pretty good outing and we wound up winning the game in the 13th inning. Any time you win a game like that, and especially when Koufax is pitching, it's a big boost. That was one of the games that we looked back on as one that helped our momentum."

By season's end, the Cardinals were in the World Series — but Hobbie was in Jacksonville where he had a 5-1 record and a bad back. He never pitched in the major leagues again.

"But hey, I won one game for the Cardinals that year and they won the pennant by one game," he said with a laugh.

He broke in with the Cubs in 1957 — long enough to get into one game and give up five runs on six hits and issue six walks in just 4⅓ innings. But he won 10 games in his first full season, 1958, and followed that with the two straight 16-win years.

"I was pitching for the Memphis Chicks in 1957 and had a 15-15 record as both a starter and a reliever. In those days, it wasn't unusual to be used as a starter and in the bullpen and I did a lot of pitching that year," he said.

"I think my break came on a day when we were playing Nashville and I won both games of a doubleheader, both in relief, and Pants Rowland saw me," he said. (Clarence "Pants" Rowland was a Cubs vice president.)

Not long after that, Hobbie was in the major leagues, joining a pitching staff that featured Dick Drott, a young fireballing right-hander and

Myron "Moe" Drabowsky, a native of Poland who later won fame as a relief pitcher for the Baltimore Oriole championship teams.

"One of the things about the Cubs in those days was we never could seem to get everybody healthy at the same time," said Hobbie.

He pitched two near no-hitters in his career, against the Cardinals in 1959 when Stan Musial got the only hit, a seventh-inning single, and against Cincinnati in 1960 when Wally Post broke it up with a seventh-inning base hit.

"Frank Robinson was my toughest out. He would stand right up on the plate — and I mean right up on it. He had the outside corner covered and he dared you to throw the ball inside on him. He was just murder on me," he said.

"More often than not, I did okay against the free-swingers. It was always the Punch-and-Judy hitters that got me. You'd be going along fine, pitching a good game and heading for a victory and then someone would dink one that would get by everybody and before you knew it, you'd lost the game."

Hobbie was on the 1961-1962 Cubs teams that didn't have a manager. Instead, the club had a rotating coaching system — a college of coaches, they called it. Coaches would rotate every few weeks from one minor league team to another with four of them — Vedie Himsl, Elvin Tappe, Lou Klein and Harry Craft — taking turns coaching the major league team.

The experiment was a disaster. The Cubs finished seventh, winning 64 and losing 90. It wasn't so disastrous for Cubs owner Phil Wrigley to drop the idea. In 1962, Tappe, Klein and Charlie Metro "coached" the team to a 59-103 ninth place finish.

"I don't think anybody on the ballclub felt comfortable with it. A team needs a manager, someone to make everything jell. That's not easy when you're dealing with 25 different personalities and it takes time. And it isn't going to happen with a change being made every few weeks," said Hobbie.

Hobbie had another unpleasant surprise as a result of a Cubs management decision.

"Bob Scheffing was my manager when I first came up and I respected him a lot. He showed confidence in me and I really developed under him. I think there was a mutual respect.

"At the end of the 1959 season, I was sitting in Scheffing's office and he told me to have a good off-season and to call him if I ever needed him for anything. I felt real good about the relationship I had with him as a player. I left the ballpark and was driving home which is about two hours south of Chicago and I heard on the radio that Bob Scheffing had been fired as manager of the Cubs. I about drove off the road. I couldn't believe it," said Hobbie.

"They brought in Charlie Grimm to manage us in 1960. Charlie was a great guy but he hadn't managed in years and he was getting older. The game had just passed him by and passed him by so far that it just wasn't going to work," he said.

(Grimm had managed the Cubs from 1932 to 1938 and from 1944 to 1949 and managed the Braves in Boston in 1952 and in Milwaukee from 1953 through 1956. But he had been relegated to the broadcast booth and had not been in uniform for five years. He lasted 17 games and had a 6-11 record. Wrigley replaced him with Lou Boudreau, a Hall of Fame player, former American League manager and at that time a Cubs broadcaster. Grimm and Boudreau switched positions in another bizarre Wrigley move, with Boudreau taking over as manager and Grimm going to the broadcast booth. Boudreau managed the Cubs to a seventh place finish. The next year, the rotating coaches came in.)

"I enjoyed playing for Lou. One thing I remember about Lou — he was always very fair with the players and that's important. That works," said Hobbie.

It was during that 1960 season that Hobbie experienced another memorable game. "I was pitching against Pittsburgh in a game at Wrigley Field and my son was born at game time: 1:30 on July 30, 1960. I found out about it in about the third inning," he said.

Hobbie said the best umpire he ever saw was Al Barlick. "He had his own philosophy about baseball and part of that philosophy was: He didn't care what your name was. Just because you had a big name didn't mean you were going to get the benefit of a call from Al — and I really liked that about him," said Hobbie.

"Look at the way it is today, with certain pitchers getting the wide strike zone — Maddux and Glavine and those guys. Al Barlick would have none of that. I remember a time I was pitching in Milwaukee — Henry Aaron's home park — and I got two strikes on him. I was going to waste a pitch but I got it a little too close to the plate and it hit the corner.

"Well, everyone knew it was supposed to be a waste pitch and Henry Aaron was the batter but none of that mattered to Al Barlick. He called it strike three and punched him out right there," he said.

"The guys who got away with a lot in my day were pitchers like Warren Spahn and Lew Burdette. They got a lot of calls because they were Warren Spahn and Lew Burdette."

Hobbie said he wouldn't want to hazard a guess as to why the Cubs have had such a long drought since the last time they were in a World Series. "If I knew the answer to that, I'd be managing them," he said.

"But one thing is for sure. The teams that dominated in my day were the ones who really knew the fundamentals because they learned them in the minor leagues. If you have a good minor league system, eventually you'll have good major league players. You don't have to teach them everything when they get to the big leagues. They've already learned. They're ready to play when they get there.

"There's a knack for finding the right players, too. You've got to have people who can not only play well but have the heart to win. I always think of Don Zimmer. Nobody gave more on the field than Don Zimmer. He was not a great ballplayer but he was an important player because of how hard he played. Teams need players like that.

"Those guys sometimes end up coaching or managing in the minor leagues and they bring that heart to those jobs too. Some even manage in the majors, like Zimmer did," said Hobbie.

He said another person who brought that kind of spirit to the ballclub — long after Hobbie's career was over — was Dallas Green. "He knew what he was doing and he did a good job with the Cubs minor league system and later as general manager," said Hobbie.

In 1984, with Green as general manager, the Cubs made their first post-season appearance since 1945, losing the National League Championship Series to San Diego, three games to two.

After his playing days were over, Hobbie worked for 25 years as plant manager of the Roller Derby Skate Corporation in Lichfield, Illinois.

Today's baseball is a different brand than the game he played, back in the days when starting pitchers were expected to try to throw complete games. Now, six innings is considered a "quality start" and relief pitchers come in and throw the ball 95 miles an hour for an inning or less.

"Watch those guys. See if they put two good years in a row together," said Hobbie. "Because I'll tell you something. Everybody has just so many pitches in them. Some have more than others, but everyone has just so many. And when it's done, it's done."

Glen Frederick Hobbie
Born April 24, 1936, in Witt, Ill.
6' 2", 195 lbs.; B-right, T-right

Year	Team	W-L	Pct.	ERA	G	IP	H	BB	SO
1957	Chi (N)	0-0	0.00	10.38	2	4.1	6	5	3
1958	Chi	10-6	6.25	3.74	55	168.1	163	93	91

Year	Team	W-L	Pct.	ERA	G	IP	H	BB	SO
1959	Chi	16-13	.552	3.69	46	234	204	106	138
1960	Chi	16-20	.444	3.97	46	258.2	253	101	134
1961	Chi	7-13	.350	4.26	36	198.2	207	54	103
1962	Chi	5-14	.263	5.22	42	162	198	62	87
1963	Chi	7-10	.412	3.92	36	165.1	172	49	94
1964	Chi-StL	1-5	.167	5.65	21	71.2	80	25	32
8 years		62-81	.434	4.20	284	1263.0	1283	495	682

Transactions:

June 2, 1964: Traded to St. Louis Cardinals for pitcher Lew Burdette.

CAL NEEMAN
Cubs Catcher, 1957–1960

> *"Back in my day, the teams that were generally at
> the top were the ones with good organizations from
> top to bottom…. The Cubs never had that."*

LAKE ST. LOUIS, Mo.—Former Cubs catcher Cal Neeman speaks softly about his major league career, like he's recounting a recent trip to the grocery store.

Neeman, 70, has a lot of respect for relief pitchers and loves to talk about a pair the Cubs had during his tenure with the ballclub.

"We had Don Elston, a right-hander, and Bill Henry, a lefty. Can you imagine how much money those guys would be making today? Wow. Henry was a tremendous athlete who set all sorts of records in college. Elston was a character — cocky but in a good kind of way.

(Elston joined the Cubs in 1957. A year later, he led the National League in appearances with 69. Henry joined the club in 1959. That year, he and Elston tied for the league lead in most appearances with 65 each — a total of 130 appearances between the two of them.)

"Back in those days, you had to face either the tying or winning run to get a save. If Elston came into a game with a two-run lead, he'd walk the first batter so he could get a save. That's the kind of guy he was. He was a tiger. He believed.

"I remember a game in St. Louis. We're up by a run in the ninth inning, There's two outs and Ken Boyer comes up with a man on second. Boyer was murder on inside pitches. He'd just kill you. Well, Elston comes in to relieve and I go out and tell him to keep the ball away from him. And Elston says, 'Aw hell, get back there — and he threw three pitches right by him, all on the inside part of the plate. And he walks off the field grinning."

Neeman keeps a newspaper clipping on his bulletin board at home that recounts a game involving Elston. "I don't know why I keep it. I guess I just get a kick out of it," he said. The story in the clipping recounts a game between the Cubs and the Giants in which Elston was the pitcher, the Cubs were winning by a run, there were two outs in the ninth and Willie Mays was on first base.

"Elston threw 11 straight pickoff throws to first base. On the 12th, he picked him off. Game over. Cubs win," Neeman said with a laugh.

Neeman played ball at Illinois Wesleyan University and was signed by the New York Yankees in 1949. "I was assigned to Class C ball in Joplin, Missouri, and I had a pretty good year. We finished second and then won the playoffs.

"In 1950, I got invited to the Yankees rookie camp. Casey Stengel ran it. He had just finished his first year with the Yankees. There were some pretty good catchers in that camp — Elston Howard, Gus Triandos, Lou Berberet and me.

"They sent me back to Joplin and I didn't want to go. Bill Dickey, the old Yankees catcher who was then a coach, said to me, 'You go there and you'll thank me.' Well, I went, and I thanked him ever since. I learned so much while I was there.

"Mickey Mantle was on that team and, to tell you the truth, he was the whole show. Then I went to Korea for the next two years. When I was in Korea, I heard that Mantle was with the Yankees. And I thought: What do you know? I'm in Korea and he's next to Joe DiMaggio in the Yankees outfield. We all knew he was good — but nobody knew he was that good," said Neeman.

He came back from Korea and played at Binghamton, New York, in 1953 and 1954, at Birmingham in 1955 and Denver, the Yankees' top farm club, in 1956. But by that time the Yankees had the great veteran Yogi Berra, a solid backup in Charlie Silvera and Elston Howard waiting in the wings. Neeman was made available to other teams, and the Cubs picked him up.

After a long haul in the minor leagues, Neeman finally got his shot. On April 16, 1957, he made his major league debut in a game against the Braves and went 1-for-3 against Warren Spahn at Wrigley Field. "You never forget your first game," he said.

Not too much later, he hit his first home run off Lew Burdette of the Braves at County Stadium in Milwaukee. "That homer put us ahead 3–2 in the ninth. In the bottom of the ninth, they loaded the bases and the game ended when someone hit a line drive to Jack Littrell at shortstop. It spun him around but he caught it. Littrell was playing short because at that time they were experimenting with Ernie Banks at third base," said Neeman.

He caught 122 games, hit .258 and hit 10 home runs for the Cubs in 1957, a year in which they tied for last place. In 1958, he appeared in only 76 games and yet hit 12 home runs and batted .259. The Cubs tied for fifth.

"My second year was very disappointing to me. I wanted to play every day and it seemed like it wasn't going to happen. I batted right-handed and the Cubs had a left-handed hitting catcher by the name of Sammy Taylor.

"I remember thinking 'Hey this guy hit .250 in Double-A and he's playing and I'm not. What's going on here? Years later, as I look back, it was okay. Sammy was a good hitter, especially good against right-handed pitching. Most of the balls I hit well I hit off mistakes.

"We had a lot of good young prospects. Dick Drott and Moe Drabowsky and Glen Hobbie were on that pitching staff and we got a left-hander, Taylor Phillips, in a trade with Milwaukee for Bob Rush. And we had hitters like Moose Moryn and George Altman and Ernie. Not a bad ballclub at all. We just couldn't get it done.

"Our manager Bob Scheffing got fired after the '59 season and nobody could believe it. He did all right after that. He went to Detroit and almost won it and then was in the front office with the Mets and built the winner there. His record speaks for itself," said Neeman.

"In 1958 and 1959, I was pretty discouraged. I remember we played the Dodgers on Opening Day in Wrigley Field and Don Drysdale struck out the first six batters and then hit a home run when he came to bat for the first time. But we hung in there and actually won the game 3–2 when Sammy Taylor hit a bases-loaded double in the ninth inning. I was happy we won but I remember thinking, 'Hell, I'll never get to play.'

"We had Earl Averill catching for us for a while and one time in Dodger Stadium he hit a grand slam home run. He came up again in the same inning with the bases loaded again and just missed hitting another one. It went foul at the last minute. I was in the bullpen at the time and when he hit that second one, we all stood up and watched it as it went foul.

"I didn't jump up like the others did, though, and Turk Lown, another one of our pitchers, asked me what was wrong. And I said, 'I'll never get to play again.' Looking back, I know that was wrong, but I was young, I had played pretty well, and I was just frustrated," said Neeman.

On May 13, 1960, the Cubs traded Neeman and second baseman Tony Taylor to the Philadelphia Phillies for first baseman Ed Bouchee and pitcher Don Cardwell. Two days later, in his Cubs debut, Cardwell threw a no hitter at Wrigley Field.

For Neeman, the trade marked the beginning of a downhill slide. He appeared in only 59 games with the Phillies in 1960 and 19 in 1961, after which he was picked up by the Pittsburgh Pirates. He played sparingly for the Pirates, Cleveland Indians and Washington Senators before calling it quits after the 1963 season.

He doesn't like to talk about his last few years in baseball. "In Washington, they wanted to send me to their farm team in Hawaii to play. I said, 'If you think I'm going to fly back and forth across the ocean'—well, I probably should have done it, but I didn't," said Neeman.

He quit and opened a health food store. "I was ahead of my time—too far ahead of my time. It failed. I even had Ernie Banks come out and take a look at it and I don't think he was impressed.

"I worked for the railroad for a while, then taught school and coached—basketball—for a couple of years. For the past 28 years, I've been associated with a company that sells maps and globes for school classrooms. I'll probably retire at the end of this year," he said.

"I don't have the strong allegiance to the Cubs that other players might have. Don't get me wrong. Chicago is big league in every way, there's no doubt about it. But I think guys who come up in an organization keep a loyalty to that organization—and I didn't come up with the Cubs.

"But I can tell you one of the things that was different about the Cubs when I was playing for them and I think it made the difference. Back in my day, the teams that were generally at the top were the ones with good organizations from top to bottom. The Dodgers had something like 37 farm clubs and the Yankees and Cardinals both had about 30. So they always had young prospects coming up to fill positions on their clubs and they could trade those prospects to fill holes, too. The Cubs never had that," said Neeman.

"Another thing that has always hurt Chicago is pitching. It's hard for pitchers to play there day after day. The wind isn't blowing out all the time but it's blowing out a lot. Now think about that. When the wind's blowing out, you can't even pitch a guy outside like you can in other ballparks. And playing all day games, like we did, means the opposing batters are seeing the ball better in Wrigley Field than in any other park. And over the course of a year, you bet it makes a difference.

"Remember — no matter how many runs you get, you still have to get them out in the eighth and ninth innings," he said, once again touting the importance of good relief pitching.

Neeman was hesitant to put the blame for the Cubs' futility on Philip Wrigley, who ran the club for nearly 50 years. "He ran it like a business which means he hired people to run it for him. People talk about how he wasn't really a baseball man, but look — Ted Turner is not really a baseball man and he seems to be doing all right.

"I met Mr. Wrigley once. He was telling me how his dad designed the park and how the park has some thrills for the fans built into it. For instance, he said, the left field and right field walls are designed so they jut back a few feet in the corners so that there are parts of left-center and right-center that aren't as deep as down the lines at Wrigley Field. He thought that added some excitement on balls hit to left and right.

"And he told me why the Cubs played so many Sunday doubleheaders which a lot of players complained about in those days. Mr. Wrigley liked them because of the number of families that came from out of town to see the Cubs play. He thought doubleheaders gave them more to see since they came so far to see the Cubs.

"Mr. Wrigley takes a lot of criticism, and I have to admit, that College of Coaches he started [in 1961-1962 in place of a manager] was a harebrained idea. But the Cubs were awful in those days. At least he had the guts to try something."

Calvin Amandus Neeman
Born Feb. 18, 1929, in Valmeyer, Ill.
6' 1", 192 lbs.; B-right, T-right

Year	Team	G	AB	R	H	D	T	HR	RBI	Ave.
1957	Chi (N)	122	415	37	107	17	1	10	39	.258
1958	Chi	76	201	30	52	7	0	12	29	.259
1959	Chi	44	105	7	17	2	0	3	9	.162
1960	Chi-Phil	68	173	13	31	7	2	4	13	.179
1961	Phil	19	31	0	7	1	0	0	2	.226
1962	Pitt	24	50	5	9	1	1	1	5	.180
1963	Cleve-Wash	23	27	1	1	0	0	0	0	.037
7 years		376	1002	93	224	35	4	30	97	.224

Transactions:

May 13, 1960: Traded with second baseman Tony Taylor to Philadelphia for first baseman Ed Bouchee and pitcher Don Cardwell.

JOHN BUZHARDT
Cubs Pitcher, 1958–1959

*"We'd make a pretty good run through the middle
of the season, but after that, we fell apart."*

PROSPERITY, S.C.— John Buzhardt was on his way out the door to eat dinner with Billy O'Dell, the left-hander who helped the Giants to the World Series in 1962.

"Billy shot some quail and pheasant and we're going to go over and help him eat it," said Buzhardt, 62, who broke in with the Cubs, then won fame with Philadelphia when he won games on each end of the Phillies' 23-game losing streak in 1961, then helped the White Sox become a pennant contender between 1962 and 1967.

"Everybody remembers Bobby Thomson's home run in 1951 that won the pennant for the Giants. Let me tell you about the Bobby Thomson home run that I remember," said Buzhardt — and I knew that O'Dell and his quail feast were going to have to wait. It was time for some old-time baseball talk.

"I'll always be indebted to Bob Scheffing because he's the man who brought me to the major leagues," he said, referring to his manager with the Cubs in 1958 and 1959.

"I had been pitching in Portland and joined the club in September. Scheffing had me pitch in relief in St. Louis and I got a couple of guys out. Then in another game, in Pittsburgh, he put me in a game in one of those right-handed, left-handed deals and I did okay.

"Then the club went to Philadelphia and I pitched to one batter and got him to hit into a double play. We scored some more runs and I got the win in that one, my first major league win," said Buzhardt.

"We came back to Chicago and Scheffing came up to me and said, 'John, you've done pretty well — I think I'm going to start you against the Dodgers.' So there I was in Wrigley Field. There was a big crowd and I was really nervous, but I did pitch pretty well.

"I had a shutout going into the ninth inning and Don Demeter hit a two-run homer off me to tie the game. In the bottom of the ninth, Bobby Thomson [now a Cub] hit a home run to win the game. That's the Bobby Thomson home run that I'll never forget," he said.

Buzhardt said the following week the Cubs went to the West Coast and Scheffing started him once again against the Dodgers.

John Buzhardt has fond memories of a Bobby Thomson home run — but it isn't the famous one.

"We played the Dodgers in the coliseum and I beat Sandy Koufax 2–1. But what I really remember about that game is that I got a single off Koufax — a line drive single to right for my first major league hit," said Buzhardt.

He finished the year with a 3-0 record for a team that finished seventh in an eight-team league with a 72-82 record. The following year, Buzhardt appeared in 31 games, starting 10 of them, and ended the year with a 4-5 record for a team that was 74-80, finishing seventh again.

Between the 1959 and 1960 seasons, both Scheffing and Buzhardt left the Cubs. Scheffing was fired. On January 11, 1960, Buzhardt was traded with veteran infielder Alvin Dark and a youngster named Jim Woods to the Philadelphia Phillies for outfielder Richie Ashburn, a future Hall of Famer but a player in the waning years of his career.

"Chicago had great fans — on both sides of the city," said Buzhardt. "No matter what you did, they always seemed to be rooting for you and they were really supportive. In Philadelphia, the fans could be cruel. They treated me okay. I lost 16 games my first year there and 18 my next year there but they always called me 'Hard Luck John' and stuck with me.

"It wasn't that way with all the players. There was Pancho Herrera — that poor boy. He came up from the minors and led the league in strikeouts. He was in trouble all year long with the fans, every time he came up. They really gave it to him," said Buzhardt.

(Herrera, a first baseman, struck out 136 times to lead the league in 1961, his first full year in the major leagues. He hit .281 and was a contender for Rookie of the Year. But he was booed unmercifully by Phillie fans. His next year, his batting average went down to .258 and he struck out 120 times, again incurring the fans' wrath. He never played major league baseball again.)

Buzhardt said he can't think of any one thing that has prolonged the Cubs' pennant drought. "There's nothing you can really put your finger on. When I was there, we had a good young pitching staff with Glen Hobbie, Moe Drabowsky, Don Elston. We'd make a pretty good run through the middle of the season, but after that we fell apart," he said.

In the two years he played for the Cubs, he said he never met Phil Wrigley, the club's owner.

"He was pretty far removed. When I was at Philadelphia, Bob Carpenter wasn't around much either. The only owner I got to know was Arthur Allyn, who owned the Chicago White Sox when I was there. He would travel with us once in a while and would come in the clubhouse.

"That was all right. The players all knew him. It didn't matter to me one way or another. I guess it didn't bother me if the owners weren't around. Look what can happen. Look at George Steinbrenner and the Yankees. He's around too much. The people you need to get to know are your managers and coaches," said Buzhardt.

In Philadelphia, he got to know his manager, Gene Mauch, very well. He said Mauch had a standing offer to pitchers. Anyone who went into the seventh inning of a ballgame with a one-run lead and got the side out, three-up, three-down for the next three innings would get a new suit, courtesy of Mauch.

Buzhardt accomplished the mission on July 28, 1961, beating the Giants 4–3. The Phillies lost the next game, and the game after that and the game after that. In fact, they didn't win again until August 20 — and Buzhardt was the winning pitcher. In between, they lost 23 straight — still a major league record. And Buzhardt is still waiting for his suit.

After the 1961 season, he was traded to the Chicago White Sox with infielder Charley Smith for aging slugger Roy Sievers. Buzhardt posted a mediocre 8-12 record in 1962 and then put together some fine seasons. He was 9-4 in 1963, 10-8 in 1964 and 13-8 in 1965. (Smith would be in the headlines years later for another trade. As a member of the St. Louis Cardinals, he was traded to the New York Yankees for home run king Roger Maris.)

Buzhardt said he had mixed emotions about leaving the Phillies, even though they were a bad ballclub. He had suffered through two miserable seasons (5-16 in 1960, 6-18 in 1961) and just about the time their young players — Herrera, Don Demeter, Don Money and others — were maturing, he was gone to Chicago.

In 1964, the White Sox got hooked up in a classic pennant race with the New York Yankees. In August, the Bronx Bombers came into Comiskey Park and lost every game of a four-game series to Chicago, including a Sunday doubleheader on August 20 in which Buzhardt beat them in the second game.

The series drew headlines across the country because of an incident after the game. Yankees infielder Phil Linz was scolded by manager Yogi Berra for playing a harmonica on the team bus going to the airport for the flight back to New York.

The Yankees put it all together after that series — and after that incident — and went on to win the pennant. But Buzhardt ranks his 4–0 shutout of them on August 20, particularly considering the importance of it in the pennant race, as one of the best games of his career.

In that same season in the National League, the Phillies, led by the young stars that Buzhardt knew would develop, sailed into the last two weeks of the season with a 6½ game lead. They proceeded to lose 11 of their next 12 and relinquished the championship to the St. Louis Cardinals.

Looking back on that 34 years later, Buzhardt thinks that what the Phillies needed down the stretch was one more reliable pitcher — perhaps the one they let go of in the Sievers trade three years earlier.

John William Buzhardt
Born Aug. 15, 1936, in Prosperity, S.C.
6' 2", 195 lbs.; B-right, T-right

Year	Team	W-L	Pct.	ERA	G	IP	H	BB	SO
1958	Chi (N)	3-0	1.000	1.85	6	24.1	16	7	9
1959	Chi	4-5	.444	4.97	31	101.1	107	29	33
1960	Phil	5-16	.238	3.86	30	200.1	198	68	73
1961	Phil	6-18	.250	4.49	41	202.1	200	65	92
1962	Chi (A)	8-12	.400	4.19	28	152.1	156	59	64
1963	Chi	9-4	.692	2.42	19	126.1	100	31	59
1964	Chi	10-8	.556	2.98	31	160	150	35	97
1965	Chi	13-8	.619	3.01	32	188.2	167	56	108
1966	Chi	6-11	.353	3.83	33	150.1	144	30	66
1967	Chi-Bal-Hou	3-10	.231	4.01	36	101	114	42	40
1968	Hous	4-4	.500	3.12	39	83.2	73	35	37
11 years		71-96	.425	3.66	326	1490.2	1425	457	678

Transactions:

Jan. 11, 1960: Traded with infielder Alvin Dark and outfielder Jim Woods to Philadelphia for outfielder Richie Ashburn.

Nov. 28, 1963: Traded with infielder Charlie Smith to Chicago White Sox for outfielder Roy Sievers.

Aug. 21, 1967: Sold to Baltimore Orioles.

Sept. 23, 1967: Sold to Houston Astros.

DICK ELLSWORTH
Cubs Pitcher, 1958, 1960–1966

"A winning attitude has to start at the top, and it just didn't with the Cubs back in those days."

FRESNO, Calif.— Dick Ellsworth's journey to the major leagues was quick. He graduated from high school in California on a Wednesday night, had about a dozen major league scouts at his house Thursday, signed with the Cubs on Friday, flew to Chicago with Ray Hayworth, head of the Cubs scouting system on Saturday, sat in uniform with the club in the dugout at Wrigley Field on Sunday, and was the starting pitcher in an exhibition game against the White Sox on Monday night. He threw a shutout.

It was an incredible week for an 18-year-old kid, but Ellsworth, now 59 and a senior partner in a real estate brokerage firm in Fresno, says his high school career helped prepare him for it.

"I was fortunate in that for three years in high school, I played for teams that dominated and we got a lot of media attention," he said.

And no wonder. Two other future major league players, Pat Corrales and Jim Maloney, were teammates. Corrales caught for nine years with the Phillies, St. Louis, Cincinnati and San Diego and later managed. Maloney, who was a shortstop on his high school team, won 136 games pitching mostly for the Cincinnati Reds and threw two no-hitters.

Ellsworth, Corrales and Maloney formed the nucleus of a high school team that won nearly 100 games in three years.

"We got a lot of media attention and there were always lots of scouts at our games. So I was comfortable talking with sportswriters and with getting a lot of attention," said Ellsworth. "Of course, it was nothing of the magnitude of Wrigley Field."

With his father's guidance, Ellsworth signed with the Cubs for $7,500, plus a bonus and the promise that he would go to spring training with the club in 1959. Then he had the spectacular week that culminated with his shutout of the White Sox.

On June 22, 1958, Ellsworth, just a few weeks out of high school, made his major league debut in Cincinnati. He got roughed up a little, allowing four hits and three walks in 2⅓ innings. Manager Bob Scheffing, hoping the youngster's confidence would not be shaken, came out and got him. Glen Hobbie relieved — and gave up a grand slam home run to the first batter, Gus Bell. That was Ellsworth's only appearance in 1958 — so his totals showed a record of no wins and one loss and an earned run average of 15.45. It was a rude introduction to the major leagues.

As promised, he went to spring training with the Cubs in 1959 but spent the year at their farm club in Fort Worth. In 1960, he came up with the Cubs in May. Ron Santo joined the club in June. The two men roomed together for four years as both developed into solid performers on lackluster Cubs teams. Ellsworth won 7 and lost 13 in 1960.

In 1961, the Cubs instituted their college of coaches, a rotating system of several coaches that produced a rotating "head coach" rather than a manager for the ballclub for the next two years.

"There was no leadership. It was tough on everybody," said Ellsworth. "For the life of me, I don't know why we did it. We were the laughingstock of baseball. I think it was the brainchild of Bob Whitlow, a retired Air Force guy who the Cubs hired as a consultant.

"With all due respect to the coaches, that's what they were. None had the qualities to be the manager of a team or they would have been managing somewhere. And the lack of leadership was reflected in how we did on the field," said Ellsworth. (The Cubs were 64-90, good for seventh place in an eight-team league in 1961, and 59-103, a ninth place finish in a 10-team league in 1962. Only the Mets, in their inaugural year, finished lower.)

The experiment with the coaches was symptomatic of a problem the Cubs experienced over the years that Ellsworth thinks kept them from being a contender — the lack of baseball expertise and the lack of the will to win in the front office.

"As gracious a man as Mr. [Philip] Wrigley was, the Chicago Cubs were not important to him," said Ellsworth. (Wrigley, head of the chewing gum company, had inherited the ballclub from his father, who had wheeled and dealed to start a legacy that came up with five pennant winners between 1929 and 1945.)

"There was no sense of Cubs pride to inspire you. Mr. Wrigley really didn't care whether we won or lost. As I look back now, having been away from the game for many years, I think of Walter O'Malley who owned the Dodgers. The Dodgers were his team. The Dodgers were his life. And I think of Horace Stoneham and the Giants. The Giants were his team. The Giants were his life.

"They hired the best possible people they could find to run their organizations, to build and develop their ballclubs and keep them competitive. That simply was not demonstrated in the Cubs organization," he said.

He pointed to what's happened since the Wrigley family sold the ballclub to the Chicago Tribune Company in 1981 — no pennants but three trips to playoffs.

"The difference now is that someone's holding them accountable," said Ellsworth.

He was 10-11 in 1961 but fell to 9-22 in 1962. He said he felt that the rotating coaching system robbed him of leadership he needed at a critical time in his development, at the ages of 21 and 22.

"We didn't have a winning attitude. We didn't feel like we had to win to uphold a tradition," said Ellsworth. It wasn't like having the responsibility to maintain the reputation of 'Dodger blue' or the 'Yankee pinstripes,'" he said.

"Veteran ballplayers joined the team like Bob Buhl from the Braves and Larry Jackson from the Cardinals and Richie Ashburn from the Phillies. They brought with them an attitude that was different than the attitude of the guys brought up in the Cubs organization. Bob Buhl was a great influence on me — and still is to this day.

"A winning attitude has to start at the top, and it just didn't with the Cubs back in those days," said Ellsworth.

In 1963, the rotating coaching system was trashed. Bob Kennedy took over as manager and led the club to an 82-80 record — its first winning record since the pennant winning year of 1945.

Ellsworth responded to the leadership he so sorely missed the previous two seasons by posting a 22-10 record and a 2.11 earned run average. The change to a full-time manager helped. So did the addition of a slider to his pitching repertoire.

In 1964, Ellsworth was involved in a game in which something happened for only the second time in the century. On September 13, he was the starter and loser in a game at Wrigley Field in which the St. Louis Cardinals scored in every inning to beat the Cubs 15–2. The Cardinals were in the process of mounting a charge in which they overtook the Phillies and won the National League pennant in the last weekend of the season. (On May 5, 1999, the Cubs were victimized again when Colorado scored in every inning in a 13–6 win at Wrigley Field.)

In 1965, Ellsworth pitched a game that epitomized the fate of the Cubs of that era. In a game against the Los Angeles Dodgers, he took a no-hitter into the ninth inning, nursing a 1–0 lead. He got the first two batters out. Then second baseman Glenn Beckert booted a ball for an error. The next batter walked. The next hitter smashed a three-run homer.

Ellsworth had thrown a one-hitter and lost the game, 3–1, losing the no-hitter with two outs in the ninth.

"Who hit the homer?" he was asked 36 years later.

The answer came quickly from his lips: "Al Ferrara." It was the only home run Ferrara hit all year.

Ellsworth spent two more years with the Cubs and then was traded to the Philadelphia Phillies on December 11, 1966, for pitcher Ray Culp. He appeared in 32 games, starting 21 of them, and finished with a 6-7 record in a season that was a nightmare for him.

"At the end of the year I went to Gene Mauch, the manager, and said, 'If you think I have any value for a ballclub, sell me or trade me.' Because I did not want to play for him any more. I had no respect for him.

"I didn't enjoy playing for him. Frankly, I don't know anybody who did. It was no fun playing for him. He was always on everybody," said Ellsworth.

He got his wish. On December 15, 1967, less than three months after his conversation with Mauch, Ellsworth was traded with catcher Gene Oliver to the Boston Red Sox for catcher Mike Ryan. It gave him a chance to play for a man he did respect, Dick Williams.

"I thoroughly enjoyed playing for Dick Williams," he said. "You always knew exactly where you stood and exactly what to expect. You knew what he expected from you. It was fun because it was structured. The Red Sox were serious about winning baseball games." They also had an owner, Tom Yawkey, who possessed the same dedication to the game as Ellsworth admired in O'Malley and Stoneham in the National League.

Ellsworth responded with a 16-7 record, his best season since the 22-10 year in 1963. Ironically, Culp, who had gone to the Cubs in the deal that sent Ellsworth to Philadelphia, was a teammate of Ellsworth's with Boston. He too won 16 games. But Jim Lonborg, the Cy Young Award winner with the Red Sox pennant winner a year earlier, slipped to 6-10 and Boston slipped to fourth place.

On April 19, 1969, the Red Sox traded Ellsworth, pitcher Juan Pizarro and slugger Ken Harrelson to Cleveland for pitchers Sonny Siebert and Vicente Romo and catcher Joe Azcue. In August of 1970, the Indians sold him to the Milwaukee Brewers where he retired a year later.

He was with the Indians on June 21, 1970, when Cesar Gutierrez set a major league record by getting seven straight hits in a game against Cleveland. Detroit beat the Indians 9–8 in 12 innings. Ellsworth pitched two innings in relief, got nicked for one of the Gutierrez hits, but did not allow a run.

(Gutierrez finished his four-year career the following year with the Tigers by getting seven hits — the same number he got in the one game in 1971.) Ellsworth's been a commercial real estate broker in Fresno ever since he retired. "I had a job waiting for me when I left baseball," said Ellsworth — the man who had a job waiting for him when he left high school, too.

Richard Clark Ellsworth
Born March 22, 1940, in Lusk, Wyo.
6' 3", 180 lbs.; B-left, T-left

Year	Team	W-L	Pct.	ERA	G	IP	H	BB	SO
1958	Chi (N)	0-1	.000	15.43	1	2.1	4	3	0
1960	Chi	7-13	.350	3.72	31	176.2	170	72	94
1961	Chi	10-11	.476	3.86	37	186.2	213	48	91
1962	Chi	9-20	.310	5.09	37	208.2	241	77	113

Year	Team	W-L	Pct.	ERA	G	IP	H	BB	SO
1963	Chi	22-10	.688	2.11	37	290.2	223	75	185
1964	Chi	14-18	.438	3.75	37	256.2	267	71	148
1965	Chi	14-15	.483	3.81	36	221.1	227	57	130
1966	Chi	8-22	.267	3.98	38	269.1	321	51	144
1967	Phil	6-7	.462	4.38	32	125.1	152	36	45
1968	Bos	16-7	.696	3.03	31	196	196	37	106
1969	Bos-Cleve	6-9	.400	4.10	36	147	178	44	52
1970	Cleve-Mil	3-3	.500	3.79	43	59.1	60	17	22
1971	Mil	0-1	.000	4.80	11	15	22	7	10
13 years		115-137	.456	3.72	407	2156	2274	595	1140

Transactions:

Dec. 7, 1966: Traded to Philadelphia for pitcher Ray Culp and cash.

Dec. 15, 1967: Traded with catcher Gene Oliver to Boston for catcher Mike Ryan.

April 19, 1968: Traded with pitcher Juan Pizarro and first baseman Ken Harrelson to Cleveland for pitchers Sonny Siebert and Vicente Romo and catcher Joe Azcue.

Aug. 7, 1970: Sold to Milwaukee Brewers.

ALVIN DARK
Cubs Third Baseman, 1959–1960

"It's pitching. It was then. It is now. You've got to have it."

EASLEY, S.C. — Alvin Dark played 14 years in the major leagues, had a .289 lifetime batting average, had 2,089 hits and played on three pennant winners. He managed in the major leagues for 13 years and had two pennant winners, one in each league.

He hasn't seen it all — but he's seen most of it. In 1959 and 1960, toward the end of his playing career, he was the third baseman for the Cubs on teams that weren't very good. "I don't blame Mr. Wrigley," said Dark, who is now 77 and out of the game for good. "He was a wonderful man — not a baseball man, but a gracious man. The fault lies with the front office men. They didn't get the job done. Look at all the managers the Cubs have had over the years.

"You've got to trust your manager and you've got to let him run the ballclub. You cannot run the Cubs from some office in downtown Chicago," said Dark, who has the distinction as a manager of being eventually fired by five different teams — the Giants, the Padres, the Indians and the A's twice, once in Kansas City and once in Oakland. Leaving no doubt about his feelings on that subject, he titled his 1980 autobiography *When in Doubt, Fire the Manager.* But he also has the distinction of being one of four managers to win pennants in both leagues — Joe McCarthy, Yogi Berra and Sparky Anderson are the others — and the first to manage All-Star teams in both leagues.

Dark was a three-sport athlete at Louisiana State University who was drafted by the Philadelphia Eagles but chose baseball for his career. He broke in with the Boston Braves, getting into 15 games in 1947. In 1948, he was the Rookie of the Year, hitting .322 for a Braves team that won the National League championship on a slogan of "Spahn and Sain and pray for rain." Warren Spahn and Johnny Sain were mainstays of a pitching staff that also got big contributions from Nelson Potter, Bill Voiselle and Vern Bickford.

On December 14, 1949, he was traded with fellow infielder Eddie Stanky to the New York Giants for Sid Gordon, Buddy Kerr, Willard Marshall and Red Webb. Nearly two years later, on October 3, 1951, Dark was a part of a Giant rally that led to one of the most famous home runs in baseball history — Bobby Thomson's "shot heard 'round the world."

It was the third and final game of a playoff series between the Giants and the Dodgers to decide the National League pennant. The teams split the first two games. The Dodgers took a 4–1 lead into the ninth inning of the third game.

Dark led off the inning with a base hit. Don Mueller followed with a single. Then Whitey Lockman hit a double, driving in Dark, but Mueller hesitated until he was sure the ball wouldn't be caught. He went from first to third on the double but broke his ankle sliding in and had to be carried off the field on a stretcher. Then Thomson hit the home run off of Ralph Branca to give the Giants the pennant.

"I'll tell you something really strange about that," said Dark. "I played for the Giants six years and played in that ballpark for many other years and that's the only ball I ever saw hit into the lower deck in left field.

"In the old Polo Grounds, the upper deck hung out over the lower deck by quite a few feet and was pretty low. So home runs hit to left field always went into the upper deck. I saw quite a few times when a ball was hit deep and the left fielder would go back and get in position to catch it — and the ball would go in the upper deck above him.

Alvin Dark said pitching was the Cubs' problem 40 years ago when he played for them — and still is today.

"Line drives to left field were generally caught or were too low to go into the lower deck. So when Thomson hit the ball that day, we're all thinking 'double, double' so we can get those two runs home to tie the game. Of course when it went out, we were all hoopin' and hollerin'. But up 'til then, I had never seen a homer into the lower deck in left field and I never saw one after that, either," said Dark.

On September 30, 1954, Dark was playing shortstop for the Giants in the first game of the World Series against the Cleveland Indians. It was in that game that Willie Mays made his famous over-the-shoulder basket catch off the bat of Vic Wertz that has been seen by millions of people on baseball highlight films.

Dark remembers something else. "I hit a line drive off of Bob Lemon in that game that the center fielder, Larry Doby, ran over for and caught in left center field just below where the upper deck hung down. He told me later I missed it by just a couple of feet. But if he hadn't caught the ball, that might have been another homer into the lower deck," he said.

Dark was involved in some celebrated trades during his career. He says trades are like billboards, telling players exactly what they're worth. He and Stanky were traded for four players in 1950. Then on June 14, 1956, Dark and catcher Ray Katt, pitcher Don Liddle and first baseman Whitey Lockman were traded to the St. Louis Cardinals for outfielder Jackie Brandt, infielder Red Schoendienst, outfielder Bobby Stephenson, pitcher Dick Littlefield and catcher Bill Sarni — lots of players but a fairly even swap.

On May 20, 1958, the Cardinals traded Dark to the Cubs for pitcher and future author Jim Brosnan — again, an even trade, one player for another player straight up. But on January 11, 1960, Dark was traded along with pitcher John Buzhardt and Jim Woods to the Philadelphia Phillies for outfielder Richie Ashburn. "When three players are traded for one, and you're one of the three, it definitely tells you what side of the hill you're on," said Dark.

He began his managerial career with the Giants in 1961—and that was the result of a trade, too. The Giants wanted Dark as their manager. He was playing for the Milwaukee Braves, the same franchise he started with, but now in a different city. The Giants traded shortstop Andre Rodgers to Milwaukee for Dark and soon named Dark as their manager.

He remained there four years, winning the pennant in 1962. He managed the Kansas City A's in 1966 and 1967, then took over the Cleveland Indians and led them to an over .500 record (rare in those days) of 86-75 and stayed with the Indians through 1971. He had his second World Series championship team at Oakland in 1974, took the A's to the League Championship Series in 1975 and had his last managerial stint with San Diego in 1977.

It was while managing the Giants in 1962 that Dark was witness to yet another great moment in championship play, this one in the seventh game of the World Series against the New York Yankees. In the bottom of the ninth inning, the Giants were losing 1–0 but had runners on second and third with two out. The runner on second was Willie Mays. Willie McCovey hit a screaming line drive that Yankees second baseman Bobby Richardson reached up for and speared to end the game.

Had the ball been hit a foot to the left or right of Richardson, it would have gone through and the Giants probably would have won the game and the World Series. Instead, they lost a heartbreaker.

Stu Miller, a Giant reliever in the bullpen that day, said if the ball had gone through, it might have set up one of the greatest plays at the plate in World Series history because Roger Maris would have been trying to gun down Mays.

"I would have bet my money on Mays," said Dark, 37 years later. "I wouldn't bet against Willie in a situation like that."

Dark was also involved in one of baseball's strangest incidents — two balls being in play at the same time. It was June 30, 1959, in Wrigley Field. Dark was playing third base for the Cubs in a game against the Cardinals. Stan Musial, the batter, took a pitch for ball four that got by catcher Sammy Taylor and rolled behind him. Taylor argued with plate umpire Vic Delmore, claiming the ball nicked Musial's bat.

Here's Dark's account of what happened next. "When the ball got by the catcher, I took off after it. I didn't know whether it hit the bat or not. It didn't matter. My job was to get that ball. It rolled back to the bench where Pat Pieper (the Cubs public address announcer) used to sit. Pat picked up the ball and I yelled at him 'drop it, drop it' and he did. While this is going on, Musial is trotting down to first base and the first base coach starts waving his arms in a whirlwind, motioning for Stan to go to second.

"I see Musial heading for second so I throw the ball to Ernie Banks, our shortstop, who is covering second. About that time, Delmore puts a new ball in play and gives it to Taylor. He sees Musial heading for second and throws the ball to Banks but the ball gets by Banks and goes into center field. Musial takes off for third and is tagged out by Banks who has the ball I threw to him. It was a mess and I really felt sorry for Vic Delmore.

[Bill Jackowski, second base umpire, ruled Musial was out because he was tagged with the ball that should have been in play. Jackowski, recalling the game in a 1994 interview, told the same story as Dark except Jackowski thought the errant throw came from Cubs pitcher Bob Anderson, who had gotten the new ball from Taylor and tried to throw Musial out.]

"I don't remember everything about it but I do remember everyone laughed at Vic Delmore. That play ruined him, and he was a great fellow and a good umpire. But he was out of the league at the end of the year and dead a year later, of a heart attack, I think," said Dark. (Delmore died June 10, 1960, at his home in Scranton, Pennsylvania.)

"If an umpire will bear down and not act like he wrote the book on the game, people will respect him. Delmore was like that. Back in those days, there were a lot of former major league players who were umpires — Babe Pinelli, Jocko Conlon, Lon Warneke. They knew the game and they knew the players.

"Beans Reardon was a good umpire. I remember one game where he was behind the plate on a day when it seemed like it was 110 degrees in the sun. Anyway, he calls a strike on one of our guys and Leo Durocher, our manager, comes out arguing. Back in those days, you could argue ball and strike counts. Anyway, Leo's arguing and he starts cussing. And Beans says to him, 'You can cuss all you want, Leo, I'm not throwing you out of the game. If I have to stay out here in this heat, so do you.' Beans Reardon — boy, he was a good umpire," said Dark.

Dark was a versatile fielder who played 1,404 games at shortstop, 320 at third base, 29 at second base, 15 at first base and 43 in the outfield during his career — and one as a pitcher.

"It was the last game of the 1953 season and we were out of it and Leo says to me, 'Hey, you wanna pitch today?'" and I said 'Sure.' Well I pitched one inning," said Dark. "I think I walked a guy and then Frank Thomas hit a home run off me. Even to this day, when I see him at card shows, he comes up to me and says, 'Hey, cuz.' And my lifetime earned run average is 18.00," said Dark.

His tone turns serious when he talks about the Cubs and the problem they've had winning a pennant. "I can tell you what the problem was — and still is. It's pitching," he said. "Here's the deal. The way you win baseball games is with your pitching. Oh, sure everything else has to be in balance. You have to have hitting and defense, but you aren't going to win it without pitching.

"Look at the Cincinnati Reds. Look at all the power they had for all of those years in the 1950s — Gus Bell, Wally Post, Ted Kluszewski, Frank Robinson. And they didn't win it. Then they won it in 1961. Why? Fantastic pitching.

"In 1947, the Giants hit 221 home runs and set a National League record. But they only had one pitcher — Larry Jansen. Oh, sure they had other good guys on their staff but they only had one real standout pitcher, so even with their 221 home runs, they didn't win it.

"Now look at the Cubs over the years. What's the problem? Pitching. It was then. It is now. For one thing, a lot of pitchers don't want to pitch for that organization. Look at the ballpark. When the wind's blowing out, nobody can pitch there. I remember in 1956 and 1957, they had some guys who could throw hard — Moe Drabowsky, Dick Drott, Glen Hobbie — but they couldn't win in Wrigley Field."

(Drabowsky won 13 as a Cubs rookie in 1957, then saw his victory totals dwindle to 9, 5 and 3. He was traded to the Milwaukee Braves in 1961, then played for Kansas City before experiencing a rebirth as a relief pitcher for the Baltimore Orioles. He was 6-0 for the Orioles in 1966 and was one the World Series stars that year. Drott won 15 for the Cubs as a rookie in 1957, then saw his win totals drop to 7, 1, 0 and 1 in the next four years. He spent two years with Houston where he won a total of 3 games and retired after the 1963 season with 27 wins in seven years. Hobbie got into one game in 1957 then won 10 in 1958, 16 in 1959 and 16 in 1960 — when he lost 20. He never won more than 7 after that and was out of baseball four years later.)

"Most teams have 10 or 12 young pitching prospects developing in the minor leagues. I can't ever remember the Cubs having that many. They just can't get good pitchers to sign, and when they do, they usually don't do well in Wrigley Field," said Dark.

"Something else is wrong with the Cubs, too. They've never put as much emphasis on the manager as they should. Like I said, you can't run the team from downtown Chicago. The manager has to run the club. He knows the players. He knows who's ready and who's not and why not. You've got to get the club into a rhythm and that's the manager's job. That's why that rotating coaching system they had in '61 and '62 didn't work. You can't get anybody in synch, doing things that way. Look how many managers they've had over the years."

(Since 1945, the Cubs have had 27 managers and three interim managers, including two years of the rotating coaches when a total of five men handled the duties.)

Dark was hesitant to talk about his best game as a major league player. "My Daddy used to tell me never to pop off, that if you had to pop off about what you had done, you hadn't done much. Let others do the popping off, he'd say.

"Now as for the best team I ever played on, that would have to be the '54 Giants, the team that beat the Indians four straight in the World Series after Cleveland won 111 games during the regular season."

Just the thought of the 1954 Giant club set in motion some more talk about the importance of pitching. "Sure, that team had Mays and Mueller, one of the best contact hitters I've ever seen. But look at that pitching staff. We had Johnny Antonelli and Sal Maglie and Jansen and Jim Hearn — and Marv Grissom and Hoyt Wilhelm in the bullpen. That's how we won it.

"And that '62 team with the Giants [when Dark was manager] with Mays, Willie McCovey and Orlando Cepeda. But look at the pitching: Billy Pierce, Billy O'Dell, Jack Sanford, Juan Marichal — and Stu Miller in the bullpen, the best relief pitcher of his day, bar none. My Oakland team in 1974 had Catfish Hunter, Vida Blue, Blue Moon Odom, Ken Holtzman, and Rollie Fingers in the bullpen.

"Those are Hall of Fame pitching staffs. Not everybody on those staffs will be in the Hall of Fame, but those are Hall of Fame staffs, wouldn't you agree?" asked Dark.

And that, he said, is what the Cubs have been lacking for lo these many years.

Alvin Ralph Dark
Born Jan. 7, 1922, in Comanche, Okla.
5' 11", 185 lbs.; B-right, T-right

Year	Team	G	AB	R	H	D	T	HR	RBI	Ave.
1946	Bos (N)	15	13	0	3	3	0	0	1	.231
1948	Bos	137	543	85	175	39	6	3	48	.322
1949	Bos	130	529	74	146	23	5	3	53	.276

Year	Team	G	AB	R	H	D	T	HR	RBI	Ave.
1950	NY	154	587	79	164	36	5	16	67	.279
1951	NY	156	646	114	196	41	7	14	69	.303
1952	NY	151	589	92	177	29	3	14	73	.301
1953	NY	155	647	126	194	41	6	23	88	.300
1954	NY	154	644	98	189	26	6	20	70	.293
1955	NY	115	475	77	134	20	3	9	45	.282
1956	NY-StL	148	619	73	170	26	7	6	54	.275
1957	StL	140	583	80	169	25	8	4	64	.290
1958	StL-Chi	132	528	61	156	16	4	4	48	.295
1959	Chi	136	477	60	126	22	9	6	45	.264
1960	Phil-Mil	105	339	45	90	11	3	4	32	.265
14 years		1828	7219	1064	2089	358	72	126	757	.289

Transactions:

Dec. 14, 1949: Traded with infielder Eddie Stanky to New York Giants for outfielder Sid Gordon, infielder Buddy Kerr, outfielder Willard Marshall and pitcher Red Webb.

June 14, 1956: Traded with catcher Ray Katt, pitcher Don Liddle and first baseman Whitey Lockman to St. Louis Cardinals for outfielder Jackie Brandt, infielder Red Schoendienst, outfielder Bobby Stephenson, pitcher Dick Littlefield and catcher Bill Sarni.

May 20, 1958: Traded to Chicago Cubs for pitcher Jim Brosnan.

Jan. 11, 1960: Traded with pitcher John Buzhardt and infielder Jim Woods to Philadelphia Phillies for outfielder Richie Ashburn.

June 23, 1960: Traded to Milwaukee Braves for infielder Joe Morgan.

Oct. 31, 1960: Traded to San Francisco for infielder Andre Rodgers. (Became manager of the Giants.)

WORLD SERIES

Year	Team	G	AB	R	H	D	T	HR	RBI	Ave.
1948	Bos (N)	6	24	2	4	1	0	0	0	.167
1951	NY (N)	6	24	5	10	3	0	1	4	.417
1954	NY (N)	4	17	2	7	0	0	0	0	.412
3 years		16	65	9	21	4	0	1	4	.323

MANAGERIAL RECORD

Year	Team	W-L	Standing
1961	SF	85-69	Third
1962	SF	103-62	First

Year	Team	W–L	Standing
1963	SF	88-74	Third
1964	SF	90-72	Fourth
1966	KC	74-86	Seventh
1967	KC	52-69	Tenth
1968	Cleve	86-75	Third
1969	Cleve	62-99	Sixth
1970	Cleve	76-86	Fifth
1971	Cleve	42-61	Sixth
1974	Oak	90-72	First
1975	Oak	98-64	First
1977	SD	48-65	Fifth
13 years		994-954	.510

LEAGUE CHAMPIONSHIP SERIES

Year	Team	W–L
1974	Oak	3-1
1975	Oak	0-3
2 years		3-4

WORLD SERIES

Year	Team	W–L
1962	SF	3-4
1974	Oak	4-1
2 years		7-5

Part III. The 1960s

Year	W-L	Pct.	Finished	Games Out	Manager
1960	60-94	.390	7th	35	Grimm/Boudreau
1961	64-90*	.416	7th	29	Himsl/Craft/Klein/Tappe
1962	59-103*	.364	9th	42.5	Tappe/Metro/Klein
1963	82-80	.506	7th	17	Kennedy
1964	76-86	.469	8th	17	Kennedy
1965	72-90	.444	8th	25	Kennedy/Klein
1966	59-103	.364	10th	36	Durocher
1967	87-74	.540	3rd	14	Durocher
1968	84-78	.519	3rd	13	Durocher
1969	92-70	.568	2nd	8	Durocher

*In 1961 and 1962, the Cubs did not have a manager. They were run by a rotating "college of coaches" instituted by Cubs owner Philip K. Wrigley.

ELVIN TAPPE

Cubs Head Coach, 1961–1962;
Cubs Catcher, 1954–1956, 1958, 1960, 1962

"Mr. Wrigley got all carried away."

Many players featured in the following pages who were with the Cubs in the early 1960s make reference to the team's "rotating coaches" system that

115

was used in 1961 and 1962. In those two seasons, the Cubs did not have a man-ager. Instead, a group of coaches rotated every few weeks, taking turns at managing the Cubs and then rotating to one of the minor league teams for a few weeks. Elvin Tappe, who was a catcher for the Cubs off and on from 1954 to 1962 and also coached in the 1960s, originated the concept. But he said owner Philip Wrigley expanded the concept far beyond what he had envi-sioned. Tappe died in October of 1998, one week before he was scheduled to be interviewed for this book. In a 1995 interview with the author, he explained his idea of rotating coaches. The full interview is included in Inside Pitch *(McFarland, 1996). In the following excerpt, Tappe explains how it was sup-posed to work.*

QUINCY, Ill. — "Why not rotate the coaches in the Cubs' minor league system so that all the young players would learn the basics the same way? That's what I asked Mr. Wrigley.

"My idea was to have a hitting instructor, a fielding instructor, a pitch-ing instructor and so on. They would rotate from one minor league team to another so all the players would have the benefit of their teaching.

"This would really help if you had a manager who had been a good pitcher in his playing days but didn't know much about hitting or a guy who was a good hitter but who didn't know how to work with pitchers.

"If you had coaches who specialized at the minor league level, then everyone would learn the relays and cutoffs and things like that the same way — the Cubs way — and they'd be much better prepared when they moved up.

"But I never intended it to be used at the big league level. Mr. Wrigley got all carried away and wanted the coaches to rotate on the Cubs, too. I said, 'All you're going to do is present an alibi for the players.' But Mr. Wrigley wanted to do it that way, and that's how it got started. Mr. Wrigley started at the top and worked his way down. That was a mistake."

Tappe said his original idea of specialized instruction in the minor leagues paid off several years later.

"Look at that 1969 team. You had Ron Santo at third. He was just a baby with the Cubs in the early 1960s. You had Don Kessinger and Glenn Beckert at short and second, both products of the system. That '69 team was a team the coaching plan developed."

The 1960 Cubs had finished seventh with a 60-94 record. The 1961 club, coached by Vedie Himsl, Harry Craft, Lou Klein and Tappe won 64 and lost 90 — almost the same record, finishing seventh again in an eight-team league. The 1962 Cubs, coached by Tappe, Klein and Charlie Metro, won 59 and lost 103, finishing ninth in a 10-team league. Only the New

York Mets, in their first season, finished lower. The Houston Colt 45s, also an expansion team in their first year, finished eighth, ahead of the Cubs. The rotating coaching system was abandoned after the 1962 season.

Rotating Coaches Record, 1961 (in order of rotation)

Vedie Himsl	5-6
Harry Craft	4-8
Vedie Himsel	5-12
Elvin Tappe	2-0
Harry Craft	3-1
Vedie Himsl	0-3
Elvin Tappe	35-43
Lou Klein	5-6
Elvin Tappe	5-11
Totals	**64-90**

Individual Coaching Records

Vedie Himsl	10-21
Harry Craft	7-9
Elvin Tappe	42-54
Lou Klein	5-6
Totals	**64-90**

Rotating Coaches Record, 1962 (in order of appearance)

Elvin Tappe	4-16
Lou Klein	12-18
Charlie Metro	43-69
Totals	**59-103**

DICK BERTELL
Cubs Catcher, 1960–1965, 1967

"While other teams were developing their minor leagues and filling weak spots in their lineups, all the Cubs did was try to get guys who could hit three-run homers."

MISSION VIEJO, Calif.— In Dick Bertell's first full season as a catcher for the Chicago Cubs, the club instituted its rotating "college of coaches" instead of having a manager.

"It was horrible," said Bertell, 63, who, as a young player, was looking for guidance and stability. "You didn't really know what kind of game you were expected to play from one week to the next.

"When you play for one manager, you learn to expect things from him and he expects things from you. There's an understanding. But you never had that with the rotating coaches," said Bertell. "Each coach had his own personality, his own way of doing things. And if you didn't fit his style, it didn't matter what you had done last week," he said.

"I remember one time we were playing in Pittsburgh and I had a real good four days against the Pirates. I was 10-for-16 or something like that with five RBIs. A new coach came along and wanted to try something different. I got benched for a week.

"And I said to myself, 'What did I do—hit myself out of the lineup?' I couldn't believe it," said Bertell.

He said the rotating coaching system is a great idea for the minor leagues. "It's a helluva system to move coaches around to teach young players specific aspects of the game. You might have a minor league manager who was a good pitcher, for example, but doesn't know diddly about being an infielder. Or you might have a catcher trying to tell you how to play the outfield.

"So, having experts move around in the minor leagues works great but it was just awful at the major league level. You can't go from having a manager who likes to bunt and hit-and-run one week to a guy who doesn't do any of that the next week. It's like a football team going from a running game to a passing game using the same players. It just doesn't work," said Bertell.

He was involved in some memorable games behind the plate for the Cubs. "You remember the real good games — and the real bad ones," he said.

"We were in LA playing the Dodgers and Dick Ellsworth had a no-hitter going into the last of the ninth inning. We got the first guy out and the next guy hit a groundball to second and (Glenn) Beckert kicked it. The next guy walked and the next guy hit a three-run homer and Ellsworth lost, 3–1, on a one-hitter.

"I went 5-for-5 against Cincinnati one time. That was probably the best hitting game I ever had. And I once threw out four Giants in a game.

"We were in Milwaukee one time and Don Cardwell was pitching for us. I was breaking in a new glove and sometimes the ball pops around in it when it's brand new. I had a ball pop out on me with a runner on third. The run scored and we lost 1–0.

"In a series against the Dodgers, I had the only items in one column of a box score two nights in a row. The first night, we had two hits and I had them both. The next night we had two errors and I had them both," said Bertell.

"On one of those errors, Maury Wills was stealing second and as the second base umpire moved in to make the call, he got in front of the play and the ball hit him. The umpire's part of the field of play so there's nothing you can do about that and it wound up being an error on me."

Bertell was part of the Iowa State University team that made it to the College World Series in 1957. A teammate was Jerry McNertney who also went on to become a major league catcher.

Bertell signed with the Cubs and played "A-ball" in Des Moines in 1957. "That was a thrill for me because that was like playing in my hometown," he said. (His college town, Ames, Iowa, is just south of Des Moines.)

In 1958, he played for Pueblo, Colorado, and then was promoted to Fort Worth, a Double-A team. The next year, he started in Fort Worth which was then a Triple-A team but he also played for Lancaster, Pennsylvania, and San Antonio. In 1960, he was a member of the Cub's Triple-A affiliate in Houston and on September 22, 1960, boarded a plane with teammate Billy Williams to join the major league team for the remainder of the season.

"I think the Cubs started to catch on in the early 1960s to what other teams had been doing for years," said Bertell. "The really good teams back then had great minor league systems and moved players up through the system to the major leagues.

"I remember talking to Jimmie Schaeffer who was a catcher and played a couple of years for the Cubs but was with the Cardinals before that. He talked about his days in the minor leagues with St. Louis. They had something like 23 minor league teams. When he first signed and was waiting to be assigned, he was something like number 970," he said.

"The Cardinals had the philosophy of 'Sign as many as you can and hope some of them make it.' And that's the way a lot of the clubs operated and they were very successful."

[Schaeffer played for the Cardinals in 1961 and 1962, joined the Cubs in 1963 and played sparingly for two years before going to the Mets. He also played for Philadelphia and Cincinnati in an eight-year, 340-game career.]

"The problem with the Cubs was Phil Wrigley," said Bertell. "He was a man who really didn't care. And he didn't give a whole bunch of thought about who was going to run his team. John Holland was our general manager. He was a nice guy but he didn't know anything. While other teams were developing their minor leagues and filling weak spots in their line-ups, all the Cubs did was try to get guys who could hit three-run homers," said Bertell.

That changed in the early 1960s, he said, when the Cubs started developing talent in their minor leagues and bringing them up to the major leagues. From that 1960 Houston Triple-A club, the Cubs brought up Bertell, Williams, Ellsworth, Ron Santo and Jim Brewer. In years to come, Ken Hubbs, Glenn Beckert and Don Kessinger would follow the same path. In 1969, the Cubs made their first legitimate run at the pennant in 24 years, with a nucleus that included Beckert, Kessinger, and Williams. (That not only proved how a good minor league system can produce good major league players, but it helped vindicate Elvin Tappe, the creator of the "rotating coaches" plan. Tappe was convinced it would help develop good big league ballplayers and thought the Cubs teams of the late 1960s were good examples.)

By 1968, Bertell had been released and was finishing out his baseball career in his wife's hometown, San Diego, which at that time was still a minor league franchise.

He had played with the Cubs for parts of six years, 1960–1965, and, ironically, had his two best years when the rotating coaches were on board, hitting .273 in 1961 and .302 in 1962.

On May 29, 1965, he was traded with Len Gabrielson to the San Francisco Giants for Harvey Kuenn, Ed Bailey and Bob Hendley. In spring training of 1966, an injury was the beginning of the end of his major league career.

"Byron Browne, a Cubbie, slid into me and tore up my knee. I spent the year at Phoenix. The next year, I was back with the Cubs. In fact, I caught Opening Day because Randy [Hundley] was hurt, but not long after that I got released and spent the rest of the season with San Diego," said Bertell.

He said Bob Kennedy, who managed the Cubs in 1963, 1964 and part of 1965 did a good job because he got the most out of his players. That may have been partly because Kennedy came along as the first full-time manager after Wrigley abandoned the rotating coaches system.

"We had struggled for so many years. In our first year with Kennedy, we went into the last weekend of the season and Kennedy told us to give it our best, that we had a chance to finish over .500 for the first time in a long time," said Bertell.

It was 1963. The Cubs finished 82-80 — their first winning season since 1946.

Bertell's return to the Cubs for that brief stint in 1967 gave him the opportunity to play for Hall of Fame manager Leo Durocher.

"What I didn't like about Durocher was that he didn't play his whole team very well. He'd have a starting eight and he'd play them every day. In the long run, that's going to kill you," said Bertell.

"Sooner or later, you're going to need those other guys and you've got to have them ready. And I didn't think Leo did that very well."

In 1966, Durocher took over a Cubs team that had finished eighth the year before. Durocher made his now famous pronouncement that "this is no eighth place team" and he was right. The Cubs finished 10th in Durocher's first year.

They experienced a 28-game gain in 1967, finishing third. But statistics bear out Bertell's point about Durocher's lack of lineup changes. The Cubs platooned several right fielders that year. But the other seven starters — Hundley at catcher, Santo at third base, Kessinger at shortstop, Beckert at second base, Ernie Banks at first base, and Adolpho Phillips and Billy Williams at the other two outfield positions — played in an average of 151 games each that year. (After Bertell filled in for Hundley on Opening Day, Hundley missed only nine games the rest of the season, a remarkable achievement for a catcher — but further evidence of Durocher's penchant for not giving many days off to his regulars.) Bertell said it's easy to say that the biggest difference in the game in the last 30 years is the money the players now make. "But look at the change that has taken place because of the big money. When I was playing, when most of us got through with the baseball season, we had other jobs. We had to have them to support our families.

"I worked at a post office, I worked in stores, I did all sorts of things because I had to work in the off-season. Then you'd go to spring training and get ready for the next season.

"Free agency's changed everything. When Brian Downing was with the Angels, he had a batting cage installed in his backyard. He took 500 swings during the winter. None of us could do that. We were all out working somewhere.

"Another thing players do now is watch videos of themselves. They can spend the winter studying their swing, or if they're a pitcher, their delivery, and work on it during the winter months.

"Some of these guys don't really need spring training like we did. They're in shape all year around because they don't have to work. That's the biggest difference I see in the game," said Bertell.

When he retired from baseball, he stayed in the San Diego area and went to work with Willamette Industries, a multi-million dollar paper company where he has worked for the past 27 years.

"Yep, I'm a paper salesman," said Bertell.

And it's a good bet he doesn't report to rotating coaches.

Richard George Bertell
Born Nov. 21, 1935, in Oak Park, Ill.
6', 200 lbs.; B-right, T-right

Year	Team	G	AB	R	H	D	T	HR	RBI	Ave.
1960	Chi (N)	5	15	0	2	0	0	0	1	.133
1961	Chi	92	267	20	73	7	1	2	33	.273
1962	Chi	77	215	19	65	6	2	2	30	.302
1963	Chi	100	322	15	75	7	2	2	41	.233
1964	Chi	112	353	29	84	11	3	4	67	.238
1965	Chi-SF	56	132	7	27	3	0	0	15	.205
1967	Chi (N)	2	6	1	1	0	1	0	1	.167
7 years		444	1310	91	327	34	9	10	188	.250

DON CARDWELL
Cubs Pitcher, 1960–1962

"You've got to have good pitchers if you're going to win in the major leagues, and especially in Wrigley Field."

CLEMMONS, N.C.— Don Cardwell took a break for a few minutes from selling cars at the Parkway Ford dealership to talk a little baseball.

Cardwell, 63, a major league pitcher for 14 years, spent almost three seasons with the Chicago Cubs and seven years later was on the New York "Miracle Mets" team that overtook the Cubs for the National League pennant.

"Stay close — and don't beat yourself. That's what you have to do," said Cardwell.

Two streaks in his career show what can happen when momentum is on your side, and when it isn't.

"In 1969, when the Mets won, I never gave up more than two runs in my last 14 starts and we won all 14 of them. I think I was the winning pitcher in four or five of them, but we won them all. That's what I mean when I say stay close and don't beat yourself," he said.

Don Cardwell threw a no-hitter in his first start with the Cubs. His philosophy for pitching was: "Stay close — and don't beat yourself."

He was 8-10 that year but had a 3.01 earned run average. Cardwell started 30 games and obviously came on strong during the pennant drive in going undefeated in those last 14 starts. "I was the pitcher on that team who wasn't Seaver or Koosman," he said, referring to future Hall of Famer Tom Seaver and left-hander Jerry Koosman, the aces of the staff. Seaver was 25-7 and Koosman finished 17-9. The Mets also had another up-and-comer on that staff, a young right-hander by the name of Nolan Ryan, who was 6-3.

That finish with the Mets represents one kind of momentum. He experienced the other kind on the 1961 and 1962 Cubs. "I had 11 or 12 ball-games where I left the game in the eighth or ninth inning with a two or three-run lead and didn't get the decision in any of them," he said.

Cardwell's two biggest days in baseball occurred nine years apart — one with the Mets and one with the Cubs. On October 11, 1969, he pitched a scoreless inning in the first game of the World Series in which the Mets disposed of Baltimore, four games to one. Cardwell relieved Seaver who worked the first five innings in the 4–1 loss. (The Mets won the next four games to win the Series, four games to one.)

"I warmed up in the first inning and my knees were shaking, I warmed up in the second, third, fourth and fifth innings and my knees were shak-ing and I came in in the sixth and had a pretty good inning and my knees were shaking," he said.

He had come a long way in a career that started when, at the age of 18, he reported to Pulaski, Virginia, a Class D ballclub in the Appalachian League. But Cardwell pitched well enough to be Rookie of the Year and was elevated to Schenectady, New York, in the Class C Eastern League in 1955. From there he moved up to Miami, a Triple-A club in the Interna-tional League where he worked in 1956.

The lowly Phillies called him up in 1957 and he was 4-8 in his rookie year as the Phillies finished sixth. He was 3-6 the next year, spending part of the season back in Miami, and 9-10 the year after that as the Phillies finished in the cellar both years.

During his years with the Phillies, Cardwell was a teammate of Robin Roberts, the great right-hander who spent most of his Hall of Fame career in Philadelphia. Cardwell said Roberts took time to talk with some of the young pitchers on the Phillies staff.

"He came to our motel one night and took me outside to talk to me about something he felt would help me. I'm sure he helped other young pitchers the same way," said Cardwell.

On May 13, 1960, he was traded to the Cubs with first baseman Ed Bouchee for infielder Tony Taylor and catcher Cal Neeman. "I joined the Cubs on Friday the 13th. That ought to tell you something," said Cardwell.

He didn't have to wait long to register the biggest game of his career. On May 15, 1960, two days after the trade, Cardwell accomplished a feat that has never been equaled in baseball history. He threw a no-hitter in his first start with a new ballclub, a 4–0 win over the St. Louis Cardinals in Wrigley Field.

"The last out came when Joe Cunningham hit a little looper into short left field that Moose Moryn made a great catch on," he said. "The only ball that was really hit hard was by Carl Sawatski that George Altman caught in right field. People say it was a great catch but Altman was about six-foot-five and he didn't have to jump to catch it. It's a good thing he was six-foot-five, though," said Cardwell.

Cardwell pitched well for the Cubs under trying circumstances. He was 15-14 in 1961, the first year the Cubs tried owner Phil Wrigley's rotating coaches system and then slipped to 7-16 in 1962, the second year of the college of coaches. The Cubs were 64-90 and 59-103 in those years.

"Nobody liked the system and it created some animosity," said Cardwell. "Guys who thought they were going to coach would make you promises if they made it — and they didn't keep the promises. Other guys thought they should have been coaching and they weren't. So there was friction.

"It wasn't a very good system and at the end of the 1962 season I went to Mr. Holland and had a little talk with him," he said, referring to Cubs general manager John Holland. "I told him I didn't like it. It was a system that didn't work.

"Mr. Holland told me that it was Mr. Wrigley's system. He said 'If you don't like it, I guess we'll just have to find another home for you.' And a week later, I got traded to the Cardinals."

The record verifies Cardwell's memory. On October 17, 1962, about two weeks after the end of the baseball season, he was traded with Altman and catcher Moe Thacker to the St. Louis Cardinals for pitchers Larry Jackson and Lindy McDaniel and catcher Jimmie Schaeffer.

A little more than a month later, Cardwell was on the trading block again. On November 19, the Cardinals shipped him to Pittsburgh with infielder Julio Gotay for shortstop Dick Groat and pitcher Diomedes Olivo.

"I was with the Cardinals only on paper," said Cardwell. "I didn't mind going to Pittsburgh because they needed pitching. As a pitcher, naturally you want to pitch, you want to start. Back in those days, starters were expected to finish what they started. You threw as hard as you could for as long as you could. It wasn't like it is today," he said.

He won 13 games in two out of three years with the Pirates but was destined to make another move — to the laughingstock of baseball, the lowly Mets. On December 6, 1966, Cardwell was traded with outfielder Don Bosch to the Mets in exchange for outfielder Gary Kolb and pitcher Dennis Ribant.

"When I was with the Pirates, we'd play the Mets and even if they were winning, we'd say, 'wait till the seventh or eighth inning — they'll go into their act,' and they usually did," said Cardwell.

"I remember one game where there was a play at the plate and the ball got away. Tug [McGraw], their pitcher, comes running in to cover the plate and of course the run scores. Tug swears at the guy who just scored but the ump thinks he's talking to him and throws him out of the game. So Tug, their best relief pitcher, gets tossed by a guy he wasn't even talking to. That was the Mets for you."

With the development of Seaver and Koosman and acquisition of players such as Tommie Agee and Al Weis from the White Sox, the Mets surged in 1969 but still found themselves 8½ games behind the Cubs in late August.

But they got hot at just about the time the Cubs went into a losing streak. "I remember we were in San Francisco, eating dinner at the Iron Horse restaurant. I think it was in August. I said to one of our coaches, Yogi Berra, 'You know what, we're gonna win this thing.' You could just feel it. And Yogi said, 'the fat lady hasn't sung yet.' Well, we continued to win and we caught 'em," said Cardwell.

The Mets pushed past the Cubs into first place in early September. On September 12, as people around the country were taking notice of the Mets' miracle, they swept a doubleheader with the Pirates.

"That was quite an afternoon. Koosman beat 'em 1–0 in the first game and drove in the only run. I beat 'em 1–0 in the second game and I drove in the only run," said Cardwell. It was part of the 14-game streak of Cardwell starts in which the Mets did not lose.

Another memorable game for Cardwell occurred a year earlier. On April 15, 1968, the Mets and Houston Astros locked horns in the longest scoreless tie in major league history — 23 innings. The Astros scored an unearned run in the bottom of the 24th to win it 1–0. At the time, it was the longest night game in major league history.

"I didn't pitch in that game but I did pinch hit," said Cardwell. The Mets used 22 players and had run out of pinch hitters. "It was going to either be me or McAndrew," he said, referring to Jim McAndrew, another pitcher. "But it turned out to be me. I had two good swings and then bunted a guy down to second."

Cardwell was sold to the Atlanta Braves in July of 1970 and retired at the end of that season.

As he looks back on his years with the Cubs, he said they simply didn't have the players to compete with other teams — and didn't go out and get them. "We had a lot of old players and a lot of bad players," said Cardwell. "Billy Williams and Ron Santo came up through the system but there weren't too many other good players coming up from the minors.

"Especially pitchers. You've got to have good pitchers if you're going to win in the major leagues and especially in Wrigley Field."

Cardwell finished his career with 102 wins and 138 losses, not bad considering the teams he played for finished eighth twice and seventh twice in an eight-team league; 10th once, ninth twice, eighth once and seventh once in a ten-team league; and fifth once in a six-team division.

The only teams to rise to mediocrity or above were the 1969 Mets, the 1957 Phillies who finished fifth; and the 1965 and 1966 Pirates who finished third — clubs that apparently followed the Cardwell credo:

"Stay close — and don't beat yourself."

Donald Eugene Cardwell
Born Dec. 7, 1935, in Winston-Salem, N.C.
6' 4", 210 lbs.; B-right, T-right

Year	Team	W-L	Pct.	ERA	G	IP	H	BB	SO
1957	Phil	4-8	.333	4.91	30	128.1	122	42	92
1958	Phil	3-6	.333	4.51	16	107.2	99	37	77
1959	Phil	9-10	.474	4.06	25	153	135	65	106
1960	Phil-Chi (N)	9-16	.360	4.38	36	205.1	194	79	150
1961	Chi	15-14	.517	3.82	39	259.1	243	88	156
1962	Chi	7-16	.304	4.92	41	195.2	205	60	104
1963	Pitt	13-15	.464	3.07	33	213.2	195	52	112
1964	Pitt	1-2	.333	2.79	4	19.1	15	7	10
1965	Pitt	13-10	.565	3.18	37	240.1	214	59	107
1966	Pitt	6-6	.500	4.60	32	101.2	112	27	60
1967	NY (N)	5-9	.357	3.57	26	118.1	112	39	71
1968	NY	7-13	.350	2.95	29	180	156	50	82
1969	NY	8-10	.444	3.01	30	152.1	145	47	60
1970	NY-Atl	2-3	.400	7.69	32	48	62	19	24
14 years		102-138	.425	3.92	410	2123	2009	671	1211

Transactions:

May 13, 1960: Traded with first baseman Ed Bouchee to Chicago Cubs for infielder Tony Taylor and catcher Cal Neeman.

Oct. 17, 1962: Traded with outfielder George Altman and catcher Moe Thacker to St. Louis Cardinals for pitchers Larry Jackson and Lindy McDaniel and catcher Jimmie Schaeffer.

Nov. 19, 1962: Traded with infielder Julio Gotay to Pittsburgh for infielder Dick Groat and pitcher Diomedes Olivo.

Dec. 6, 1966: Traded with outfielder Don Bosch to New York Mets for pitcher Dennis Ribant and outfielder Gary Kolb.

July 12, 1970: Sold to Atlanta.

WORLD SERIES

Year	Team	W-L	Pct.	ERA	G	IP	H	BB	SO
1969	NY (N)	0-0	.000	0.00	1	1	0	0	0

BOB BUHL
Cubs Pitcher, 1962–1966

"While other teams were developing teams through their farm systems, the Cubs were changing the director of their farm system. They just couldn't seem to get it together."

WINTER HAVEN, Fla.— Bob Buhl's debut with the Chicago Cubs in 1962 came at the end of a whirlwind 24-hour saga that started with him, as a Milwaukee Brave, having a frank conversation with his manager — and ended with him across the continent in a Cubs uniform.

Buhl was a star pitcher for the Braves from 1953 to 1962 who won 72 and lost only 35 between 1956 and 1960. But at the start of the 1962 season, he wasn't being used as much as he liked, so he did something that served him well several other times in his career. He spoke up.

"Birdie Tebbetts was my manager then at Milwaukee. We were on a flight to Philadelphia to play the Phillies when I went up and sat down next to him and said, 'Birdie, if you're not going to use me, why don't you trade me?' And he was real nice about it and he said, 'All right, son' or something like that.

"And the next day, I got traded to the Cubs. Just like that. It was that fast. So I had to catch a flight to Los Angeles where the Cubs were playing. I got there in the morning and Lou Klein, who was the head coach at the time, welcomed me and said, 'You're pitching tonight.'

"So I went out that night and pitched eight pretty good innings and had a 2–1 lead. Don Elston came in and pitched the ninth and I had my first win as a Cub," said Buhl.

Buhl was a high school standout who even as a teenager wasn't afraid to challenge a system he thought was being unfair to him. His first close encounter with the baseball establishment came shortly after he graduated from high school in Saginaw, Michigan.

"I signed while I was still in high school with Madisonville, Kentucky, in Class D. It was in the White Sox organization and I had a pretty good year," said Buhl, who is now 70 years old. "I think I won 18 and lost 8."

The year was 1946 and Buhl had attended a White Sox tryout camp in his hometown of Saginaw. He threw one inning and was offered the contract that landed him in Madisonville. The $100 a month was tough to live on, he said, but he figured after the good year he had, the White Sox would move him up and he would make substantially more.

"The next year I was moved up to Class C at Waterloo for $200 a month. For some reason or other, Johnny Mostil, the manager, didn't think much of me and I overheard him say that I would never make the majors," he said.

Buhl was convinced other players were making more than he was and that he was being treated unfairly. But he was young and inexperienced and didn't know what to do.

"About that time, I read in the newspaper about a Cleveland Indians pitcher who was signed while he was still in high school. He had been declared a free agent because of that. So I sent a telegram to Happy Chandler telling him my situation." (Chandler was the commissioner of baseball and frowned on high school students being wooed and signed by major league teams without being told all of their options.)

"He sent me back a telegram declaring me a free agent and telling me I could sign with any team besides the White Sox or the Cleveland Indians. The Indians had been accused of tampering and that's why they couldn't bid on me.

"I signed a three-year contract with the Braves and was assigned to Saginaw which was all right because it was my hometown," he said. His pay: $800 a month. Later that same day, a scout for the Detroit Tigers offered him a $50,000 bonus — but it was too late. He was a Brave.

"The next year, 1949, I went to Hartford, Connecticut, in the Eastern League and went to spring training in 1950 with the Braves Triple-A team, the Milwaukee Brewers, but was not getting much playing time," he said.

Once again, brashness played a part in moving his career along. Buhl, who admits to being confident and cocky as a youth, asked his manager, Bob Coleman, to send him somewhere where he would play. He wound up with Dallas, a Double-A team in the Texas League. It was there that he met Charlie Grimm, the former Cubs star and, until the previous year, the Cubs manager. He was later to be Buhl's first manager in the major leagues.

"Charlie was terrific. He used to say 'you got a ball, you got a bat, you got a glove — go get 'em.' And we did," he said.

Buhl had a so-so year, winning 10 and losing 14 while striking out about as many as he walked. But he showed constant improvement, so much that the Boston Braves wanted him to report to the major league team on September 1.

Buhl said by that time he had developed a tremendous loyalty to Grimm, and the Dallas ballclub was in the playoffs. He asked for and received permission to finish the year with Dallas and report to the Braves for spring training in 1951.

The result: Dallas lost in the playoffs; Buhl went home and was drafted into the Army in December. It would be 1953 — more than two years later — before he would again pitch in the big leagues. Another consequence: By turning down the chance to pitch for the Braves in September of 1950, he deprived himself of two years of pension money.

"The Braves were a real close team in those days. There weren't any loners. We played hard and we chummed around with one another after the games," said Buhl.

"I roomed with Eddie Mathews for 9½ years and we were good friends who really helped each other," he said. Buhl would tell Mathews what pitches he'd throw, if he were facing Mathews, to get him out and Mathews would talk to Buhl about what pitches he'd expect if he were hitting against him.

"I'd go out to eat all the time with Warren Spahn and Lew Burdette. Spahn was a good guy and Burdette was real character," said Buhl. "Any time one player played a practical joke on another, Burdette always got blamed for it," he said.

"Ed Bailey, the old catcher, had the best line about Burdette. He said they ought to take him, pack him up and put him in a cage and let him out on game day. We used to call him Bird Cage Burdette."

Buhl said Mathews and Henry Aaron had a friendly competition over the years, trying to outdo one another in home runs and runs batted in. It was not a bitter rivalry, he said, but one that helped each of them to strive for loftier goals. (In 1998, Mark McGwire of St. Louis and Sammy Sosa of Chicago, though not teammates, had a similar friendly rivalry that was said to have helped them both as each broke Roger Maris' single-season home run record.)

Spahn and Burdette overshadowed Buhl on the Braves pitching staff in the mid–1950s. Buhl was 13-8 in his rookie year in 1953. Spahn was 23-7. Burdette was 15-5.

On April 17, 1953, Buhl replaced Vern Bickford in the starting rotation because Bickford had a stiff neck. On a cold day in Milwaukee, Buhl beat Leo Durocher's Giants 8-1. At one point in the game, Durocher tried to rattle the rookie by having a runner on third try to steal home. Buhl saw what was happening and fired a fastball inside, backing the batter out of the way — and clearing the way for the tag of the baserunner sliding in.

In 1954, Buhl slumped to 2-7, his worst year in professional baseball. Spahn was 21-12. Burdette was 15-14. The next year, Buhl was 13-11, Spahn was 17-14 and Burdette was 13-8.

In 1956, the Braves made their first charge at a championship, losing out to Brooklyn by one game. Buhl bounced back to go 18-8, but once again, he was in the shadows of Spahn, 20-11, and Burdette, 19-10.

The Braves won their first championship in 1957 with Spahn leading the way at 21-11. Buhl had his best major league season, finishing at 18-7. Burdette was 17-9 and won three games in the World Series to lead the Braves past the Yankees. Buhl was shelled in his only World Series appearance.

"I didn't mind Spahn and Burdette getting the attention they did because we were all good friends and were part of a team. That's what made us so good," said Buhl.

The 1956 season, while one of Buhl's best, held a major disappointment for him. Grimm, who had been one of his mentors in the minors and in the major leagues, was fired early on, with the club barely over .500 at 24-22. Under new boss Fred Haney, the Braves won their next 11 games and remained hot the rest of the year, nearly catching Walter Alston's Dodgers.

After the World Series championship in 1957, the Braves started strong in 1958 but Buhl got hurt early on. He was on the disabled list for much of the season but came back strong in the stretch drive and finished with a 5-2 record.

"I wasn't used much and I didn't pitch at all in the World Series even though I was ready. I remember the guys wondering why I didn't play and I really don't have an answer for it now," he said. "The only thing I can say is that I wasn't the manager."

He had several more decent seasons with the Braves before being traded to the Cubs on April 30, 1962, for pitcher Jack Curtis. Buhl arrived in time to be part of the second year of the Cubs' bizarre rotating coaches system.

"It was weird because it seemed like each coach expected something different, wanted something different so it was kind of hard to adjust to," said Buhl. "One had one idea on how to do things and another had another idea. It was an experiment that didn't work, but I got along with them all."

He said the Cubs' two stars, future Hall of Famers Ernie Banks and Billy Williams, never said much about the coaching system and just tried to go about their business. "Everyone was unhappy but nobody complained," said Buhl.

He set a major league record that year that had nothing to do with his pitching. Buhl went to the plate 70 times without a hit. "My problem was that I couldn't hit a curve. And I don't exaggerate. *I couldn't hit a curve*," he said.

But Buhl got paid to pitch and he led the staff in wins with 12, and also in innings pitched and earned run average for a team that won 59 and lost 103.

That team featured George Altman at first base who later became one of the first American stars in Japanese baseball; Ken Hubbs at second base who won the Rookie of the Year Award and was killed two years later in a plane crash; Banks at shortstop; young up-and-comer Ron Santo at third; and Williams in the outfield.

"Lou Brock was an outfielder on that team and he hadn't blossomed yet. He wasn't hitting real well, and playing the outfield was an adventure. He was young and really just hadn't matured yet," said Buhl.

"The Cubs are famous for trading Brock to the Cardinals for Ernie Broglio," he said, referring to what many have called the worst trade in baseball history. Brock went on to get 3,000 hits, set base-stealing records, and help the Cardinals to three World Series in a 19-year career. Broglio won 10 games in the next three years for the Cubs and then was out of baseball.

"Ernie had won 20 games for the Cardinals — and the Cubs needed pitching. Brock hadn't matured yet, so it didn't look like a bad deal at the time. Ernie hurt his shoulder and was never the same after that," said Buhl.

(For the record, a few more players were involved in the Brock-Broglio deal. On June 15, 1964, Brock and pitchers Paul Toth and Jack Spring were traded to the Cardinals for Broglio, veteran pitcher Bobby Shantz and outfielder Doug Clemens.)

Buhl said one of the differences between the Braves and the Cubs — the difference between a good team and a not-so-good team — is their systems in evaluating and developing young ballplayers.

"The Cubs have a good organization. Everybody says that. They just never put it all together. I don't think playing all day games has much to do with the fact they never won the pennant. The way I look at it, you're either in shape or you're not.

"The Cubs always seemed to fold in July. I don't think it had anything to do with conditioning. You gotta have the ballplayers and the Cubs never seemed to have them. The only way you can do that is to have good scouts and good minor league players. While other teams were developing teams through their farm systems, the Cubs were changing the director of their farm system. They just couldn't seem to get it together.

"Look at the Braves today and what they've been able to develop. They brought guys up and what they didn't have in their farm system they made deals to get.

"When they first got to Atlanta, they didn't have diddly. And they were down for many years. They hired me to help out in the minors. I remember going to Bill Lucas, the farm director, in 1976, after going all over and looking at their prospects.

"He asked me what I thought, and I said 'they aren't worth a damn.' He acted kind of shocked and told me these guys were signed by Braves' scouts. And I said, 'you better go get some new scouts.' I didn't last long in that job but I wasn't wrong," said Buhl.

The formula for winning is simple, he says. If you don't have the players, you better develop them or go get them. The Braves have done that in recent years. The Cubs, for many years, lagged well behind the best teams in the league in getting the players they needed.

Buhl said all pitchers do the same thing when they arrive at Wrigley Field on game day. "You get to the park and the first thing you do is look at the flag. And no matter which way it's blowing, you say 'Oh, boy' because you know already what kind of an afternoon you're going to have," he said.

While Grimm was his favorite manager, the man who made him into a major league pitcher was his first pitching coach with the Braves, Bucky Walters. "He taught me the slider. In the major leagues, the ball has to break two ways or you aren't going to make it. And Bucky Walters showed me how."

His most colorful manager: Charlie Dressen with the Braves. "As long as you liked Charlie's cooking, you'd get along okay with him."

His toughest out: Ted Kluszewski of Cincinnati. "Boy was he big— and boy could he hit. He hit everything off me hard and long. Musial and Mays were tough outs, too. I used to have a goal of trying to hold Musial to a double. And Willie, heck, he gave everybody fits.

"One of the differences between Mays and Aaron is that Mays was always flashier. Mays would always take the extra base if given the chance. Henry would take what he was given."

Buhl made one more stop in the major leagues. On April 21, 1966, at the age of 38, he was traded, along with Larry Jackson, another aging Cubs pitcher, to the Philadelphia Phillies for two established ballplayers —

outfielder Adolpho Phillips and first baseman John Herrnstein—and a young, unknown pitcher, Ferguson Jenkins. The following season, Jenkins began a Hall of Fame career with the Cubs.

When his baseball career was over, Buhl said he took a year off and then got into the construction business.

He called today's player salaries "outrageous" and that they've changed people's attitude about the game. "I saw Bud Selig [baseball commissioner] in Milwaukee a while back and asked him how it happened," said Buhl, whose top pay was $32,000. He said 'it just got out of hand' and he was right about that."

He said when he was playing, he had to have a job in the off-season to support his family and had to figure out a way in the regular season to maintain a home in Michigan and pay his expenses in Milwaukee. "Today it's easy. Then, it wasn't," said Buhl.

"Today's players are different. At first they wanted long-term contracts. Now, if they could, they'd be free agents every year," said the man who started his career as a free agent.

"I'll tell you how it was when I was playing," he said, his voice quickening with a sense of excitement. "Every day was a new day, another game—and I couldn't wait to get out there."

Robert Ray Buhl
Born Aug. 12, 1928, in Saginaw, Mich.
6' 2" , 180 lbs.; B-right, T-right

Year	Team	W-L	Pct.	ERA	G	IP	H	BB	SO
1953	Mil	13-8	.619	2.97	30	154.1	133	73	83
1954	Mil	2-7	.222	4.00	31	110.1	117	65	57
1955	Mil	13-11	.542	3.21	38	201.2	168	109	117
1956	Mil	18-8	.692	3.32	38	216.2	190	105	86
1957	Mil	18-7	.720	2.74	34	216.2	191	121	117
1958	Mil	5-2	.714	3.45	11	73	74	30	27
1959	Mil	15-9	.625	2.86	31	198	181	74	105
1960	Mil	16-9	.640	3.09	36	238.2	202	103	121
1961	Mil	9-10	.474	4.11	32	188.1	180	98	77
1962	Mil-Chi	12-14	.462	3.87	35	214	210	98	110
1963	Chi	11-14	.440	3.38	37	226	219	62	108
1964	Chi	15-14	.517	3.83	36	227.2	208	68	107
1965	Chi	13-11	.542	4.39	32	184.1	207	57	92
1966	Chi-Phil	6-8	.429	4.96	33	134.1	160	40	60
1967	Phil	0-0	.000	13.50	3	2.2	6	2	1
15 years		166-132	.557	3.55	457	2586.2	2446	1105	1268

Transactions:
April 30, 1962: Traded to Chicago Cubs for pitcher Jack Curtis.
April 21, 1966: Traded with pitcher Larry Jackson to Philadelphia for outfielders Adolpho Phillips and John Herrnstein and pitcher Ferguson Jenkins.

WORLD SERIES

Year	Team	W-L	Pct.	ERA	G	IP	H	BB	SO
1957	Mil	0-1	.000	10.80	2	3.1	6	6	4

DON KESSINGER
Cubs Shortstop, 1964–1975

"Day ball made a difference. It took a lot out of me."

OXFORD, Miss.— It was a busy week for Don Kessinger, associate athletic director at the University of Mississippi. The Ole Miss football team was getting ready to go to the Independence Bowl with a brand new head coach, hired in a hurry after Rebels coach Tommy Tuberville left at the end of the season — but before the bowl game — to take over a coaching job at Auburn.

"It's been a time of a lot of scheduled meetings and a lot of unscheduled ones," said Kessinger, who played 12 years with the Chicago Cubs, managed the Chicago White Sox for part of a season, and returned to his alma mater to coach the Ole Miss baseball team for six years before taking the job of associate athletic director in 1996.

So, football was on his mind on this day, but he squeezed in some time to talk about baseball and his days with the Chicago Cubs.

Kessinger was an All-American baseball player at Ole Miss and still holds the school record for career batting average, .407. In 1964, his senior year, Kessinger — he was "Donnie" in those days — hit .429, second highest in Ole Miss history. Charlie Conerly, who went on to a stellar career as a National Football League quarterback, showed he could play a little baseball, too, with his .451 batting average in 1948.

Kessinger's career at Ole Miss was good enough to earn him a contract with the Chicago Cubs. "Timing is everything," said Kessinger, 56, as he reflected on the luck he encountered. "The Cubs were between short-

Don Kessinger, who was part of the Cubs' great 1969 team, says he wilted in the heat that summer in Chicago.

stops. Ernie Banks was being moved over to first base and they had played Andre Rodgers but were looking to fill that slot," he said. "I went straight from Ole Miss to Double-A ball at Fort Worth. The next year I went to spring training with the Cubs, got sent down and then came back up at the end of the year."

Kessinger started to bloom into an everyday ballplayer with the Cubs at the time that Leo Durocher, the feisty, veteran manager came on the scene. Durocher, a firebrand player in the 1920s and 1930s, had managed the Dodgers and Giants and had a reputation for two things — stirring up trouble and winning.

In 1947, he was suspended for a year by Commissioner Happy Chandler for associating with gamblers. In 1954, when he was manager of the Giants, his team went to the World Series and swept the Cleveland Indians, a club that had won 111 games during the regular season. Now, 12 years later, "the Lip" was back, managing a team that finished over .500 just once in the past 21 years.

"I learned more baseball from Leo Durocher than from anyone else," said Kessinger. "It turned out to be both a blessing and a curse that I just happened to play the position that Leo used to play — because he spent a lot of time with me. He would chew me out but he helped me. He helped me a lot," said Kessinger.

"There were a lot of things about Leo I respected. He wasn't worried about what people thought. And he didn't go by the book. He'd go by his instinct and by his experience so he'd do a lot of things that other managers wouldn't think of doing.

"For instance, when a guy like Dick Groat was up and there would be a man on first, Leo would sense that the hit-and-run was on. He'd yell at me not to cover the bag if the runner took off. He'd shout, 'he's gonna make contact, he's gonna make contact' because Dick Groat was a good contact hitter. If the runner takes off and I cover the bag, Groat will shoot one through the hole. Leo knew that — so he'd go against the book. And he was right most of the time but even when he wasn't, you'd have to respect him.

"One thing that was different about Leo — he didn't believe in private conversations. If he had something to say to you, he'd say it in front of everybody. You might as well have been having a team meeting in the clubhouse — and a lot of guys didn't like that. There were guys who'd listen to his radio show to see if they were playing that day."

In Durocher's first year with the Cubs, 1966, they finished tenth. "We were a pretty bad team," said Kessinger. "Everybody was young. He played a lot of young guys and we took our lumps." But better days were ahead.

"We picked up Ferguson Jenkins from the Phillies and the young guys were getting some experience and you could see things starting to turn around. We finished third in 1967 and in 1968," he said.

Jenkins, who had a 6-8 record playing for the Phillies and Cubs in 1966, was 20-13 in 1967, the first of six straight 20-win seasons for him.

And then, 1969 — a year that will live in infamy in the hearts of Cubs fans. The Cubs led the Eastern Division of the National League most of the season and had an 8½ game lead in late August over the second place New York Mets. But the Mets put on a late season surge at just about the time the Cubs went into a fade — and once the momentum switched, it never reversed itself.

"I thought that from 1968 to 1972, we were as good as any team in baseball. Heck, there were three Hall of Famers on that team [Jenkins, Ernie Banks and Billy Williams]. Had we won in '69, we might have won two or three more pennants," said Kessinger.

He said there were several factors to the Cubs collapse. "First, the Mets played unbelievable baseball down the stretch. At the same time, we were playing less than .500 ball. We played all day games in Chicago and 1969 was a very hot summer. I think when you come right down to it, we didn't have as much left down the stretch."

(Weather statistics for Chicago in the summer of 1969 verify Kessinger's recollections. Highs were consistently in the high 80s and low 90s in August.)

"As an athlete, sometimes you have to reach back for that little extra, for that little reserve to get you through, and in the summer of '69 it just wasn't there," he said. "I don't blame Leo. I don't blame him at all. A lot of people do because he played the regulars for so many games. But if he had asked me or any of the others if we wanted to come out, we would have told him no. We were just playing so well. 'Ole Mo' just got on their side, and when that happens, it's hard to get it back.

"You know how it is in sports — when the breaks are going the other guys' way, they always recover the fumble," he said.

Kessinger said it's difficult to pinpoint a reason why the Cubs haven't played in a World Series in more than 50 years. "There's probably a lot of factors, depending on when you played. As for Don Kessinger, I got tired of playing day ball all the time. From a family standpoint, it was great. I could go home at night and be with my wife and kids. But from a professional standpoint, it took a lot out of you.

"I'd lose 10 to 12 pounds playing in Wrigley Field in the summer, and I didn't have that much to lose," he said. (He lost 20 pounds, going from 175 to 155 in the summer of 1969.) "When I played for other clubs and played more night games, I really noticed the difference. I had something left; it wasn't all taken out of me."

Kessinger has remained consistent in his views about what happened in 1969 — that it was not Durocher's fault; that he wore out toward the end of the year; that teams playing night games have an advantage over teams playing day games; and that the Mets got hot at the right time.

He explained the difference between day games and night games by saying someone who plays three hours of tennis every afternoon during the summer is going to wear out faster than someone who plays three hours of tennis every night. And the same is true with baseball, said Kessinger.

His 1969 statistics are evidence that he is right, at least with respect to his own play. He reached base in each of the Cubs' first 41 games, during which the Cubs posted a 27-14 record. From September 4 to September 23 that year, Kessinger hit .148, robbing him of a possible .300 season. He finished at .273. During that same September stretch, the Cubs lost 11 out of 12.

On October 28, 1975, Kessinger was traded to the St. Louis Cardinals for pitcher Mike Garman and minor league infielder Bobby Hrapmann. "If anything, St. Louis was hotter than Chicago in the summertime, so playing night games there made a difference for me, a difference I really noticed," he said.

His next move was back to Chicago. On August 20, 1977, he was traded to the White Sox where he played sparingly the rest of that season and in 1978 before taking over as manager for part of the 1979 season.

"When I came back to Chicago, this time on the south side, again I noticed how much easier it was playing night games, this time in the same city where I had played most of my career. So I can't speak for everybody, but for Don Kessinger, day ball made a difference. It took a lot out of me," he said.

Kessinger said another factor that might have held the Cubs back was the indifference of owner Philip K. Wrigley, who inherited the Cubs from his father but made his fortune in the chewing gum business.

"We were always told that Mr. Wrigley was extremely interested in us. But in my day, he was never around. We'd hardly ever see him at the ballpark and he never ever went on road trips to watch us play. But I have to be honest. We were treated good. I just don't think the interest was there, especially compared to how other owners took an interest in their teams," he said.

Kessinger said the greatest game he ever played in occurred on September 9, 1965, when the Cubs' Bob Hendley hooked up in a pitching dual with Sandy Koufax of the Dodgers. "Koufax threw a perfect game and Hendley allowed just one hit, a little flair off the end of the bat that went over the first baseman's head into right field," he said. "The winning run in that game scored when our catcher threw the ball into left field."

The record shows that Kessinger is right on all counts. Lou Johnson got the hit off Hendley, a double. But he was left stranded. Earlier in the game, he walked, stole second and when he attempted to steal third, Cubs catcher Chris Krug threw the ball into left field. That's how Johnson scored the only run.

Looking back on that remarkable game years later, Hendley quipped, "It seemed like every time I turned around, that guy [Johnson] was on base."

Kessinger says: "That was the greatest single performance I've ever seen. I think Koufax struck out the last seven batters. If you didn't get to him early, you didn't get to him," said Kessinger.

(Kessinger's memory was close to perfect. Koufax struck out the last six batters — Ron Santo, Ernie Banks and Byron Browne in the eighth, and Chris Krug, Joe Amalfitano and Harvey Kuenn in the ninth.)

Santo, the Cubs third baseman, tells the story that before that game, someone on the Cubs bench said that Koufax was tipping off his curveball when he was in the stretch — and that hitters should watch for it that night. Of course, Koufax never went into a stretch that night.

Kessinger said he's heard a lot of stories about that game over the years and then contributed one of his own.

"When Kuenn came up to pinch hit with two out in the ninth inning, he walked past Amalfitano, our third base coach, and said, 'Wait right there. I'll be right back.' And Koufax struck him out to end the game.

"I'll tell you something else about that night. That late-arriving LA crowd didn't see much. The game only lasted about an hour and a half. They got there and turned around and went home," said Kessinger.

He was the Cubs leadoff man for most of his years in Chicago. He and Glenn Beckert set the table for Williams, Banks and Santo, the team's big run-producers. In 1969 and 1970, Kessinger scored 109 and 100 runs, respectively. His best year with the Cubs was 1969 when he hit .273 with 181 hits, including 38 doubles.

He played more games at shortstop, 1,618, than any other Cub and also has the most assists for a Cubs shortstop, 5,346, and took part in the most double plays at his position, 982. Though Kessinger only played with the Cubs into the 1975 season, he holds the club record for most games played during the 1970s — 937.

Kessinger played in six All–Star Games and was 2-for-2 in the 1970 game in Cincinnati, the game that ended with Pete Rose barreling over Cleveland catcher Ray Fosse to score the winning run.

He was in other memorable games for the Cubs, who always seemed to be on the losing end. On September 13, 1964, he was a rookie, called up at the end of the season, and watched from the bench for most of the game as the Cardinals scored in every inning to beat the Cubs 15–2.

"I got in the game late, after it had gotten out of hand. It wasn't pretty," said Kessinger.

On September 5, 1969, Kessinger had an "oh-fer" (0-for-2) in a game against the Pirates, but so did most of the rest of the Cubs. Chicago got only four hits off Pittsburgh's Steve Blass that day — and Billy Williams got all four of them, two doubles and two home runs.

"Nothing Billy Williams did with a bat surprised me," said Kessinger. "He was just a fine hitter, that's all you can say."

Kessinger's two sons, Keith and Kevin, followed in their father's footsteps at the University of Mississippi. They both set hitting records there and signed major league contracts. Kevin Kessinger signed with the Cubs but a back injury cut short his career. Keith Kessinger played nine years of pro ball.

"Keith got a cup of coffee in the major leagues, about a month with Cincinnati. But he hit a home run," said Papa Kessinger.

While Don Kessinger has the Ole Miss record for batting average, Keith holds the record for most at-bats and Kevin holds the record for most hits. Both sons got a chance to play for their father, who had a record of 185-153 in six seasons as head baseball coach.

But on this day, after Don Kessinger devoted part of his morning to reminiscing about Cubs baseball, his energies and thoughts jumped back to the present task at hand — Ole Miss football ... and the bowl game and the coaching vacancies ... and all those unscheduled meetings.

Donald Eulon Kessinger
Born July 17, 1942, in Forrest City, Ark.
6' 1", 170 lbs.; B-both, T-right

Year	Team	G	AB	R	H	D	T	HR	RBI	Ave.
1964	Chi (N)	4	12	1	2	0	0	0	0	.167
1965	Chi	106	309	19	62	4	3	0	14	.201
1966	Chi	150	533	50	146	8	2	1	43	.274
1967	Chi	145	580	61	134	10	7	0	42	.231
1968	Chi	160	655	63	157	14	7	1	32	.240
1969	Chi	158	664	109	181	38	6	4	53	.273
1970	Chi	154	631	100	168	21	14	1	39	.266
1971	Chi	155	617	77	159	18	6	2	38	.258

Year	Team	G	AB	R	H	D	T	HR	RBI	Ave.
1972	Chi	149	577	77	158	20	6	1	39	.274
1973	Chi	160	577	52	151	22	3	0	43	.262
1974	Chi	153	599	83	155	20	7	1	42	.259
1975	Chi	154	601	77	146	26	10	0	46	.243
1976	StL	145	502	55	120	22	6	1	40	.239
1977	StL-Chi (A)	98	253	26	60	7	2	0	18	.237
1978	Chi	131	431	35	110	18	1	1	31	.255
1979	Chi	56	110	14	22	6	0	1	7	.200
16 years		2078	7651	899	1931	254	80	14	527	.252

Transactions:

Oct. 28, 1975: Traded to St. Louis Cardinals for pitcher Mike Garman and infielder Bobby Hrapmann.

Aug. 20, 1977: Traded to Chicago White Sox for pitcher Steve Staniland.

PAUL POPOVICH

Cubs Infielder, 1964; 1966–1967; 1969–1973

"The Dodgers always had a strong farm system....
When they had a void they needed to fill, they'd go
down there and there would always be somebody in
their minor league organization to fill it. The Cubs
never seemed to have that."

NORTHBROOK, Ill.— Paul Popovich says the 30th anniversary of the Chicago Cubs' sudden plunge out of a pennant race didn't bring any new attention to that fateful 1969 collapse. Not from his standpoint, at least.

"I get asked about that every year," said Popovich, 58, who was a utility infielder on the 1969 team that finished second to the New York Mets after leading the league most of the year.

The Cubs had an 8½ game lead in August but played less than .500 ball the rest of the way while the "Miracle Mets" soared past them to their first championship.

"What I always tell people is this: That Met team was a lot better than people ever gave them credit for," said Popovich. "They beat us, but they also beat Atlanta in the playoffs and then they beat a very good Baltimore Oriole team four out of five in the World Series.

"They had the best pitching in the big leagues with Tom Seaver and Jerry Koosman and Tug McGraw and others. We didn't lose it. They won it. They got hot at the right time and that's what it takes," he said.

"Momentum is a funny thing. It can happen to an individual just like it can happen to a team. You can be hitting really well and feel like you're really in a groove and every thing you hit is a line drive, everything you hit is dropping in somewhere.

"And then suddenly you haven't changed anything but you can't buy a hit. You've lost your momentum and you don't know how or why. You just have. That's what happened to us in '69," said Popovich.

He has fond memories of Cubs manager Leo Durocher. "He was real hard-nosed but I enjoyed playing for him. He was very competitive and you never knew quite what to expect. He made it exciting every day. It was fun to come to the ballpark.

"Leo got criticized a lot for playing the regulars every day, not giving them enough rest and having a set lineup, but I think that's unfair. I know he tried everything he could to get me in the lineup," he said.

Popovich came up with the Cubs for one game in 1964 and two games in 1966. In 1967, he appeared in 49 games. His 2 RBIs in 159 at-bats that year is a major league record for fewest RBIs for a player with more than 150 at-bats. In November, he was traded with Jimmy Williams to the Dodgers for outfielder Lou Johnson.

He was a regular with Los Angeles in 1968 and part of 1969. In June of 1969, Cubs second baseman Glenn Beckert broke his hand — and Durocher needed someone to fill in. Popovich was one of the lesser names in a three-way deal but was the key player as far as the Cubs were concerned.

The Dodgers traded Popovich and Ron Fairly to Montreal for Maury Wills and Manny Mota. Fairly became one of the Expos most popular players, Wills returned to the city where he was once a base-stealing champion and Mota was to set pinch-hitting records for the Dodgers.

But in the second half of that trade, Popovich was traded to the Cubs for outfielder Adolpho Phillips and pitcher Jack Lamabe. Phillips' departure created a vacuum in center field that Durocher never did fill satisfactorally, but he got his second baseman.

Popovich hit .312 in 60 games for the Cubs, giving him a .284 average for the season, by far his best in the majors. The record bears out his claim that Durocher tried to work him into the lineup anywhere he could. In addition to playing 49 games at second base for the injured Beckert, he played shortstop in 10 games, third base in six games and center field in one.

He was unlucky in coming up with the Cubs at a time when they had one of the greatest infields of all time: Ron Santo at third, Don Kessinger at short, Beckert at second and Ernie Banks at first — all All-Stars at one time or another.

But Popovich doesn't think he was the victim of bad timing. "The most important thing to me, to anyone who plays baseball, is to make it to the big leagues. You don't care what you do. You're there and that's the only thing that counts," he said.

For Popovich, it had been a long road. "I signed with the Cubs in 1960 and was assigned to their Double-A team in San Antonio. I'll never forget my first road trip. It was a 26-hour bus trip to Mexico. We played a lot of Mexican teams in those days. But 26 hours on a bus was a long haul. I was 19 then, and at 19, it doesn't bother you much. It would bother me today," he said.

He spent 1961 in San Antonio and then was sent to Wenatchee, Washington, for the 1962 season. "It was hot in San Antonio, hotter than I've ever been anywhere else. Our manager [in 1960] was Grady Hatton and he used to have morning workouts in all that heat and then we'd play at night and then work out again the next morning in the heat. It was tough," said Popovich.

"In 1961, we had revolving coaches in San Antonio just like they had on the Cubs and it didn't work any better in San Antonio than it did in Chicago," he said.

After stops in Amarillo and Salt Lake City, the Cubs decided to give him a quick look.

On April 19, 1964, he made his major league debut in a game against the Phillies at Wrigley Field. "I came up to the plate and my knees were shaking. I made up my mind I was going to swing at the first pitch and I did and hit one right up the middle for a base hit. I remember the pitcher was a left-hander. I think it was Dennis Bennett," said Popovich, who was a switch hitter. That was his only big league appearance in 1964.

He spent the rest of that season and all of 1965 and 1966 in Salt Lake City and then came up to the majors to stay in '67.

Popovich played for Walter Alston at Los Angeles and then for Danny Murtaugh at Pittsburgh after the Cubs traded him to the Pirates in April of 1974.

"Alston and Murtaugh were much different than Durocher in that they were both low-key. Walter Alston knew how to get his point across, though. When he wanted to, he didn't have any trouble showing you who was boss.

"I feel very fortunate to have played for three of baseball's best managers in Durocher, Alston and Murtaugh," said Popovich.

For Pittsburgh in 1974, he appeared in three games and got three hits in five at-bats in the league championship series that the Pirates dropped to Cincinnati.

"That was a great Pirate team with just loads of hitting. Willie Stargell, Dave Parker, Al Oliver, Richie Zisk, Manny Sanguillen, Rennie Stennett. Boy, could they hit," he said.

Popovich said he noticed something about the Dodgers for sure, and to some extent, the Pirates, that he thought was lacking with the Cubs in those days.

"The Dodgers always had a strong farm system," he said. "They could always reach down there and bring up a star. When they had a void they needed to fill, they'd go down there and there would always be somebody in their minor league organization to fill it. The Cubs never seemed to have that. They just didn't have the capability of finding the player they needed.

"I don't know why things were like that. All the teams had scouts and they were all scouting pretty much the same players. But the Dodgers seemed to get them and the Cubs didn't."

Popovich said his greatest memories from his major league career are: Making the playoffs with the Pirates; the emotional downfall of the 1969 Cubs; hitting a grand-slam home run for the Cubs at Wrigley Field off Jerry Reuss of the Cardinals in 1971; and playing behind Don Drysdale when Drysdale pitched 58 scoreless innings in 1968, a major league record at the time.

Popovich, in his typical role, played second base, shortstop and third base during Drysdale's streak, which started with a 1–0 shutout against the Cubs at Wrigley Field on May 14, 1968, and continued with shutouts against St. Louis, Houston twice, San Francisco and Pittsburgh. The Phillies finally nicked him for a run on June 8.

"It was very inspiring but it was a little nerve-wracking, too," said Popovich. "I think there was more pressure on the fielders than there was on Don. None of us wanted to be the one to make the error that would break the scoreless string.

"Boy, that Drysdale. You talk about being a competitor. He and Bob Gibson. There were no tougher competitors than those two guys.

"When Drysdale had his streak going, I couldn't wait to get to the ballpark. Typically, I'd leave to go to the park at about four o'clock. On nights when Drysdale was pitching, I'd leave at three. I remember we were playing Pittsburgh on the night he threw his sixth shutout. And I remember going to the ballpark and seeing the traffic backed up for miles. And

Los Angeles is noted for its late-arriving crowds so that was really something," said Popovich.

His lifetime statistics pay homage to his versatility, to his acceptance of his role as a utility player for most of his career. Popovich played 358 games at second base, 139 games at shortstop, 49 at third base, 1 in the outfield (center field for Durocher in 1969) and 165 as a pinch hitter.

He retired from baseball after the 1975 season and worked for several years as an instructor in the Dodger organization. Now he is semi-retired but helps give batting lessons at Club 41, an all-purpose sports club in suburban Chicago, where he helps kids between the ages of 8 and 21...

...And probably answers questions about the summer of '69.

Paul Edward Popovich
Born Aug. 18, 1940, in Flemington, W. Va.
6', 175 lbs.; B-right, T-right

Year	Team	G	AB	R	H	D	T	HR	RBI	Ave.
1964	Chi (N)	1	1	0	1	0	0	0	0	1.000
1966	Chi	2	6	0	0	0	0	0	0	.000
1967	Chi	49	159	18	34	4	0	0	2	.214
1968	LA	134	418	35	97	8	1	2	25	.232
1969	LA-Chi	88	204	31	58	6	0	1	18	.284
1970	Chi	78	186	22	47	5	1	4	20	.253
1971	Chi	89	226	24	49	7	1	4	28	.217
1972	Chi	58	129	8	25	3	2	1	11	.194
1973	Chi	99	280	24	66	6	3	2	24	.236
1974	Pitt	59	83	9	18	2	1	0	5	.217
1975	Pitt	75	40	5	8	1	0	0	1	.200
11 years		682	1732	176	403	42	9	14	134	.233

Transactions:

Nov. 30, 1967: Traded with outfielder Jim Williams to Los Angeles for outfielder Lou Johnson.

June 11, 1969: Traded with outfielder Ron Fairly to Montreal for infielders Maury Wills and Manny Mota.

June 11, 1969: Traded to Chicago Cubs for outfielder Adolpho Phillips and pitcher Jack Lamabe.

April 1, 1974: Traded to Pittsburgh Pirates for pitcher Tom Dettore and cash.

LEAGUE CHAMPIONSHIP SERIES

Year	Team	G	AB	R	H	D	T	HR	RBI	Ave.
1974	Pitt	3	5	1	3	0	0	0	0	.600

RICH NYE

Cubs Pitcher, 1966–1970

"For many years, what other teams got through their organizations, the Cubs tried to get through trades. And when you trade to fill spots on your ballclub, you almost always trade young players."

WESTCHESTER, Ill.— "Baseball is a psychological game," says Rich Nye, 55, now a veterinarian but in the late 1960s a promising young left-handed pitcher for the Chicago Cubs.

As he looks back on his baseball career now, he concedes that the way he was treated by Cubs manager Leo Durocher had an effect on him.

He is frank in his comments about Durocher and about the Cubs organization in general, but that should not be construed as bitterness. He is not a bitter man. To the contrary, Nye appreciates the opportunity he had to play in the major leagues. But he is frank about missed opportunities, too.

"I was 13-10 in 1967 and that's still the Cubs record for most wins by a rookie. Kerry Wood tied it in 1998 when he was 13-6," said Nye, whose specialty now is treating birds and snakes and other exotic animals.

(Nye is nearly right. The Cubs rookie record for wins is actually held by Dick Drott who won 15 in 1957. Nye holds the Cubs rookie record for a left-hander.)

It was in that same 1967 season that Nye's elbow started giving him trouble. "There were times I went out there and didn't know whether I could even lift my arm," he said. He got through the season all right and battled through 1968 with periodic arm problems but managed a 7-12 record.

At the start of 1969, he and the entire Cubs team had high hopes. They had finished third in 1968 and were confident they could make a run for it in 1969. They had an All-Star infield of Ron Santo at third, Don Kessinger at short, Glenn Beckert at second and future Hall of Famer Ernie Banks at first. Another future Hall of Famer, Billy Williams was in left field and a third Hall of Famer, Ferguson Jenkins, was the ace of a starting rotation that also included Bill Hands and Ken Holtzman.

One of the missing ingredients that spring was a fourth starter. Nye had a shot at it as did young right-hander Joe Niekro.

"Joe got a couple of starts early on because the Cubs wanted to show-case him — and it worked. They wound up trading him to San Diego for Dick Selma. So that fourth spot, instead of being between Niekro and me was now between Selma and me," said Nye.

The Cubs started the season strong and were to be in first place for five months straight. An early test of their strength was a four-game series against the Mets in New York in late April. Jenkins and Hands won the first two games. Then came a doubleheader, the Cubs' third twin bill in seven days — a killer for a pitching staff. Durocher decided to go with Selma and Nye.

"Selma pitched the first game and really got rocked. But the Cubs got him some runs and he won, even though he didn't look very good," said Nye. The Cubs had now taken the first three games of the series with Nye pitching the finale.

"I had a great game, threw eight shutout innings, but we didn't score either. Cleon Jones hit a three-run homer in the ninth and we lost 3–0. Still, I figured I did my job. I pitched a pretty good ballgame, even though I lost, compared to Selma, even though he won.

"Well, Selma went into the rotation and I didn't start again for 10 days. And I just figured they didn't have me in their plans. Part of the game of baseball is confidence and when you sense they've lost confidence in you, you start to lose it in yourself.

"Leo never said anything to me. I was just a smart-alec college kid to him. And I wasn't going to say anything to him. When you have a manager like Leo, you're not going to say anything to rock the boat. You have to figure, I was about number 740 when I was drafted by the Cubs so I was just extra fortunate to even be there. I knew that.

"Now, Kenny Holtzman — he'd stand up to Leo. He'd swear at him and call him names. But he was Kenny Holtzman, a guy some people were comparing to Sandy Koufax. Me — I had no false images of myself," he said.

Nye played baseball at the University of California–Berkeley and signed with the Cubs after he graduated in 1966. He played in a rookie league for three weeks and then five weeks in a special summer league.

"Niekro played in that same league. If they have plans for you, they'll move you along, and they moved Niekro up. I had been playing in the rookie league in Idaho, then over to the summer league in California where I played for Ray Perry, the man who signed me.

"One day before a game, he walked me out to the outfield and told me, 'Now don't tell anybody, but you're gonna get called up.' Don't tell anybody? I was so excited. But Ray just wanted to keep it quiet until it was all official. I had had a good year. I struck 95 in about 65 innings and I knew Ray had been building me up as some sort of phenom.

"As it happened, the Cubs were on a West Coast swing and I met the team in San Francisco but I didn't pitch in that series. It didn't matter. I looked around Candlestick Park and thought: Here I am. I grew up in California and had seen all these Giant players for years and now I was on the same field with them. It was quite a feeling.

"I got my first start against the Cardinals in St. Louis. They had quite a lineup — Orlando Cepeda, Joe Torre, Tim McCarver, Julian Javier and on and on. They'd been in the World Series in 1964 and would be again in '67 and '68. I pitched 7⅔ innings and held them scoreless and then I gave up a three-run homer in the eighth.

"It's funny, the things you remember. I got a hit in that game and I was standing on first base next to Orlando Cepeda and I just started talking to him. I told him I was really excited to meet him. I have no idea whether he understood anything I said," said Nye.

He pitched a total of 17 innings in 1966, winning none, losing two but finishing with an earned run average of 2.12. The next year, he won the 13 in his first full season, then struggled through the mediocre 1968 season with a 7-12 record.

Next came the infamous 1969 season when Nye was a part of a team that couldn't hold onto an 8½ game lead it enjoyed in late August.

"If I was to make one observation, unfortunately the problem was Leo Durocher and his leadership. He had blinders on when it came to the team concept. He used the same players day in and day out and wore them out.

"We started to slide in late August, just about the time the Mets were getting hot, and Leo didn't do anything to build up our team. He just kept sending the same guys out there. In the bullpen, he just kept ringing up [Phil] Regan. It was obvious he didn't have confidence in anyone else. And then when one of the rest of us did have an opportunity, we just weren't sharp."

Nye said he and other relief pitchers who weren't being used sometimes got up and started warming up on their own — just so they would be mentioned from time to time on radio and television.

"We had all those day games at Wrigley Field and that was a hot summer. But there was no platoon system. Not even close. And you know, the way we were going that year, anyone who played would have blended with the rest. We would have kept on winning. Because we knew we were going to win every day. There was talent there. But a lot of guys just came and sat every day. He just didn't use us," said Nye.

(Nye appeared in 35 games in 1967, starting 30. In 1968, he appeared in 27 with 20 starts. In 1969, though he had spent his entire career as a starter, he started only five games and relieved in 29 others.)

"Look at the Chicago Bulls during their great years. They won because Phil Jackson knew how to get everybody involved. Everybody felt like they were contributing. Theirs was always a true team effort, even with all the stars they had.

"Leo didn't do that. He stuck with the same guys. They started to wear out and the Mets caught us and beat us. I never held any animosity toward the Mets. I know some of the guys did for a while and I know the fans did," he said.

Nye agrees with others who played on the 1969 team that had the Cubs won it, they might have been champions for several years to come. They would have established themselves as winners and developed the confidence of winners. But it didn't happen.

The tide can turn in a hurry in baseball, not only for teams, but for players. On December 4, 1969, the Cubs traded Nye to the Cardinals for outfielder Boots Day.

"I had a lousy spring with the Cardinals. I broke camp with them and got into about six games but didn't do well. They sold me to Montreal and the Expos assigned me to their Triple-A farm team," said Nye.

So, about six months after playing on a team that almost won the National League championship, he found himself back in the minor leagues. "I was there for about a month. I pitched against the Orioles Triple-A team and they had guys like Bobby Grich and Don Baylor. I did okay. I pitched six innings, struck out nine and gave up one infield hit. But when I was warming up before the game, I felt a little pinch in my shoulder. After the game, I couldn't lift my arm for a month.

"Montreal brought me back up and I had three or four good starts and then the arm started bothering me again. Our manager, Gene Mauch, told me point-blank he didn't like sore-arm pitchers. Well, I had seen some doctors and was put on all sorts of medications and was told not to pitch for a while.

"On August 5, 1970, the Giants were in town. I was sitting on the bench and Mauch says, 'Nye, go down and get loose.' And I'm thinking — doesn't he know what the doctors said — or didn't the doctors tell him — or what's going on?

"I came into that game to pitch to Willie McCovey. There was nobody out and Willie Mays was on first base. McCovey hit a frozen rope line drive to Bobby Wine at shortstop and he turned it into a double play. Then I struck out Jim Ray Hart. The reason I remember the date is that's the last time I ever pitched in the major leagues," he said.

"I quit baseball and went to vet school. When I opened my veterinary practice, I started with dogs and cats but had the desire to do something different. So now I do nothing but birds and exotics and I'm really enjoying myself," said Nye.

The year of 1969 was just one season where the Cubs came up short. What about all of the others dating back to 1945?

"There's never been the pressure on the Cubs to win, even from top management, like there has been for other clubs," said Nye. "A winning tradition — that's a huge factor. For years, when you looked at the Cubs, you thought 'loser.' Then, look at the Yankees. Look at the Dodgers. Even today, when I imagine ever pitching in Dodger Blue, that would have been something.

"But the Cubs have never built that tradition. Why? Look at their organization and compare it with others. The strong teams over the years have always had strong minor league organizations. For many years, what other teams got through their organizations, the Cubs tried to get through trades. And when you trade to fill spots on your ballclub, you almost always trade young players.

"The Dodgers had the best organization from the ground floor all the way up. When I was in the rookie league in California, do you know who was managing the Dodgers' rookie team — the lowest rung on the ladder? Tommy Lasorda. He was inspiring players even way back then.

"And he was teaching them how to play baseball the Dodger way. Working on fundamentals — bunting, hit-and-run, moving a runner along, all the things that add up to being a winner, and things you don't have to teach them when they reach the big leagues. The Cubs farm system was simply nothing like what Dodgers and a lot of other good teams had back then.

"There's another aspect to tradition," said Nye. "The Cubs do absolutely nothing for their alumni. I've been involved in one Old-Timers Game and that was in 1977 when they were doing something to honor Ernie Banks. But other than that, nothing. A lot of us stay in touch and see each other from time to time but it's nothing organized by the Cubs.

"Look at what they do in New York. They honor their former players. They even televise their Old-Timers Games.

"But the Cubs don't do it and there's a certain sadness to that. Because, after all, we were a part of it."

Richard Raymond Nye
Born Aug. 4, 1944, in Oakland, Calif.
6' 4", 185 lbs.; B-left, T-left

Year	Team	W-L	ERA	G	IP	H	BB	SO
1966	Chi (N)	0-2	2.12	3	17	16	7	9
1967	Chi	13-10	3.20	35	205	179	52	119
1968	Chi	7-12	3.80	27	132.2	145	34	74
1969	Chi	3-5	5.09	34	69	72	21	39
1970	StL-Mont	3-2	4.14	14	54.1	60	26	26
5 years		26-31	3.71	113	478	472	140	267

Transactions:

Dec. 4, 1969: Traded to St. Louis Cardinals for outfielder Boots Day.
May 15, 1970: Sold to Montreal.

JOE NIEKRO
Cubs Pitcher, 1967–1969

"All those day games in the heat — it really takes a toll on you."

PLANT CITY, Fla.— Joe Niekro was 10-7 as a 23-year-old rookie for the Chicago Cubs in 1967 and followed that by winning 14 games in 1968. In 1969, he was ready to be a mainstay on the pitching staff. Then, a strange thing happened. Less than a month into the season, he was traded.

"Yosh Kawano, the equipment manager, told me," said Niekro, 54, who won 221 games in his 21-year career, 197 of them after he left the Cubs.

"I must have gotten in Leo's doghouse," he said, referring to Leo Durocher, the Cubs' feisty manager. "I was very surprised when I heard the news. To this day, I have no idea why they traded me."

On April 25, 1969, Niekro, along with pitcher Gary Ross and shortstop Francisco Libran went to San Diego for pitcher Dick Selma. While Selma was helping the Cubs contend for the Eastern Division title, Nieko was 8-17 with an awful Padres team.

With the Cubs, he had appeared in four games, starting three of them, and had an 0-1 record and a 3.72 earned run average at the time of the trade.

"I only pitched about nine innings in spring training that year for some reason," said Niekro. "Then on the fourth day of the season, Joe

Becker, our pitching coach, put two balls in my locker. That was the signal that I was pitching that day. I went 10 innings against Montreal at Wrigley Field and I think we won it in the 11th.

"Later, when we went up to Montreal, I lost 3–2. I pitched seven innings on a Sunday. Then we went to Pittsburgh and I was sitting in the dugout on Tuesday and I think Bill Hands is pitching for us. They get a couple of men on and Leo looks at me and says, 'go warm up.' I couldn't believe it. I had just pitched seven innings on Sunday. I didn't even have my baseball shoes on.

"So I go down to the bullpen and throw about seven pitches and all of a sudden, boom, I'm in the game facing Willie Stargell. He hits a home run and two days later, I'm traded, and Yosh tells me about it," said Niekro.

"They had about a six or seven game lead when I got traded and you saw what happened after that," he said, obviously joking about the situation.

The Cubs maintained a six-to-seven game lead most of the 1969 season but slumped in September at about the same time the Mets surged. The Cubs finished second to New York, 8½ games back. Had Niekro remained with the Cubs, he might have made the big difference in 1969 and for many years to come.

Back in his early days, Niekro fooled around with a knuckleball, a pitch that he later used to good advantage for much of his career. But Durocher and the Cubs coaching staff frowned on young pitchers throwing a knuckler.

"I threw one in a game once to Mike Shannon of the Cardinals and he hit it out of the ballpark. Leo came out and told me to save that pitch for Toledo. I got the message.

"But I hold no hard feelings toward Leo Durocher. He was a great manager. He knew baseball inside and out. I had the pleasure of playing for two of baseball's best managers — Leo and Billy Martin with the Yankees. Both knew the game and both were very intense. And both were winners," he said.

He also has high praise for the last manager he played for, Tom Kelly of the Minnesota Twins. "Kelly is a player's manager, not intense like Leo or Billy Martin, but he knows how to get the best out of what he has. We won the pennant and the World Series in 1987 and I'm not sure we had the best team man for man. But we got the most out of what we had.

"When I came to the Twins, I was older than Kelly. He called me 'Pops.' But we got along real well and I still have a lot of respect for him," he said.

Niekro signed with the Cubs in 1966 and went to their rookie league team in Idaho where he pitched one game. He then went to Quincy, Illinois, and then to Dallas–Fort Worth for the remainder of the season.

He went to spring training with the Cubs in 1967 and made the team. In that 10-7 rookie year, he had seven complete games and two shutouts. He followed that with his 14-win season in 1968, a year in which he threw another shutout and had two saves in five relief appearances.

Niekro only spent one year in San Diego. On December 4, 1969, he was traded to the Detroit Tigers for pitcher Pat Dobson and infielder Dave Campbell. In his three seasons with the Tigers, he compiled a 21-22 record. On August 7, 1973, he was sold to the Atlanta Braves where he was a teammate of his brother, future Hall of Famer Phil Niekro. He was used primarily in relief for two years.

On April 6, 1975, Niekro was sold to the Houston Astros for $25,000, one of the best bargains in Houston's history. Niekro pitched 11 years for the Astros and is still their all-time winningest pitcher with 144 wins. He holds their single-season record for wins with 21 in 1979 and followed that with a 20-win season in 1980.

He is second on Houston's all-time list in complete games, innings pitched and shutouts, with only Larry Dierker ahead of him in all three categories. He helped Houston to a Western Division championship in 1980 and to a divisional playoff series in the strike-shortened 1981 season.

The 1980 league championship series (LCS) between Niekro's Astros and the Philadelphia Phillies is remembered as one of the great playoffs in baseball history. The Phillies won it in five games, but the last four went extra innings.

Niekro pitched 10 shutout innings in game three and the Astros pushed across a run in the 11th on Joe Morgan's triple and Denny Walling's sacrifice fly to win it 1–0. It was one of the classic games of Niekro's career — a shutout in a pressure-packed situation.

"It was a good game, but a better one was the game that got us there," he said. "All we had to do was win one of our last three games of the season to win our division. We were three games up on the Dodgers and that's who we played to end the season. And they swept us. So we had to play the Dodgers — at Dodger Stadium. I pitched and we won 7-1," he said.

The date was October 6, 1980. The game was played before a crowd of 51,127 fans at Dodger Stadium. The victory gave Niekro a 20-win season. But the playoff game proved costly to Houston because Niekro had to rest until the third game of the league championship series. Without a playoff game, he probably would have started two LCS games — and that could have made the difference for the Astros.

In 1982, Niekro narrowly missed having the best earned run average in the National League. That, too, went down to the last day of the season. "I needed to pitch a shutout and Steve Rogers at Montreal needed to allow two runs. I pitched my shutout, he allowed one run and he won the ERA title," said Niekro. (Rogers won by seven-tenths of a percentage point — 2.40 to Niekro's 2.47.)

The glory years for Niekro came more than a decade after the Cubs had traded him for Selma, who played only one more year with the Cubs and won 13 games over the next five years with three other teams before retiring.

"I really don't know what's kept the Cubs from getting over the top all of these years," said Niekro. "When I was there, they didn't have lights. All those day games in the heat — it really takes a toll on you. Even when you're not playing. You're just sitting out there in the bullpen with the sun beating down on you.

"I know it had an effect on the regulars who were out there day after day after day. Even your feet get hot in those black shoes," he said. "Chicago and St. Louis in the summertime get really hot.

"The Cubs have great fans. There are a lot of fans who love their teams when they're winning. Cubs fans love the Cubs all the time and they have a lot of fun at the ballpark. You know, they really started something with Harry Caray singing 'Take Me Out to the Ballgame' during the seventh inning stretch and now that Harry's gone, they're carrying it on with guest singers. I watch it down here in Florida on WGN. Did you see Mike Ditka singing? He better stick to football. But the point is, the fans love the Cubs and they're really into it," said Niekro.

He said he'd have to rate among his biggest thrills the nine times he pitched against his brother during their careers. He won five, Phil won four. And he hit a home run off his brother once, in 1976 — the only home run of Joe Niekro's career. That home run accounted for Niekro's only run batted in for the entire season.

What did Phil Niekro say about it? "He didn't say anything, but he doesn't send me Christmas cards anymore," said Joe, laughing again.

The Niekros hold two major league records: most total seasons played by two brothers — 46; Phil played 25 and Joe played 21; and most wins by two brothers — 539; Phil had 318 and Joe had 221.

In 1979, the Niekro brothers tied for the National League lead in wins with 21. They each won their 21st game on September 30, the last day of the season.

After he retired as an active player, Joe Niekro coached for the Portland Beavers in the Twins organization for two years and coached one year in the Colorado Rockies farm system.

Now, he said, he spends much of his time watching his children play — and they range in age from 24 years to 15 months.

His 20-year-old son, Lance, is a third baseman on the Florida Southern college team and will soon be eligible for the major league draft. As for the youngest Niekro, little Joseph, his father sees potential.

"He's throwing pretty good already," said Niekro.

The 1964 trade in which the Cubs traded Lou Brock to the St. Louis Cardinals for Ernie Broglio is considered by many observers to be among baseball's worst trades upon analysis of how the trade impacted both teams.

The 1969 trade in which Joe Niekro went to San Diego for Dick Selma can be put under a similar microscope. Selma spent only one year with the Cubs and was 10-8 — his best year in the major leagues. He was traded to Philadelphia after the 1969 season and spent five more years in the big leagues, winning 13 games.

After leaving the Cubs, Niekro spent 18 more years in the major leagues. Here are some of his accomplishments:

• 197 more major league victories (after 24 with the Cubs.)
• Houston Astros winningest pitcher with 144 victories.
• Houston Astros second-highest in complete games, innings pitched, and shutouts.
• Winner of 1980 sudden-death playoff game versus Los Angeles Dodgers.
• 0.00 earned run average in 10 innings in 1980 league championship Series versus Philadelphia Phillies.
• Member of the 1987 Minnesota Twins World Series championship team.

Joseph Franklin Niekro
Born Nov. 7, 1944, in Martins Ferry, Ohio
6' 1", 185 lbs.; B-right, T-right

Year	Team	W-L	ERA	G	IP	H	BB	SO
1967	Chi (N)	10-7	3.34	36	169.2	171	32	77
1968	Chi	14-10	4.31	34	177.1	204	59	65
1969	Chi-SD	8-18	3.70	41	221.1	237	51	62
1970	Det	12-13	4.06	38	213	221	72	101
1971	Det	6-7	4.50	31	122	136	49	43
1972	Det	3-2	3.83	18	47	62	8	24
1973	Atl	2-4	4.13	20	24	23	11	12
1974	Atl	3-2	3.56	27	43	36	18	31

Year	Team	W–L	ERA	G	IP	H	BB	SO
1975	Hous	6-4	3.07	40	88	79	39	54
1976	Hous	4-8	3.36	36	118	107	56	77
1977	Hous	13-8	3.03	44	181	155	64	101
1978	Hous	14-14	3.86	35	203	190	73	97
1979	Hous	21-11	3.00	38	264	221	107	119
1980	Hous	20-12	3.55	37	256	268	79	127
1981	Hous	9-9	2.82	24	166	150	47	77
1982	Hous	17-12	2.47	35	270	224	64	130
1983	Hous	15-14	3.48	38	263.2	238	101	152
1984	Hous	16-12	3.04	38	248.1	223	89	127
1985	Hous-NY	11-13	3.80	35	225	211	107	121
1986	NY (A)	9-10	4.86	25	126	139	63	59
1987	NY-Minn	7-13	5.33	27	147	155	64	84
1988	Minn	1-1	9.75	5	12	16	9	7
22 years		221-204	3.59	702	3585	3466	1262	1747

Transactions:

April 25, 1969: Traded with Gary Ross and Francisco Libran to San Diego for pitcher Dick Selma.

Dec. 4, 1969: Traded to Detroit Tigers for pitcher Pat Dobson and infielder Dave Campbell.

Aug. 7, 1973: Sold to Atlanta Braves.

April 6, 1975: Sold to Houston Astros for $35,000.

Aug. 30, 1987: Sold to Minnesota Twins.

DIVISIONAL PLAYOFF SERIES

Year	Team	W-L	ERA	G	IP	H	BB	SO
1981	Hous	0-0	0.00	1	8	7	3	4

LEAGUE CHAMPIONSHIP SERIES

Year	Team	W-L	ERA	G	IP	H	BB	SO
1980	Hous	0-0	0.00	1	10	6	1	2

WORLD SERIES

Year	Team	W-L	ERA	G	IP	H	BB	SO
1987	Minn	0-0	0.00	1	2	1	1	1

ARCHIE REYNOLDS
Cubs Pitcher, 1968–1970

*"With the Cubs, it's always something. They just
never seem to have the right combination and
they've always had a shortage of pitchers."*

TYLER, Texas — On August 15, 1968, Archie Reynolds made his major
league debut, pitching for the Chicago Cubs in the second game of a doubleheader at Crosley Field in Cincinnati. He started, pitched pretty well,
and had the lead when he was taken out for a relief pitcher.

But he didn't go five innings and besides, the game was suspended
after seven innings because the Reds had to catch a flight.

The significance of this is that for Reynolds, his first major league
appearance is about as close as he ever came to winning a major league
game. And if you were a young pitcher working for Leo Durocher, you
simply had to impress or you would be ignored.

Reynolds, 53, said, "I pitched pretty well in Cincinnati. A week later,
I started against Montreal, and was a little wild. Also, there were some mis-
plays in the field. We lost the game. A few days later, I was in the bullpen.
Not long after that, I got sent back to Triple-A.

"We always compared Leo to George Allen, the coach of the Washington Redskins who won championships using old-timers. Leo loved veteran players and didn't have much confidence in young players.

"I went to spring training camp with the Cubs in '68 and I had a good
spring. Several of us had a shot at the last spot on the squad before we left
camp. I had one bad outing but it was at the end of camp, and the next
thing I know, I'm in San Antonio. I was 13-2 there and back with the Cubs
in August," said Reynolds.

"In 1969, I went to camp again and had a good spring. I thought I
was going to make the team. I was a sinker-slider pitcher which was perfect for Wrigley Field. I only had one bad outing again and I remember it
well. It was a miserable, rainy day in Tucson. But it didn't matter. In trying to make Leo's team, if you had a bad outing, you were done. And I
wound up in Tacoma.

"It was a strange situation for me. I was young and I was in awe of
Leo. I not only knew of him from his days managing the Giants, but I
remembered him as a broadcaster on the *Game of the Week* on television.
I was in the presence of a baseball legend.

"But Leo was the kind of guy that if he got on an elevator with you, and you were the only two on the elevator, he was the friendliest guy in the world. If there were others on the elevator, he'd ignore you and act as if you didn't even exist. Why? I don't know. That was just Leo."

Reynolds signed with the Cubs out of junior college in 1966 and was assigned to Treasure Valley in the rookie league where he was 9-3, made the All-Star team and led the league in earned run average. Two other pitchers on that rookie team were Joe Niekro and Rich Nye, both future major league hurlers who would eventually compete with Reynolds for a spot in the Cubs pitching rotation.

In 1967, Reynolds was assigned to Dallas–Fort Worth in the Texas League and had a 6-7 record with a 3.00 earned run average when he left for six months of active duty in the military reserves.

Reynolds got into only seven games with the Cubs in 1968 and had an 0-1 record with a 6.75 earned run average. He gave up 14 hits and issued seven walks in 13⅓ innings. He was sent down to San Antonio, where, with regular work, he registered a 13-2 record with a 2.00 earned run average. That earned him a return trip to the Cubs spring training camp.

In 1969, he got into only two games, had an 0-1 record again and again suffered from control problems, walking seven and giving up 11 hits in seven innings. His ERA was 2.57. He spent most of the year in Tacoma.

"In 1970, I had another good spring and this time I made the team. And then I didn't get into a game until about May 15. We were in Atlanta and Leo had gotten thrown out of the game and so had our pitcher, Kenny Holtzman.

"Pete Reiser, the acting manager, brought me in to replace Holtzman. That's how I finally got into a game. Once you got into Leo's doghouse, it was hard to get out. Reiser always said he couldn't understand why Leo didn't give me 10 starts. Then, if I don't make it, fine, I had my shot. But I never got that chance.

"When Reiser called on me in that game in Atlanta, I had to face Henry Aaron with the bases loaded — and he was the first guy I had faced in a long time without a batting cage around him. Fortunately, I think he grounded out," said Reynolds.

"Leo had a double standard. Paul Popovich used to say there were the regulars and the irregulars. Rich Nye would sit in the bullpen and try to analyze it. He was a college graduate and was real smart and he couldn't figure it out.

"Leo used the same veteran players so often that when we'd get off a plane or arrive at the ballpark, there were only a handful of players that any of the fans recognized. For the rest of us, they didn't even know our names.

"In 1968, I wore uniform number 39, but in '69 when Dick Selma came over from San Diego, he wanted 39. So I got number 48. That uniform got to be kind of a joke because it always seemed to go to the guy who was going to be sent down next. I wore it. Jim Colborn wore it. Joe Decker wore it. If you wore 48, you knew you weren't going to last long," he said.

"When pitchers toss a ball back and forth before a game, a lot of times they'll fool around with a new pitch. We used to stand in the outfield and throw knuckleballs to each other. Mine didn't do anything. It was like most people's. It just floated straight with nothing on it. Now Joe Niekro— he could really throw one. But in those days, the Cubs management didn't want any young pitchers throwing knuckleballs. They were absolutely against it. So Niekro didn't throw it until he got traded. And then he made a pretty good living throwing it from time to time for about 20 years.

"I make no excuses. My problem was, when I got a chance, I didn't perform. And Leo had no patience with people like me. I had heard that Leo was telling people in 1970 that I would never pitch for him again. But he never said anything to me," said Reynolds.

"And there were a lot of trade rumors. John Holland, our general manager was quoted in the newspaper as saying, 'Everybody wants the guy we're not using but nobody wants to give us anything for him.' I knew who he was talking about."

On July 9, 1970, the Cubs traded Reynolds to the California Angels in a strange deal.

"We were playing Montreal. Before the game, I got a message to go up to John Holland's office. When I got there, he started telling me about how the Cubs were going to make some personnel changes and I was one of them.

"He told me he hated to do it because I had always been one of Mr. Wrigley's favorites which was just a song-and-dance that I'm sure he told anybody he traded. But like I said, it was kind of a strange deal and here's why. The Cubs needed a left-hander and the Phillies were interested in me. John Quinn was general manager of the Phillies and his son, Jack, was the general manager of Hawaii, the Angel farm club.

"I cleared waivers and, in effect, was optioned to Hawaii. In return, Juan Pizarro, a real good left-hander with major league experience who had been pitching in Hawaii, went to the Cubs. I think the idea was that someday, John Quinn in Philadelphia would get me from his son's club in Hawaii but that never happened.

"I had become so frustrated in Chicago that I was excited to leave. I caught a flight and started the next night in Hawaii for Chuck Tanner who was the manager there. And the next year, 1971, I got the most work I ever got in the major leagues.

"Lefty Phillips was the California manager. Lefty was a great guy but there was no discipline. We had some real characters on that team — Alex Johnson, Chico Ruiz and some others. We even had an incident with a gun in the clubhouse that got a lot of publicity. There was just not the professionalism there that we had in Chicago and I say that even with all the problems I had with Leo."

In 1972, the Angels shipped Reynolds to Milwaukee, his last stop in the major leagues. "I'll tell you something about Milwaukee in those days. If you had ever been 'up' in the major leagues, you knew you weren't 'up' any more if you played for the Brewers. They were a long way from 'up,'" said Reynolds.

He played for Evansville in 1973, went to spring training with the Brewers in 1974 and was sold to Mexico City in the Mexican League. "As a ballplayer, there's a definite message there, when a major league team sends you to Mexico City," he said. "I called Jack Quinn and managed to finish the '74 season in Hawaii," he said. In another year, he was out of baseball altogether.

Since that time, he has sold insurance, spent five years in Saudi Arabia working for a Louisiana oil company, got divorced and remarried, operated a bar for nine years and is now selling mobile homes in Tyler, Texas.

From his experience playing with the Cubs and from many years of watching them, Reynolds said it's hard to say why they haven't made it to the top. "In our day, we blamed it on the heat, playing all of those day games, the same thing they used to say in Texas about the Rangers. But I'll tell you something. Day games are an advantage. You have the opportunity to go home and get a good night's sleep every night — if you go home.

"So I don't think playing all those day games, or playing in Wrigley Field has much to do with it. I think if you took the Braves team and put them in Wrigley Field, they'd still win. With the Cubs, year after year, it's always something. They just never seem to have the right combination and they've always had a shortage of pitchers.

"The fans at Wrigley Field are just great — and those who think that might be part of the problem may have something there. Because win or lose, everyone's happy at the end of the day if you go to the ballgame at Wrigley Field. That might be the Red Sox's problem, too. There's not that burning desire, that tradition to live up to, the feeling that you have to win. Because the Cubs fans will be there, win or lose.

"But more than anything else with the Cubs, it's just never quite having the right people to get the job done," said Reynolds.

His lifetime record as a big league pitcher is 0-8. "I don't talk about it much because hardly anybody down here knows I was once in the major leagues," he said. "But do I think about it? Sure. Even 30 years later, I can say it would have been nice to get a win, to have just one. Because I came so close.

"There was that suspended game in Cincinnati. And there were other chances. When I think about it now, it's frustrating. I pitched 3⅔ innings in relief against St. Louis in a game against St. Louis that went about 15 innings. I think it was Al Hrabosky's first appearance with the Cardinals [in 1970, Hrabosky's rookie year]. But I didn't get a decision.

"In my next start, I lost 3–1 to Nolan Ryan in a game where he threw a one-hitter against us. In 1972, in my first start for Milwaukee, I shut out Oakland for seven innings but didn't get the decision — and that was that great Oakland team that won the World Series three years in a row.

"Yeah, I had some good games here and there, but you know what I didn't have in my major league career?

"I never had a 10-to-5 lead."

Archie Edward Reynolds
Born Jan. 3, 1948, in Glendale, Calif.
6' 2", 205 lbs.; B-right, T-right

Year	Team	W-L	ERA	G	IP	H	BB	SO
1968	Chi (N)	0-1	6.75	7	13.1	14	7	6
1969	Chi	0-1	2.57	2	7	11	7	4
1970	Chi	0-2	6.60	7	15	17	9	9
1971	Cal	0-3	4.67	15	27	32	18	15
1972	Mil	0-1	7.11	5	19	26	8	13
5 years		0-8	5.75	36	81.1	100	49	47

Transactions:

July 9, 1970: Traded to California for pitcher Juan Pizarro.

Part IV.
The 1970s, 1980s, 1990s

Year	W-L	Pct.	Finished	Games Out	Manager
1970	84-78	.519	2nd	5	Durocher
1971	83-79	.512	3rd (tied)	14	Durocher
1972	85-70 (s)	.548	2nd	11	Durocher/Lockman
1973	77-84	.478	5th	5	Lockman
1974	66-96	.407	6th	22	Lockman/Marshall
1975	75-87	.463	5th (tied)	17.5	Marshall
1976	75-87	.463	4th	26	Marshall
1977	81-81	.500	4th	20	Franks
1978	79-83	.488	3rd	11	Franks
1979	80-82	.494	5th	18	Franks/Amalfitano
1980	64-98	.395	6th	27	Gomez/Amalfitano
1981	38-65 (s)	.369	6th	21.5	Amalfitano
1982	73-89	.451	5th	19	Elia
1983	71-91	.438	5th	19	Elia/Fox
1984	96-65	.596	1st	+ 6.5	Frey
1985	77-84	.478	4th	23.5	Frey
1986	70-90	.438	5th	37	Frey/Vukovich/Michael
1987	76-85	.472	6th	18.5	Michael/Lucchesi
1988	77-85	.475	4th	24	Zimmer
1989	93-69	.574	1st	+ 6	Zimmer
1990	77-85	.475	4th	18	Zimmer
1991	77-83	.481	4th	20	Zimmer/Altobelli/Essian
1992	78-84	.481	4th	18	Lefebvre

Year	W-L	Pct.	Finished	Games Out	Manager
1993	84-78	.519	4th	13	Lefebvre
1994 (s)	49-64	.434	5th	16.5	Trebelhorn
1995 (s)	73-71	.507	3th	12	Riggleman
1996	76-86	.469	4th	12	Riggleman
1997	68-94	.420	5th	16	Riggleman
1998	93-70 (w)	.574	2nd	10	Riggleman

(s) strike-shortened season
(w) earned playoff berth as wild card entry

LARRY GURA
Cubs Pitcher, 1970–1973

"The front office did some strange things. There were rumors that you'd be gone if someone didn't like the way you looked or the way you dressed."

LITCHFIELD, Ariz.— Larry Gura says he was the "player to be named later" in the deal in which Ferguson Jenkins was traded to Texas in 1973.

It was obviously a complicated set of circumstances since Gura was actually traded two months before Jenkins was — but circumstances were always complicated for young Cubs pitchers in those days.

"Leo wanted experienced pitchers," said Gura, 51, who went from Arizona State University to the Cubs Triple-A affiliate at Tacoma in 1969. In 1970, he went to spring training with the Cubs and made the team.

"But it was an up-and-down roller coaster with Durocher. He didn't trust young pitchers. He wanted experience. But how are you going to get experience if no one gives you a chance?

"When you got a chance, if you pitched badly, you'd go to the bottom of his list. And the only way you'd make it back to the top is if enough other guys pitched badly. That's exactly the way it was with Leo Durocher," said Gura.

"One year, I was with the Cubs for three months and had six innings of work. It's a little hard to impress someone when you're doing that. Another thing about those days — you never knew your role, and that made it tough, too. I was a starter in the minors but Leo used me a lot in relief. You never knew what you were going to do.

"There's a whole different mentality to being a starter. You have time to psyche yourself up for a game and you can establish a pattern, a flow, a routine as the game goes along. With relief pitching, it's completely different. It's right now. You don't have hours to prepare, you have minutes. The mental preparation isn't the same at all.

"And the bad part with Leo for us young pitchers was that you never knew. One time we were playing a doubleheader and we knew ahead of time that me or Jim Colborn or Joe Decker was going to work the second game but we didn't know which one of us.

"Someone asked Leo before the first game who was pitching the second game and he said 'Don't worry about it.' So that was that. Then, between games, I opened my locker and there were two balls inside — the signal that you're starting the next game. I asked Leo about it and he said, 'I didn't want to scare you.' Scare me? The established pitchers were in a rotation. They had a routine. They prepared themselves mentally and physically. Me? I was a kid and that's how Leo treated me."

Gura said his first appearance in the major leagues was a typical Durocher maneuver. "We were playing the Braves in Atlanta. I was in the bullpen and I had just gotten up to throw a few, just to loosen up. All of a sudden I'm in the ballgame facing Rico Carty, Orlando Cepeda and Henry Aaron, two future Hall of Famers and a batting champion, all right-handed hitters. [Gura was a left-hander.]

"I said to myself, 'Oh, great, this is a good way to start your career. I got Aaron and Cepeda but I contributed to Carty's 32-game hitting streak," said Gura.

"I got my first win in Montreal. I actually got a start and we got some runs early. Joe Becker, our pitching coach, came out to the mound in the third or fourth inning and I said, 'don't you dare take me out of this game.' In those days, the infielders could all come in to the mound so Santo, Kessinger, Beckert and Jim Hickman all heard me and, to tell you the truth, I think they were kind of impressed with my aggressiveness. At any rate, I stayed in the game and I think we won, 11–3."

Gura had three starts with the Cubs in 1970 and worked in relief in 17 games, posting a 1-3 record. He worked exclusively in relief in 1971 and 1972, appearing in only six and seven games, respectively, with no wins or losses. Then in 1973, he appeared in 21 games, starting seven, and posting a 2-4 record.

On August 31, 1973, he was traded to the Texas Rangers for pitcher Mike Paul and spent the rest of the year in the minor leagues. Jenkins was traded to the Rangers on October 25 for infielders Bill Madlock and Vic Harris. So if the Jenkins deal was arranged in advance, Gura could have been a part of the overall deal, a "player to be named later" so to speak, but traded first.

At any rate, it was in Texas that he had his first encounter with manager Billy Martin. "I pitched one inning in spring training and he sent me out [to the minors]. He told me I needed to work on my control," said Gura. "My control? That was always my strong point. And he had a pitching staff of David Clyde, Jim Bibby and others who couldn't hit the broad side of a barn. But he sent me to Spokane." He never threw a pitch in a regular season game for the Rangers.

On May 8, 1974, Gura was traded to the Yankees for catcher Duke Sims — a move that Gura thought would be a turning point in his career. "Bill Virdon was the manager there and he gave me my first real shot. I got called up in September. He put me in the starting rotation right away and I went 5–1.

"I beat Nolan Ryan 2–1 in New York and then we went to Chicago and I got beat in my next start on a Sunday. I remember sitting next to Whitey Ford [Yankees pitching coach] on the bus on the way to the airport and I said, 'If I was with the Cubs, I wouldn't pitch for four weeks.' And Ford said to me, 'You're pitching Friday.'

"I really appreciated the confidence Virdon had in me and was looking forward to the next season. But then — Virdon gets axed and who do they bring in to manage? Billy Martin. I went to him right away to try to square things, to let him know the past was the past as far as I was concerned. And he told me, 'Things are fine.'

"Then he went from a five-man to a four-man starting rotation and guess who got left out. I went to talk with him about it. I told him, 'Look, right now I'm pitching better than Catfish [Hunter] so what's going on?'

"I didn't mean anything by it. During a baseball season, all pitching staffs go through periods where one guy is pitching better than another. It happens all the time. It's part of baseball. But I think Billy thought I was saying I was a better pitcher than Catfish.

"Anyway, the next year, I go to spring training and Billy comes up to me and says, 'You're my fifth starter.' A month later, I got traded to Kansas City."

On May 16, 1976, the Yankees sent Gura to the Royals in exchange for catcher Fran Healy. And finally, he had found a home. He pitched 10 years for the Royals and became a mainstay in their starting rotation in 1978 when he compiled a 16-4 record with a 2.72 earned run average. He was an 18-game winner in 1980 and again in 1982.

Gura won 111 games in a Royal uniform and lost only 78. His .590 winning percentage is the highest in team history. He ranks fourth all-time in team wins, innings pitched and shutouts despite the fact he didn't become a starter with them until he was 30 years old.

He also helped them get to the league championship series four times and into the 1980 World Series. "We didn't quite beat the Phillies that year but getting into the World Series is every ballplayer's dream," said Gura.

He said the best game he ever pitched was a one-hitter against Toronto. "Alfredo Griffin got a broken-bat hit over shortstop or I'd have had the no-hitter," he said.

The one-hitter was his best game — but not his biggest game. That came toward the end of the season in 1976. "We were tied for the division lead with Oakland and I got the start against them and beat them. I remember when Whitey Herzog told me I was going to start and what a thrill it was. [It was one of two starts he had all year.] He even asked me who I wanted as my catcher and I said John Watham.

"I heard that when Harry Caray [a White Sox broadcaster in those days] saw on the scoreboard that the battery for that game was Gura and Watham, he said, 'How in the world is Kansas City going to win that game?' But we did. We broke the Oakland dynasty." (The A's had won the American League West championship five years in a row and won the World Series three consecutive years during that stretch.)

Gura said while he is grateful to Virdon and Herzog for giving him the chance he needed, he wouldn't have minded staying with the Cubs if the circumstances had been different. "For one thing, I loved the day games. I don't really see that as being part of their problem.

"The front office did some strange things. There were rumors that you'd be gone if someone didn't like the way you looked or the way you dressed. I'm not talking about Mr. Wrigley because he didn't have much to do with the club. It was the people he had working for him, or at least that's what we always heard.

"At Kansas City, Mr. Kaufman let everyone do their job in the front office — and he had good people working for him — and look at the success they had.

"There were other strange things in Chicago. Why did they put that basket on the outfield wall. That was a short ballpark as it was and of course that just made it shorter," he said. (In 1970, the Cubs installed wire fencing that extends out from the outfield walls and serves as a "basket" that fly balls fall into, just short of the outfield wall. Balls hit into the basket are home runs.)

"You hear a lot about the great fans at Wrigley Field and most of them are. But I remember when they booed Ron Santo's son at a father-son game when Santo was in a slump. And I remember how, even when we'd have a seven or eight game lead, the fans would come up to you and say, 'When are you going to blow it?'

"The media would be that way, too. You'd lose a couple of games and they'd be all over you, like 'Here they go again.' It's the same as putting an idea in your mind. You know, when you're on the golf course and someone says, 'Don't hit it in the water'—you know where you're next shot's going to go.

"I'm not blaming the fans or the media. I'm just saying it was different in Chicago than in Kansas City, for example. In Kansas City, when we'd start to lose, everyone would say, 'Don't worry about it. You'll get 'em tomorrow.' And you know, that's a whole different atmosphere.

"There were some good times in Chicago. I remember sitting in the bullpen and watching Ernie Banks hit his 500th home run. It brought tears to your eyes, it really did. And playing with guys like Banks and Jenkins and Billy Williams.

"And Fergie Jenkins winning 20 games all those years in that ballpark. How'd he do that? It was great. I enjoyed those years.

"I made my best fielding play when I was with the Cubs, my Lou Brock play. Brock, of course, was with the Cardinals and you know how fast he could run. Well, he hit a high chopper over the mound against me. The ball went way up in the air and past me. Kessinger came running in from short but he was never going to get there.

"I ran out with my back to the plate and caught it over the shoulder, Willie Mays style, and then turned and threw him out at first," he said.

With all of the special times he had in baseball — the one-hitter against Toronto, the big victory over Oakland, the four division championships and the World Series appearance, Gura seems to only have one lingering regret.

"I'd like to have a videotape of that Lou Brock play," he said.

The Cubs' trade of Larry Gura to Texas for Mike Paul in 1973 deserves a closer look. Paul had pitched four years for Cleveland and was in his second year with Texas when he was traded to the Cubs for Gura on August 31, 1973. He had a lifetime record of 27-46.

Paul was 0-1 with the Cubs for the rest of the 1973 season and appeared in only two games in 1974, pitching one inning in relief, allowing four runs on four hits and a walk, for an earned run average of 36.00 He never pitched in the major leagues again.

Gura was 3-7 in limited service with the Cubs over four years. After leaving the Cubs, he spent 13 more years in the major leagues. Here are some of his accomplishments:

- 123 more major league wins; only 90 more losses.
- Kansas City Royals lifetime leader in winning percentage among starters with .590.
- Threw a one-hitter against Toronto Blue Jays.
- Had three-year span (1976–1978) where he won 28, lost 9.
- Helped Kansas City Royals to four division championships.
- Member of 1980 American League All-Star squad.
- Member of 1980 American League championship team.

Lawrence Cyril Gura
Born Nov. 26, 1947, in Joliet, Ill.
6', 170 lbs.; B-left, T-left

Year	Team	W-L	ERA	G	IP	H	BB	SO
1970	Chi (N)	1-3	3.79	20	38	35	23	21
1971	Chi	0-0	6.00	6	3	6	1	2
1972	Chi	0-0	3.75	7	12	11	3	13
1973	Chi	2-4	4.85	21	65	79	11	43
1974	NY (A)	5-1	2.41	8	56	54	12	17
1975	NY	7-8	3.51	26	151.1	173	41	65
1976	KC	4-0	2.29	20	63	47	20	22
1977	KC	8-5	3.14	52	106	108	28	46
1978	KC	16-4	2.72	35	221.2	183	60	81
1979	KC	13-12	4.46	39	234	226	73	85
1980	KC	18-10	2.96	36	283	272	76	113
1981	KC	11-8	2.72	23	172	139	35	61
1982	KC	18-12	4.03	37	248	251	64	98
1983	KC	11-18	4.90	34	200.1	220	76	57
1984	KC	12-9	5.18	31	168.2	175	67	68
1985	KC-Chi(N)	0-3	9.50	8	24	41	10	9
16 years		126-97	3.76	403	2046	2020	600	801

Transactions:
Aug. 31, 1973: Traded to Texas for pitcher Mike Paul.
May 8, 1974: Traded to New York Yankees for catcher Duke Sims.
May 16, 1976: Traded to Kansas City for catcher Fran Healy.

Divisional Playoff Series

Year	Team	W-L	ERA	G	IP	H	BB	SO
1981	KC	0-1	7.36	1	3.2	7	3	3

LEAGUE CHAMPIONSHIP SERIES

Year	Team	W-L	ERA	G	IP	H	BB	SO
1976	KC	0-1	4.22	2	10.2	18	1	4
1977	KC	0-1	18.00	2	2	7	1	2
1978	KC	1-0	2.84	1	6.1	8	2	2
1980	KC	1-0	2.00	1	9	10	1	4
4 years		2-2	4.18	6	28	43	5	12

WORLD SERIES

Year	Team	W-L	ERA	G	IP	H	BB	SO
1980	KC	0-0	2.19	2	12.1	8	3	4

PETE LaCOCK
Cubs First Baseman, 1972–1976

"You have to build a team around that ballpark, especially with pitching and defense. I'm not sure the Cubs always did that."

OVERLAND PARK, Kan.—"I'm the answer to a trivia question," Pete LaCock said with a laugh, taking a break from baseball lessons he gives at The Old Ballgame, a sports academy.

"I hit the last pitch Bob Gibson ever threw in his major league career. It was a grand-slam home run on Bob Gibson Day in St. Louis. He used to kid about it and say that if I hit one off him, he knew he was through.

"I hit another one off of him earlier in my career in a game I think we won 3–2," said LaCock, 47, who played five years with the Cubs and four with the Kansas City Royals.

(Gibson recalls the incident differently. In his 1994 autobiography, he says the Cardinals brought him in for a rare relief appearance against the Cubs, two days after Bob Gibson Day, and he gave up the bomb to LaCock. He said Red Schoendienst, the Cardinal manager, came out to get him and he gladly gave him the ball. He called the LaCock homer "the absolute limit in humiliation" in a season in which he won 3 and lost 10.)

LaCock came up with the Cubs in 1972 when Billy Williams broke his ankle and the Cubs needed a left-handed hitting outfielder. "I think my reaction was 'it's about time' or something like that," he said. LaCock signed with the Cubs right out of Taft High School in Woodland Hills, California, the same school where Larry Dierker played a few years before him and Robin Yount played a few years after him.

LaCock spent four years in the minors, winning the Triple Crown in one of those years, before earning his shot when Williams hurt his hand.

On September 6, 1972, he made his debut in a starting role against the Philadelphia Phillies. "I went 2-for-3 off of Wayne Twitchell and drove in three runs. It was a good day," said LaCock. He got into four other games that year and finished with a .500 batting average — 3-for-6 including 1-for-1 as a pinch hitter. None of that made much of an impression on his manager.

"Leo Durocher really didn't know who I was," he said. "Fergie [Jenkins] used to laugh about it. Leo could just never remember my name. He probably thought to himself: Let's give this long-haired freak a chance to show what he can do."

Four days earlier, LaCock was on the bench when Milt Pappas of the Cubs threw a no-hitter against the San Diego Padres — and had a perfect game for 8⅔ innings.

"Bruce Froemming was the umpire and he called ball four on a 3-and-2 pitch with two out in the ninth inning," said LaCock. "Garry Jestadt was the next hitter and he got him out to get the no-hitter."

(Pappas was infuriated over the ball-four call on the previous hitter. He reportedly confronted Froemming about it in the next day or two and asked him how he could do that on a call that could have gone either way. Froemming is said to have told Pappas, "If I had called it the other way, I wouldn't have been able to sleep," to which Pappas replied, "How have you slept after all the other lousy calls you've made?")

LaCock had better years with the Royals than he did with the Cubs. For Kansas City, he hit .303, .295 and .277 in 1977 through 1979. In his best year with the Cubs, he hit .229 in 1975.

"I got to play more in Kansas City," said LaCock. "That makes a big difference. With the Cubs, I was more of a spot starter. Plus, Wrigley Field is a great ballpark but it's a tough place to play. It's hot during the day and you never know what the wind is going to be doing.

"I had an apartment right outside of Wrigley Field. The first thing I did when I got up in the morning was check to see which way the wind was blowing, because you always knew what kind of a game you were going to have. If the wind was blowing out, it was going to be 18–16. If it was blowing in, it was going to be 2–1.

"I saw Dave Kingman hit the hardest ball that's ever been hit. If someone tells me they've seen one hit harder, I would challenge them on it. The ball went over the brownstones across the street from the left field bleachers. The wind wasn't blowing out that day; it was blowing up," said LaCock. (Kingman played for the Giants at the time.)

"Jose Cardenal, our left fielder, came running in at the end of the inning and he couldn't stop talking about it. He kept saying, 'The ball heet so hard, eet look like vitamin.'"

In one of LaCock's most memorable games with the Cubs, he was more of a spectator even though he was playing right field. On September 16, 1975, he could do little but watch as the Pirates beat the Cubs, 22–0 at Wrigley Field. In that game, Pittsburgh's Rennie Stennett became the first major league player to get seven hits in a nine-inning game. He got two hits in an inning twice in that game — and that's a major league record, too. A third record is the final score — the most lopsided shutout in history.

"So many of them were going around the bases, I thought they were bringing their families with them," said LaCock.

He said he couldn't pinpoint specific reasons why the Cubs have had such a long drought from winning the pennant. "Day baseball may be part of it. It takes a lot out of you and it's a hard adjustment to go from night ball to day ball like the Cubs had to do all the time," he said.

"Another thing is the ballpark. You have to build a team around that ballpark, especially with pitching and defense. I'm not sure the Cubs always did that. Even in their good years, they seemed to be one pitcher short."

On December 8, 1976, LaCock was in a three-way trade involving the Cubs, the Royals and the New York Mets. LaCock was traded to Kansas City for outfielder Sheldon Mallory who was then peddled to the Mets for catcher Jim Dwyer.

At Kansas City, LaCock played for Whitey Herzog. "The guy knows how to win. He's intense. He makes a lot of moves. But he gets a lot of respect. He got my respect. He's a winner."

LaCock hit .333 in league championship series play with the Royals, getting four hits in 12 at-bats in 1977, 1978 and 1980. He was a defensive replacement in the 1980 World Series for Kansas City but did not come to bat.

When LaCock was with the Cubs, one of the priorities for players during their off-time was to visit children in hospitals. That experience gave him a perspective that has carried on long after his baseball career ended.

"After I left the Cubs and was in Kansas City, a nurse called and asked me if I would come visit some kids with cancer. These kids were terminally ill. I did it and I was astounded. They are remarkable. They are inspiring. They are the most courageous people I have ever met in my life," he said.

LaCock's wife, Janna, is executive director of the Mid-America Chapter of the Leukemia Society of America. In 1992, she began a program called "Team in Training" in which runners from all over the country compete in endurance events to raise money for leukemia research.

It has raised $50 million and has expanded over the years to include walking, cycling and triathlons in addition to running events. Competitors earn money for the fight against leukemia through pledges from supporters.

The triathlon includes swimming, biking and running. LaCock himself has competed in the Ironman Triathlon — a grueling ordeal that involves a 2.4 mile swim, 112 miles of biking and a 26.2 mile run. In 1996, he competed in Kailua, Hawaii, a little more than a year after undergoing an angioplasty to correct a blocked artery around his heart.

LaCock said triathlon competition has given him tremendous respect for athletes who compete in events that require so much time for preparation and are totally dependent on individual achievement.

"In baseball, you have a bad game and you can play well the next day," he said. "But with Olympic athletes, you train for four years and can lose by a fraction of a second.

"I do it [triathlons] because it's a challenge," said LaCock. "Life is a bunch of challenges. I've always liked challenges and I like to set goals for myself. I never would have played baseball if I wasn't goal-oriented."

But his focus in the charity triathlons and in Team in Training is not on the winning or losing but on the kids who benefit from the events, said LaCock, who has two healthy daughters.

His father is Peter Marshall, a singer and nightclub performer who won fame in television as the host of the popular game show *Hollywood Squares.*

"He's doing fine," said LaCock. "He's 73 years old and last year did 40 concerts with Les Brown and His Band of Renown."

Marshall, who still plays golf and tennis, teamed with his son a few years ago to sponsor a charity golf tournament to help pay off a Ronald McDonald house and he went to Hawaii in 1996 to entertain at the Ironman Triathlon festivities in which his son was competing.

LaCock said he's amazed at the salaries ballplayers are drawing today but doesn't begrudge them one penny of it. "I don't think there's a case on record where a player put a gun to an owner's head and said 'pay me.' The money is there," he said.

LaCock retired from major league baseball at the age of 28. He looks back on his career with pride, particularly his years with the Cubs.

"How could I not have enjoyed it? First of all, it was such a first-class group of guys: Don Kessinger, Glenn Beckert, Billy Williams, Fergie Jenkins, Randy Hundley, Ernie Banks, Ron Santo— all wonderful people.

"Baseball in Wrigley Field is untouchable," he said. "The fans are great and the field is wonderful. When I was playing first base there, I used to have conversations with people in the first row. And when you're in the bullpen, the fans bring you food and talk with you all the time.

"And have you ever noticed — there's never any fights at Wrigley Field. When I was playing there, I don't think the policemen even wore guns. The fans would get to know your route home when the game was over. I used to pull up to stop lights and fans would run up to the car and want autographs.

"It wasn't that way over on the south side, at Comiskey Park. It's funny. It's the same city but a whole different atmosphere from the one ballpark to another.

"To me, Wrigley Field is like a great old church and playing there is a religious experience. I used to stand in the batter's box and think: Babe Ruth put his feet exactly where my feet are. Now, that's a special feeling and I got to experience it. I'm the luckiest man alive."

Ralph Pierre LaCock II
Born Jan. 17, 1952, in Burbank, Calif.
6' 2", 200 lbs.; B-left, T-left

Year	Team	G	AB	R	H	D	T	HR	RBI	Ave.
1972	Chi (N)	5	6	3	3	0	0	0	4	.500
1973	Chi	11	16	1	4	1	0	0	3	.250
1974	Chi	35	110	9	20	4	1	1	8	.182
1975	Chi	106	249	30	57	8	1	6	30	.229
1976	Chi	106	244	34	54	9	2	8	28	.221
1977	KC	88	218	25	66	12	1	3	29	.303
1978	KC	118	322	44	95	21	2	5	48	.295
1979	KC	132	408	54	113	25	4	3	56	.277
1980	KC	114	156	14	32	6	0	1	18	.205
9 years		715	1729	214	444	86	11	27	224	.257

Transactions:

Dec. 8, 1976: Traded to Kansas City for outfielder Sheldon Mallory; Mallory was then traded to the New York Mets for catcher Jim Dwyer to complete the three-team trade.

League Championship Series

Year	Team	G	AB	R	H	D	T	HR	RBI	Ave.
1977	KC	1	1	0	0	0	0	0	0	.000
1978	KC	4	11	1	4	2	1	0	1	.364
1980	KC	1	0	0	0	0	0	0	0	.000
3 years		6	12	1	4	2	1	0	1	.333

World Series

Year	Team	G	AB	R	H	D	T	HR	RBI	Ave.
1980	KC	1	0	0	0	0	0	0	0	.000

Whitey Lockman
Cubs Manager, 1972–1974

"Some people think playing all days games, like they used to, and then going on the road and playing at night, messes up your biorhythms and they may be right."

SCOTTSDALE, Ariz.— Whitey Lockman has been in baseball longer than the Cubs' pennant drought. He broke into professional baseball as a 16-year-old in 1943. Today, at age 72, he scouts for the Florida Marlins.

He is a soft-spoken man who punctuates many of his sentences with a chuckle that is the vocal equivalent of the twinkling of an eye.

For parts of three seasons, he was manager of the Chicago Cubs. "I took over for Leo [Durocher] in '72 and had them in 1973 and part of 1974. We had some good ballplayers back then — Ferguson Jenkins and Milt Pappas and Burt Hooton and Rick Reuschel on the pitching staff..."

He ticked off the names from the past as quickly as if he was giving the names of his children.

"...Billy Williams, Glenn Beckert, Don Kessinger, Ron Santo, Rick Monday and Randy Hundley — that was a pretty good team. I don't know why we didn't win it; the only thing I can figure is mismanagement," he said, offering that infectious chuckle.

The Cubs, who had become a contender under Durocher, were

floundering in Leo's sixth season, and were in fourth place, just two games above .500 at 46-44 when the decision was made to make a change. Lockman came on and led the team to a 39-26 record the rest of the way. The Cubs finished second, but a distant second, 11 games behind the Pittsburgh Pirates.

The next season was one of the strangest in National League history, with five teams having a chance at the Eastern Division championship going into the last weekend of the season.

The Mets, with Yogi Berra as manager and Willie Mays in his last big league season, won the title with an 82-79 record. The Cubs finished fifth with a 77-84 record but just five games out of first. Jenkins, Hooton and Reuschel all won 14 games — but all lost more than 14.

"The thing that threw a monkey wrench into that race was how well the Montreal Expos did," said Lockman. "Here they were in about their fifth year and they were right in the race, all the way to the finish."

Gene Mauch's Expos finished fourth, two games ahead of the Cubs, chiefly because of a young relief pitcher, Mike Marshall, who won 14 games and saved 31 of Montreal's total of 79 wins that year.

Between the 1973 and 1974 seasons, the Cubs traded Jenkins to the Texas Rangers for infielders Bill Madlock and Vic Harris. Madlock eventually won two batting titles with the Cubs but the immediate result for the Cubs was that they were without their ace and had to find some other way of winning the 20 games Jenkins usually won. They didn't and Lockman lost his job. Jenkins had won 20 or more games six years in a row before slipping to 14 in 1973.

While the Cubs sank to last place with a 66-96 record in 1974, Jenkins led the American League in wins with 25 and went on to win 115 games in eight seasons in the American League before the Cubs got him back in 1982.

Lockman was fired 93 games into the 1974 season as the Cubs could manage only a 41-52 mark. They were 25-44 for Lockman's replacement, Jim Marshall, the rest of the way.

"The one thing we didn't have in my years in Chicago was good middle relief. We were fairly strong everywhere else but that weakness hurt us," said Lockman.

He signed with the New York Giants right out of high school and was sent to Jersey City, New Jersey "I stayed there 10 days and didn't get into a game. I don't know why they sent me there in the first place. Then I went to Springfield, Massachusetts for part of the season and then they sent me back to Jersey City. I played there the rest of '43 and all of the 1944 season.

"My manager there was Gabby Hartnett, an ex–Cubbie. What a

wonderful man he was. He was a great guy and he really knew the game. Genial. That's what I would call him. He might have been just the right type of guy for a 16-year-old like me to have as a manager. I wasn't scared. I was excited to be there," said Lockman.

He was called up to the Giants in mid-season 1945 — and hit a home run in his first major league at-bat. "July 5, 1945. The pitcher was George Dockins, D-O-C-K-I-N-S, of the Cardinals. Some things you don't forget," he said.

He played on Giant pennant winners in 1951 and 1954 and was one of manager Alvin Dark's coaches on the Giants' 1962 pennant winner.

Had it not been for Lockman, Bobby Thomson may not have hit "the shot heard 'round the world"—the home run that won the 1951 championship in the third game of the playoffs against the Brooklyn Dodgers.

The Giants went into the bottom of the ninth inning, trailing 4–1. Brooklyn's big right-hander Don Newcombe appeared to be in control. But Dark led off the bottom of the ninth with a base hit and Don Mueller followed with a single.

Then Lockman doubled, scoring Dark and moving Mueller over to third — and prompting Dodger manager Chuck Dressen to make a pitching change.

He brought in Ralph Branca to face Thomson, and the result of that match-up has put the names of both Branca and Thomson in baseball history books. And it was Lockman's double that set it up.

"Mueller broke his ankle sliding into third base. To this day, I don't know why he slid," said Lockman. "He had been on first and I hit a stand-up double. The only thing I can figure is he must have held up, thinking the ball was going to be caught and then had to hustle into third. They carried him off on a stretcher. He missed the World Series and that was a shock to us, not having him in the lineup."

Lockman had been an outfielder for six years when Durocher moved him to first base in 1951, a position he played for the rest of his career. "They brought up some kid who thought he could play center field. Why they moved me to first and kept Willie Mays in center field is a mystery to me," said Lockman, chuckling again.

On June 14, 1956, the day before the trading deadline, the Giants traded Lockman, along with Dark, catcher Ray Katt and pitcher Don Liddle to the St. Louis Cardinals for outfielders Jackie Brandt and Bobby Stephenson, infielder Red Schoendienst, pitcher Dick Littlefield and catcher Bill Sarni. He spent only half a season with the Cardinals and then was traded back to the Giants on February 26, 1957, for pitcher Hoyt Wilhelm.

He made the transition with the Giants from New York to San Francisco and then was sold to the Baltimore Orioles on February 14, 1959.

Four months later, he was traded to Cincinnati for another first baseman, Walt Dropo, and finished his career with the Reds in 1960. Lockman had a career batting average of .279.

He has more than 50 years of experience and perspective on major league baseball, but in analyzing the Cubs, he said there are no easy answers.

Regarding their inability to get into the World Series, he said it was probably a combination of things. "Look, 1969 was a freaky thing, and to some degree, so was 1973. They could have easily won it in either of those two years. Sometimes, things just don't work out, whether you call it luck or whatever you want to call it.

"Some people think playing all days games, like they used to, and then going on the road and playing at night messes up your biorhythms and they may be right. I don't know.

"Some people blame the ballpark because it's so small and with the wind and everything, it's hard on pitchers, but I don't know. Ebbets Field in Brooklyn was a tough place to pitch in and the Dodgers seemed to do all right over the years. So I don't think that's necessarily the answer.

"Some people blame Phil Wrigley. It's very difficult for me to say anything negative about Mr. Wrigley. He was a kind and gracious man and he enjoyed the game. He didn't pay as much attention to it from a business standpoint as other owners did, that's true. But I don't think it's true that he didn't care," said Lockman.

After Lockman's last year as a player in 1960, he coached for his old teammate, Dark, with the Giants from 1961 to 1964, then joined his old Giant manager, Durocher, as a coach when Leo took over the Cubs in 1966. He managed in the minor leagues until 1970 and then worked in player development for the Cubs for two years until he replaced Durocher as the Cubs manager.

In 1976, Lockman hooked on with Montreal and served as a scout for the Expos for the next 15 years. In 1992, he joined the expansion Florida Marlins organization as a scout and remains with them today.

"World champions in 1997," he proudly reminds people — and the familiar chuckle reappears.

Carroll Walter Lockman
Born July 25, 1926, in Lowell, N.C.
6' 1", 175 lbs.; B-left, T-right

Year	Team	G	AB	R	H	D	T	HR	RBI	Ave.
1945	NY (N)	32	129	16	44	9	0	3	18	.341
1947	NY	2	2	0	1	0	0	0	1	.500
1948	NY	146	584	117	167	24	10	18	59	.286

Year	Team	G	AB	R	H	D	T	HR	RBI	Ave.
1949	NY	151	617	97	186	32	7	11	65	.301
1950	NY	129	532	72	157	28	5	6	52	.295
1951	NY	153	614	85	173	27	7	12	73	.282
1952	NY	154	606	99	176	17	4	13	58	.290
1953	NY	150	607	85	179	22	4	9	61	.295
1954	NY	148	570	73	143	17	3	16	60	.251
1955	NY	147	576	76	157	19	0	15	49	.273
1956	NY-StL	118	362	27	94	7	3	1	20	.260
1957	NY (N)	133	456	51	113	9	4	7	30	.248
1958	SF	92	122	15	29	5	0	2	7	.238
1959	Bal-Cin	90	153	17	37	6	2	0	9	.242
1960	Cin	21	10	6	2	0	0	1	1	.200
15 years		1666	5940	836	1658	222	49	114	563	.279

Transactions:

June 14, 1956: Traded with infielder Alvin Dark, catcher Ray Katt and pitcher Don Liddle to St. Louis for outfielders Jackie Brandt and Bobby Stephenson, infielder Red Schoendienst, pitcher Dick Littlefield and catcher Bill Sarni.

Feb. 26, 1957: Traded to New York Giants for pitcher Hoyt Wilhelm.

Feb. 14, 1959: Sold to Baltimore Orioles.

June 23, 1959: Traded to Cincinnati for infielder Walt Dropo.

MANAGERIAL RECORD

Year	Team	W-L	Standing
1972	Chi (N)	39-26	Second
1973	Chi	77-84	Fifth
1974	Chi	41-52	Fifth
3 years		157-162	

DAVE LAROCHE
Cubs Pitcher, 1973–1974

"The biggest thing that hurt the Cubs in my days was playing all day games at Wrigley Field. It probably seems like a little thing, but it isn't when you go through it."

FORT SCOTT, Kan.—In Dave LaRoche's first year with the Chicago Cubs, he experienced something that not many Cubs players have in the past 50 years: his team was in a pennant race in the last week of the season.

"It was kind of a funny year where a lot of teams were bunched up and we had a shot at it until about Friday of that last week," he said. "Then, on the last day of the season, the Mets clinched it against us at Wrigley Field. Because of rainouts, we had to play a doubleheader and they clinched it by winning the first game," he said.

It was a crazy year. The Mets were the only team in the Eastern Division to finish over .500 at 82-79. Their final winning percentage of .509 is the lowest ever for a division champion. And they went on to win the league championship series and took Oakland to seven games before losing the World Series.

Reminiscent of their late-season sprint in 1969, the Mets went 23-9 over their last 32 games to climb over the Pirates, Cardinals, Expos and Cubs. LaRoche remembers correctly that the Cubs were eliminated on Friday of the last weekend of the season.

All of this late season excitement was new to LaRoche, who played on a California Angels team that finished 12 games out in 1970 and 25 games out in 1971 and a Minnesota Twins team that finished 16 games out in 1972.

Another quirky thing about 1973—LaRoche came to the Cubs in a deal that sent veteran right-hander Bill Hands to Minnesota. Hands had been part of the Cubs team that had challenged for the championship three years in a row in the Leo Durocher era. Trading him was the first of several transactions over the next few years where the Cubs traded the aging nucleus of their pennant contenders in order to rebuild.

Yet, here they were, in 1973, back in a pennant race. And LaRoche was a part of it.

"We had a real good team that year. We had some holdovers from the '69 team that almost won it—Randy Hundley, Glenn Beckert, Don Kessinger, Ron Santo and Ferguson Jenkins and we had a young pitching staff other than Jenkins and Milt Pappas. I think that was the year that Jenkins broke his string of consecutive 20-win seasons," said LaRoche, 51, who now coaches junior college baseball in his wife's hometown of Fort Scott, Kansas.

(He was right about Jenkins, who had six straight 20-win seasons until he slipped to 14-16 in 1973. After the season, the Cubs traded him to the Texas Rangers where he won 25 games in 1974.)

"One thing that year with the Cubs that I had never experienced before — as soon as we lost a game in August, the media started saying, 'Here they go again.' You would hear it, you would read it all the time. For us newcomers, we thought: What do you mean? We just got here.

"We had some key players who hadn't been there in '69 when everyone thought the Cubs should have won it. We had Rick Monday and Jose Cardenal and Burt Hooton and Rick Reuschel. And Joe Pepitone was at first base.

"We all heard it and read it — are they going to blow it again? You get tired of hearing it and you try not to pay any attention to it, but you know, it works on

Dave LaRoche said playing day games with the Cubs was a difficult adjustment for him.

you. You had to be careful not to start believing it," he said.

LaRoche broke in with the California Angels in 1970 and also pitched for the Minnesota Twins, the Cubs, and the Cleveland Indians, then was back with California and finished up with the New York Yankees. He won 65, lost 59 and had 126 saves over the course of his career.

He grew up in Southern California and signed with the Angels as an outfielder. He played two years as a minor league outfielder but in 1969 his El Paso team came up short of pitchers because of some injuries. LaRoche, who had pitched in high school, returned to the mound to help his team out. A year later, he was pitching in the major leagues.

"It was pretty quick," he said. "I remember my first game like it was yesterday. I know people use that expression a lot, but in my case it's true."

It was May 11, 1970. The Angels were playing the Boston Red Sox in Anaheim.

"I came in in the 12th inning of a tie ballgame. Carl Yastrzemski was the batter. The count went to 3-and-2 on him and our catcher, Joe Azcue, called for a slider. Well now, in the minor leagues, I had never thrown a 3-and-2 breaking ball but this wasn't the minor leagues anymore. I figured if he had guts enough to call it, I had guts enough to throw it. So, I did and Yastrzemski hit a little roller between first and second. Our first baseman, Tom Silverio went over to try to field it but went too far. The second baseman picked it up and threw it to me covering first and we got him. It was a 4-1 putout to end the inning.

"We scored in the bottom of the 12th to win the game. So in my major league debut, I pitched one-third of an inning, made a putout and got a win. And the only batter I faced was Carl Yastrzemski. That was a pretty good night," said LaRoche.

(That was the only day in Silverio's three-year career that he played first base. Ordinarily, he was an outfielder.)

On November 30, 1971, LaRoche was traded to the Minnesota Twins for infielder Leo Cardenas. He spent one year with the Twins and then was involved in the trade with the Cubs. On November 30, 1972, exactly one year after his first trade, LaRoche went to the Cubs in exchange for pitcher Bill Hands (a 20-game winner in 1969), pitcher Joe Decker and pitcher Bob Maneely.

A little more than two years later, the Cubs traded LaRoche and outfielder Brock Davis to Cleveland and got pitcher Milt Wilcox in return. Then he went back to California on May 11, 1977, along with pitcher Dave Schuler for outfielder–first baseman Bruce Bochte and pitcher Sid Monge.

While with Cleveland, he witnessed Frank Robinson's dramatic debut as the major league's first black manager. Robinson, who was a player-manager, homered in his first at-bat. "It was amazing," said LaRoche. "He hardly had any spring training because he was managing. He came up and hit the first pitch for a home run, as I recall, and just missed hitting a second one his next time up."

LaRoche was in the bullpen in Cleveland in 1977 when Indian starter Dennis Eckersley threw a no-hitter. Eckersley later became one of the all-time great relief pitchers with the Oakland A's and St. Louis Cardinals.

In his second tour of duty with the Angels, LaRoche played on the 1979 team that made it to the league championship series, then lost to the Baltimore Orioles, three games to one.

"Seven out of our nine offensive players, counting the designated hitter, had career years that year — and Rod Carew wasn't one of them. He hit .318, but he hit .333 the year before and .388 the year before that — so .318 would be a career year for most guys but it wasn't for Rod Carew. Don

Baylor had his MVP year that year and we also had Bobby Grich and Joe Rudi, although Rudi was hurt a lot of the year.

"We had great pitching — Nolan Ryan, Frank Tanana and a kid named David Frost who didn't pitch long in the big leagues but had a good year for us and started one of the league championship games. Tanana had hurt his arm by that time in his career and was making the transition from fastball pitcher to control pitcher.

"When Tanana was in his prime, he was unbelievable. In 1977, he had a string of 14 straight complete games and the only two he lost were 1–0 on Dennis Eckersley's no-hitter [for Cleveland] and 3–2 to Vida Blue [for Oakland]."

In 1980, LaRoche was traded to the New York Yankees and made an appearance for them in the 1981 World Series in which the Yankees lost to the Dodgers, four games to two. In 1983, his last year in the majors, his manager was Billy Martin.

"Early in his career, he was always ahead one or two innings as a manager. He had a reputation for that. It was hard to match him. By 1983, he was always behind, always making moves later than he should have. We noticed it a lot in the bullpen. Sad to say but I think the hard life had taken its toll. I really do," said LaRoche.

As for the Cubs' troubles over the years, LaRoche said, "The biggest thing that hurt the Cubs in my days was playing all day games at Wrigley Field. It probably seems like a little thing, but it isn't when you go through it.

"It's hard to get your body regulated to the routine. When you're on the road, you might play six out of seven games at night. You're out late, you sleep in, you have a big lunch and you go to the ballpark.

"When the Cubs are home, you don't have lunch. You basically go all day on just breakfast. It was hard to get used to and I know it took its toll on me and probably on other guys," he said.

"That, and what I mentioned earlier, the media getting all over us in August if we lost a game — that we were blowing it again. Like I said, that can work on you and I never experienced it anywhere else I ever played."

But La Roche said he has special memories of his days with the Cubs. "They have great fans and at the time, that was unique to me. I had played for California and the Twins, two teams that really didn't have a tradition. The Cubs had been around forever.

"Playing for the Cubs was my first experience with a rivalry, too. Their rivalry with the Cardinals was amazing. When you went to St. Louis or if we played them in Wrigley Field, it was sometimes hard to tell which was the home team because so many fans for both teams showed up.

"I later experienced that a little with the Red Sox and the Yankees but I thought the Cub-Cardinal rivalry was really something when I was there," he said.

LaRoche said he also liked the uniqueness of Wrigley Field. "It used to be that each ballpark was a little different, had some character all its own. When the new ballparks were built, it was as if all of them came from the same design. If you woke up some night and you were at second base and you looked around you, you'd really have to think about where you were," said LaRoche.

After finishing his major league career, he coached in the majors and minors through 1995 and then went back to Kansas where he helped coach at the high school level before taking on similar duties at the local junior college.

On the night we talked, LaRoche was home, watching the New York Yankees playing the Orioles on television.

"The Yankees provided me with some thrills even in the years I didn't play for them," he said.

"One year when I was with Cleveland, they brought me in to pitch against the Yankees with the bases loaded and nobody out — and I struck out the side."

Does LaRoche remember who he struck out?

"Chris Chambliss, Graig Nettles and Sandy Alomar, Sr.," he responded without hesitation. "Anything you do for or against the Yankees is always memorable."

LaRoche has good reason to stay in touch with what's happening in professional baseball these days. His son, Jeff, is a left-hander with the Kane County (Ill.) Cougars, a farm club of the Florida Marlins.

David Eugene LaRoche

Born May 14, 1948, in Colorado Springs, Colo.

6' 2", 200 lbs.; B-left, T-left

Year	Team	W-L	ERA	G	IP	H	BB	SO
1970	Cal	4-1	3.42	38	50	41	21	44
1971	Cal	5-1	2.50	56	72	55	27	63
1972	Minn	5-7	2.84	62	95	72	39	79
1973	Chi (N)	4-1	5.83	45	54	55	29	34
1974	Chi	5-6	4.79	49	92	103	47	49
1975	Cleve	5-3	2.19	61	82.1	61	57	94
1976	Cleve	1-4	2.25	61	96	57	49	104
1977	Cleve-Cal	8-7	3.51	59	100	79	44	79

Year	Team	W-L	ERA	G	IP	H	BB	SO
1978	Cal	10-9	2.81	59	96	73	48	70
1979	Cal	7-11	5.55	53	86	107	32	59
1980	Cal	3-5	4.08	52	128	122	39	89
1981	NY (A)	4-1	2.49	26	47	38	16	24
1982	NY	4-2	3.42	25	50	54	11	31
1983	NY	0-0	18.00	1	1	2	0	0
14 years		65-58	3.53	647	1049.1	919	459	819

Transactions:

Nov. 30, 1971: Traded to Minnesota for infielder Leo Cardenas.

Nov. 30, 1972: Traded to Chicago Cubs for pitchers Bill Hands, Joe Decker and Bob Maneely.

Feb. 25, 1975: Traded with outfielder Brock Davis to Cleveland for pitcher Milt Wilcox.

May 11, 1977: Traded with pitcher Dave Schuler to California for catcher Bruce Bochte, pitcher Sid Monge and $250,000.

LEAGUE CHAMPIONSHIP SERIES

Year	Team	W-L	ERA	G	IP	H	BB	SO
1979	Cal	0-0	6.75	1	1.1	2	1	1

WORLD SERIES

Year	Team	W-L	ERA	G	IP	H	BB	SO
1981	NY (A)	0-0	0.00	1	1	0	2	0

RICK WRONA

Cubs Catcher, 1988–1990

"They know they're going to fill that ballpark whether they win or lose. There's really no pressure to win."

TULSA, Okla.— When the Chicago Cubs won the National League's Eastern Division in 1989, they surprised the baseball world, said Rick Wrona, a backup catcher on that team.

Rich Wrona experienced something not many Cubs have in the past 50 years — post-season play.

When they lost in the league championship series to the San Francisco Giants, nobody was surprised because people don't expect the Cubs to win, he said.

Wrona, who now paints houses in Tulsa, has some special memories of his relatively short time with the Cubs — memories many players never got a chance to have in lengthy careers in Chicago.

"I'll never forget the night of the first playoff game at Wrigley Field," said Wrona, who retired from baseball at the age of 35. "I was standing on the dugout steps, waiting to run out on the field when my name was announced. Ron Santo, the old Cubs third baseman came up to me and said, 'Man, you'll never forget this day. Just think of all the men who played so many games on this field and never got the chance to do what you're doing tonight. When you go out there tonight, you're representing all of them.'

"Of course, Santo was one of the players who never got in the playoffs or a World Series, so he really spoke from the heart. I tell that story a lot," he said.

The Cubs lost to the Giants, three games to one. In the fourth game, with the Cubs on the brink of elimination, Mike Bielecki took a 1–0 lead into the eighth inning, got into some trouble, and was relieved by Mitch Williams, "The Wild Thing" as he was affectionately called, who had been the ace of the Cubs bullpen all year.

"He came in to face Will Clark with the bases loaded and got him

0-and-2 right away," said Wrona. "He threw him an eye-high fastball that Clark somehow got around on — I still don't know how — and ripped it up the middle. It about spun poor Mitch's cap around. It scored two runs and that was the ballgame," said Wrona.

In 1993, Williams, pitching for the Philadelphia Phillies, gave up an even more famous hit. Pitching against Toronto in the sixth game of the World Series, Williams was protecting a one-run lead when he gave up a two-run homer to Joe Carter that clinched the series for the Bluejays — the only World Series in history that was won with a come-from-behind home run.

"People thought Mitch was hard to catch but he really wasn't because he hardly ever bounced a pinch. Sure, he threw the ball 100 miles an hour, but a ball thrown 100 miles an hour is actually pretty easy to catch," he said.

Wrona was the Cubs' fifth round draft choice after playing three years at Wichita State University (1983–1985). Wrona and Rafael Palmeiro, a first round draft choice from Mississippi State University, were sent up to the Cubs A-ball farm team in Peoria after about a week at a mini-camp.

Wrona was with Peoria for a month before being shipped to Winston-Salem, another A-ball farm team where he backed up future Cubs catcher Damon Berryhill. He spent the 1986 season at Winston-Salem but went to Pittsfield, Massachusetts, a Double-A team, in 1987. While the Cubs major league team was finishing last in 1987, Pittsfield, loaded with future major league players, won the Eastern League championship.

"That was a great team. We had Mark Grace, Hector Villanueva, Dwight Smith, Jeff Pico, Mike Harkey, Doug Dascenzo, Rolando Roomes and me. All of us wound up in the big leagues. But what brought that team together was our manager, Jim Essian, who had major league experience and treated us as if we were in the majors.

"In 1988, I started with Pittsfield and then got sent up to Iowa, the Cubs Triple-A team. In September, I got called up to the Cubs. They needed someone to back up Berryhill. They were trying to get rid of Jody Davis — and they did by the end of the season. They sent him to Atlanta," said Wrona.

He made his major league debut on September 3. "I got sent up as a pinch hitter for someone which must have meant we had a big lead or I was part of a double switch or something. Anyway, I faced John Franco who was the Rolaids Relief Pitcher of the Year and battled him to a 2-and-2 count. Then I hit a line shot that ricocheted off the mound right to Davey Concepcion at shortstop and he threw me out by a mile. Years later, I told Concepcion that story and he said, 'Hey, I'm sorry man.' There was no need for him to be sorry. I was just making conversation.

"In the next game I got in, I faced Danny Jackson, who was the Cy Young Award winner and he got me out. Then in my first major league start, I faced Randy Johnson who was pitching for Montreal back then and I went 0-for-4. So, for the season, I was 0-for-6 — against the relief pitcher of the year, the Cy Young Award winner and the future Cy Young Award winner," said Wrona.

"I had some problems with our manager, Don Zimmer, that year only I don't think I realized it. When I came up, I was trying to be one of the guys, acting like a veteran, instead of a rookie, and Zimmer didn't like it. It would be stuff like when the veterans would clown around — they wouldn't do it when the manager was around.

"Then I'd horse around and it would be in full view of Zimmer and he didn't go for it. The rookie was having a little too much fun. I gave a guy a hot foot one time and Andre Dawson came up to me and said real quietly, 'you need to not be doing that.' That was a veteran trying to keep a rookie out of trouble."

(A fabled Zimmer exchange with rookies occurred in 1989 when Jerome Walton crossed the plate and excitedly stopped and bumped elbows with Dwight Smith, who was the next hitter. Zimmer took them both aside and said, "Save that stuff for Iowa.")

Wrona said some of his embarrassing moments as a rookie weren't his fault. "The veterans liked to set me up. One time during a nationally televised game, Goose Gossage struck up a conversation with me in the dugout, about elk hunting, of all things. I was really impressed. Here's this veteran chitchatting with me. But while he's talking with me, Al Nipper's behind me quietly putting shaving cream on my cap. Gossage wasn't making conversation. He was just trying to distract me.

"So now my cap is full of shaving cream, unbeknownst to me, and suddenly the call goes out — I need to get a pitcher ready. I race out of the dugout to go down to the bullpen and shaving cream is just flying all over the place off the top of my cap. And of course, everybody's laughing.

"When I came to spring training in 1989, I had heard that Zimmer had been unhappy with me the year before. So I hustled all spring. I hustled all over the place, trying to impress him. When they made the decision to send me down, he called me into his office and said, 'You know, last year you were a rookie SOB. This year, I hate to let you go. But you'll be back.' He was really encouraging and I really appreciated that.

"On August 25, I was playing golf in a cornfield in West Des Moines, Iowa, when I got the word that the Cubs had called me up. I got to Chicago and took a cab to the ballpark and got there in about the middle of the game. I came up as a pinch hitter in extra innings and got a hit and wound up scoring the winning run. The fans went nuts and the press made a big deal out of me getting there late and still doing well and it was quite a night," said Wrona.

"That 1989 season was something special. I saw Zimmer last winter and he gave me a hug and asked me how I was doing. I think everyone on that team knows how special it was, even though we didn't get to the World Series." (As a Yankees coach, Zimmer has been in the World Series twice in the 1990s. As a player, he helped the Dodgers win two National League pennants.)

"Zimmer told me he had changed his uniform number to 50 to signify his 50 years in baseball. He said he was thinking about retiring so he could go back to St. Petersburg, Florida, and help coach his twin grandsons. Then Joe Torre got sick, and look who's the acting manager of the Yankees — Don Zimmer." (Torre, the Yankees manager, missed part of the 1999 season because he was being treated for prostate cancer.)

Wrona said Dawson played with incredible pain at the end of his career. "It was ridiculous, how badly his knees hurt him. He would come in early and have his knees taped — and I mean, a lot of tape — and then he would go out for batting practice and get all sweated up and come in and have to be completely retaped all over again before the game.

"Then after the game, he would come in and get on the training table and they would ice his knees down. He would lay there on the table and sign hundreds of autographs on balls and pictures while they worked on his knees. He was a quiet leader. He never complained. But he was hurting all the time," said Wrona.

"Ryne Sandberg had a totally different personality than what he showed in public, once you got to know him. He and I became good friends but when I first met him, I thought: Who is this guy? He never says 'hi' to anyone.

"Well, he kind of took Doug Dascenzo and me under his wing and we had a good time, but we knew a Ryno that the public never knew. One time in Montreal, we went with him on a subway ride. He knew where he was going, but we didn't. At one of the subway stops, he got off and so, of course, we got off. Then just as the subway door was closing and it was about to take off, Ryno dove back on and took off without us.

"Another time, he did the same thing only this time he acted like he was bending over to tie his shoe and instead he flopped back on the subway and left us standing there.

"He would do things all the time and just chuckle about it. If you fell asleep on a plane, when you woke up you were likely to find your sportcoat filled with silverware and packets of cream and sugar — and there would be Ryno, chuckling.

"But he was a great ballplayer and excellent at helping young ballplayers. One thing about Ryno that was different than anybody else. He would not only tell you about opposing pitchers. He'd tell you about umpires.

"When he talked about pitchers, he'd tell you things like 'Look out for this guy — his fastball comes up and in' or 'When he throws you this pitch, it's going to look waist-high but it will drop out of sight so don't swing at it. He could almost draw you a picture of how a certain guy was going to pitch to you — and it really helped me.

"With umpires, he'd say things like, 'Eric Gregg's behind the plate tonight. Swing at anything with two strikes.' Or he might say about another umpire, 'This guy doesn't give a rookie a break so be ready to swing at anything close.' He knew the umpires just like he knew the pitchers.

"It wasn't that the umpires are bad, like most of them are in the minor leagues. It's that major league umpires all have their own style and if you can learn their style, it will help you. Sandberg knew that," he said.

Wrona hit .283 in 38 games for the Cubs in 1989. It was to be his longest stint in the major leagues. The Cubs had three good, young catchers in Wrona, Berryhill and Joe Girardi and another one, Villanueva, waiting in the wings.

In 1990, Grace, the Cubs' All-Star first baseman, went into one of the worst slumps of his career — and Wrona paid for it. "Villanueva was a catcher who could also play first base. When Grace was struggling, they brought up Hector, who hit with a lot of power, to play first base and to catch. And I finished the season in Des Moines," said Wrona.

"In 1991, I was a free agent and went to camp with the Milwaukee Brewers. They were looking for a backup catcher to B. J. Surhoff. Rick Dempsey was on that team. He was in his forties but he could still play. I got released on April Fool's Day but it wasn't funny."

Wrona had a roller coaster career for the next seven years, with stops in Nashville, a Cincinnati farm club; Nashville again when it was a Chicago White Sox farm club (getting into four games with the White Sox in 1993 after they released Carlton Fisk); the Milwaukee Brewers in 1994; Triple-A teams of the Cleveland Indians, St. Louis Cardinals and Philadelphia Phillies in 1995–1996; back with the White Sox organization in Triple-A in 1997; and a stint with the Texas Triple-A farm club in Oklahoma City in 1998.

Wrona said it's difficult to say why the Cubs haven't been in the World Series for so long. He said maybe it's because the team doesn't have the same pressures that other teams face.

"They know they're going to fill that ballpark whether they win or lose. There's really no pressure to win. Nothing is ever expected of the Cubs. Look at the White Sox in the same city. They had Frank Thomas, Albert Belle and Robin Ventura. They were expected to win and they did for a while but they still didn't draw many fans, or at least not like the Cubs draw.

"The Cubs don't have a winning tradition to fall back on or to live up to. For the fans, going to the ballpark is an event, like going to the county fair. Have a good time and don't expect too much. Maybe that's been a factor over the years. I don't know," said Wrona.

He's painting houses now with his brother in Tulsa and looking for more permanent work. But he doubts that it will be in baseball. "Now I'm coaching my kid's second grade team, and that's right where I want to be," said Wrona, tired of the minor league grind and reaching the age, he said, where his knees might start feeling like Andre Dawson's did.

Baseball is a game in which players often succeed because they fill a void in the lineup. If there is no void, it's almost impossible for them to succeed.

Wrona's last year in the major leagues is a classic example. Milwaukee had Surhoff and Dempsey and hence no void at the catching position. Wrona, trying to make the team, got up 10 times and had 5 hits for a batting average of .500. All five hits were for extra bases — four doubles and a home run. But it wasn't good enough. There was no void. The Brewers released him.

Wrona is not bitter. He knows how it goes. That's baseball. But he has a special perspective on his final season. "I led the American League in hitting that year," he said.

Richard James Wrona
Born Dec. 10, 1963, in Tulsa, Okla.
6' 1", 185 lbs.; B-right, T-right

Year	Team	G	AB	R	H	D	T	HR	RBI	Ave.
1988	Chi (N)	4	6	0	0	0	0	0	0	.000
1989	Chi	38	92	11	26	2	1	2	14	.283
1990	Chi	16	29	3	5	0	0	0	0	.172
1992	Cin	11	23	0	4	0	0	0	0	.174
1993	Chi (A)	4	8	0	1	0	0	0	1	.125
1994	Mil (A)	6	10	2	5	4	0	1	3	.500
6 years		79	168	16	41	6	1	3	18	.244

Year	Team	G	AB	R	H	D	T	HR	RBI	Ave.
1989	Chi (N)	2	5	0	0	0	0	0	0	.000

GARY SCOTT
Cubs Third Baseman, 1991–1992

"How do you let a guy like Maddux go?"

DARIEN, Conn.— Gary Scott's rise to the major leagues was incredibly fast, maybe too fast, he says now in retrospect.

Scott, 30, is in the oil transport business. "We help move oil from Point A to Point B. It's interesting work. I'll probably be doing it for a long time. It's not like putting on a cap and uniform everyday and getting dirty playing baseball — but it's close," he said with a laugh.

Scott played baseball at Villanova University and, after his junior year, was the Chicago Cubs' first pick in the second round of the 1989 draft. He played that summer with Geneva, New York—"short season A-ball," he calls it — for players signed after school was out. In 1990, he played for the Cubs farm team in Winston-Salem, North Carolina, this time full-season A-ball, where he hit .300, had 17 home runs, 90 runs batted in, and was minor league Player of the Year.

The following April, he was the Opening Day third baseman for the Chicago Cubs.

"It was kind of fast. Not many guys make that kind of a jump, from A-ball to the big leagues. But they had a void there at third base for quite some time. Even if I wasn't quite ready, I think their thinking was, 'we've got enough guys around him to carry him.' Look at the infield we had: Mark Grace at first, Ryne Sandberg at second, Shawon Dunston at short and then me at third," said Scott.

He was right about the void at third base. Sandberg played third in his first full year with the Cubs in 1982. They acquired Ron Cey from the Dodgers who played third base from 1983 through 1986. Then the parade started. It included Keith Moreland, Manny Trillo, Vance Law, Domingo Ramos, Luis Salazar, Chico Walker and Jose Vizcaino before Scott had his shot. Since then, Steve Buechele, Jose Hernandez, Todd Zeile, Howard

Johnson, Kevin Orie, Gary Gaetti, Tyler Houston and Shane Andrews have all played third.

For Scott, it turned out to be a tough move up to the big leagues. "I equate it to going to college. You have four years to grow. You don't just jump from your freshman to your senior year. There's a maturing process that helps you get to your senior year," he said.

"I skipped both Double-A and Triple-A and went right to the big leagues which seemed like a good idea at the time. If I had played Double-A and Triple-A, would I still be in the major leagues today? Who knows?

"The manager Don Zimmer came up to me two weeks before the end of spring training and said, 'you're my Opening Day third baseman.' The Cubs had won the division in '89 and we had Grace and Sandberg and Andre Dawson and Greg Maddux and we thought we had a legitimate chance of competing. It looked like I could blend in real well," said Scott.

"Grace was a big help to me. He kind of took me under his wing. In spring training, he came up to me and said to make things easier for me, why didn't I just live with him when we went back to Chicago. What does a 21-year-old kid say to that? So I roomed with 'Gracie' when we were home," he said.

Opening Day of 1991 in Wrigley Field was cold and windy, not unusual for April in Chicago. "When I was named minor league Player of the Year, the Cubs brought me up to throw out the first pitch of one of their ballgames. That was the first time I had ever been in Wrigley Field. Opening Day 1991 was the second time," said Scott.

"We were playing the Cardinals. My first time up, I hit a line drive and their third baseman, Todd Zeile, made a diving catch to get me out. And I thought: So this is what life is like in the big leagues."

But there were not enough line drives off Scott's bat, and two months into the season, he was sent down to the Cubs Triple-A farm team in Des Moines.

"My fielding was fine but everyone knew I'd be okay there. Listen, if you can catch a groundball in A-ball, you can do it in the major leagues — maybe even better in the majors because the fields are better.

"But hitting is different in the major leagues. Take Sandberg, for instance. If a pitcher made a mistake on him, he hit it. He was the best I ever saw at hitting a hanging breaking ball. Me, I might foul it straight back. When Ryno got a hanger it was 'see you later.' In all the times I saw him bat, I never saw him miss one.

"That's important too, especially in the big leagues. If a pitcher throws a mistake, you've got to be right on it. You can't foul it off because the pitcher knows it was a mistake and he's not going to give it to you again. He's going to go to his nasty stuff.

"In the major leagues, you may get one good pitch to hit in an at-bat. You better be ready for it, and you better hit it," Scott said.

So in June of 1991, he was sent to Des Moines. "I wasn't there too long and I broke my hand and that was it for me for the season," he said.

Scott had another shattering experience in Des Moines. "A couple of days after I was sent down, Zimmer got fired in Chicago. I was shocked. I liked Zim. I thought he was a great guy. They moved Jim Essian up from Iowa to replace him and then they had to move some other guys around and before it was over, I think Iowa had three managers that year.

"Zimmer was a fierce competitor and definitely from the old school. He believed in baseball as war and that each game was a battle. He didn't like you talking with players on the other team and he would let you know.

"When we would do our running before a game, with most teams you run across the outfield grass even while the other team is out there. Zimmer always thought there was a chance you might talk with one of the players on another team. So he had us run from third base to the left field wall and back so there would be no chance of fraternizing.

"Sometimes, when I was on first base, I'd look over in the dugout and there would be Zim glaring at me, making sure I didn't talk with the first baseman. It was kind of funny, really. Like in an exhibition game, and I'm on first base and Mark McGwire says 'hi' and I don't say anything and McGwire's probably thinking: Who does this rookie think he is, not speaking to me? But that's the way it was when you played for Zimmer.

"To me, he was a general and a father figure and a friend all wrapped into one, and that's hard to do. I really liked the guy," said Scott.

In 1992, Scott came back up with the Cubs, this time with Jim Lefebvre as manager. "We brought George Bell over from the American League and again, we thought we had a shot," he said. But once again, Scott had trouble sticking with the big club. He went back and forth to Des Moines several times and by the end of the year, he was live bait for expansion teams. He was picked up by the Florida Marlins in November. But that was just the start of his travels.

"Between November of 1992 and 1997, I was with nine organizations — the Cubs, the Marlins, the Reds, the Twins, the Giants, the Braves, the Mets, the Padres and the Mariners. In the spring of 1997, I was playing in Mexico and the team I played for had a working agreement with the Cleveland Indians, so technically I was in the Indians organization, too, and that makes 10. It's always nice to be in double figures," he said, laughing again.

It was in 1997 that he decided a career change would be best. "I got tired of bouncing around. You don't have any roots. You're always with new guys — and yet you're always the new guy," he said.

So he quit baseball and took a job with a real estate company in Hilton Head, South Carolina, making land deals. He stayed with that for about a year before hooking up with the oil company.

He looks back fondly on his years with the Cubs, his time with Zimmer and the relationship he had with some of the greatest players of the last 20 years.

"Sandberg was a quiet leader. He was real quiet at first. He's the kind of guy who likes to feel everybody out and won't let you get real close to him. He does the same with everybody. He looks at you from afar before he lets you into his world. But like I said, he never missed a hanging curveball.

"Andre Dawson was quieter than Ryno. A silent observer. But Dawson didn't have to say anything to make people respect him. He would sometimes come in the clubhouse before a game and spend two hours working on his knees and was in a great deal of pain.

"And then he'd say whether he could go today or whether he couldn't. And when he could, he'd go out there and play like nothing was wrong and everyone knew how much pain he was in.

"At the end of his career, he would walk and run like he was on stilts because he just couldn't bend his knees. But he gave it everything he had and we all respected him for the way he went about his job.

"Greg Maddux was really likeable. He had a great sense of humor and he was a student of the game. When he wasn't pitching, he'd always be in the dugout watching players on the other team, studying the hitters and trying to learn a thing or two that he could use the next time he faced them," said Scott.

He said he really couldn't be much of a judge on why the Cubs have failed to get into a World Series for 53 years, but he noticed something in 1998 that might be a tip off to past troubles.

"I saw the Cubs play in Houston at the end of the 1998 season. They lost two out of three to Houston to end the season, but the Giants lost on the last day and that put them in a playoff. They beat the Giants to become the wild card team and then lost three in a row to the Braves to knock them out of it.

"When I saw them in Houston in that last weekend, I was wondering — how would they have done over the years if they had kept Greg Maddux? How do you let a guy like Maddux go?"

(Maddux came up with the Cubs in 1986 and was 2-4 in limited service. In 1987, he suffered through a last-place season with the rest of the club and wound up 6-14. In 1988, his career took off. He was 18-8 in 1988; 19-12 in 1989, when the Cubs won the division championship; 15-15 in 1990; 19-12 in 1991; and 20-11 in 1992 when he won the Cy Young Award. But the Cubs failed to come to terms with Maddux after the 1992 season and he signed with Atlanta. He was 20-10 in 1993, 16-6 in 1994, 19-2 in 1995, 15-11 in 1996, 19-4 in 1997 and 18-9 in 1998. He has won three Cy Young Awards and has helped the Braves to three World Series appearances.)

"As far as I know, Maddux would have stayed with the Cubs. Was money the problem? How much have they spent on other free agents since Maddux left? Here's how important Maddux is. Let's say he wins 20 games. But he also has the ability to make your other pitchers even better.

"So let's say they each win two or three more games just because of Maddux's presence. Now you're not talking about 20 wins, you're talking about potentially 40 wins with Maddux there. How do you let a guy like that get away? I don't know.

"But if things like that happened in the past, that's why the Cubs haven't been there and other teams have."

Gary Thomas Scott
Born Aug. 22, 1968, in New Rochelle, N.Y.
6', 175 lbs.; B-right, T-right

Year	Team	G	AB	R	H	D	T	HR	RBI	Ave.
1991	Chi (N)	31	79	8	13	3	0	1	5	.165
1992	Chi	36	96	8	15	2	0	2	11	.156
2 years		67	175	16	28	5	0	3	16	.160

Part V. Statistics

The Chicago Cubs won 98 games en route to the National League championship in 1945. In 1946, they slipped to third but finished 11 games above .500. That was the last time they finished over .500 until 1967, a drought in which they finished exactly at .500 once, in 1952, and under .500 the 19 other years. During that time, they never finished higher than fifth and finished either seventh or eighth (in an eight-team league) nine times. From 1962, when the National League expanded to 10 teams, through 1966 the Cubs finished ninth, seventh, eighth, eighth and tenth.

Then they had a string of six consecutive years, 1967–1972, of being over .500 and finishing no lower than third. They finished below .500 again in 1973 and did not emerge again to the plus side of .500 until 1984 when they won the National League Eastern Division championship. They won the division title again in 1989 and earned the wild card spot in 1998. Between those years, they finished over .500 only twice.

Add it all up and it totals more than 50 years without a pennant and under .500 for most of that time. Why?

Any analysis of the Cubs' futility over the last 55 years would be flawed without looking at four factors that made the Cubs different than any other club:

(1) For all 55 years, they played all of their home games in Wrigley Field. They are the only team in the National League that has not moved to another city or moved into a new ballpark during that period.

(2) For 42 of those years, they played all of their home games during the day. They were the only team in the National League to play all of their home games in daylight.

(3) For 32 of those years, the Cubs were under the ownership of Philip K. Wrigley and remained in Wrigley family ownership for four more years after his death in 1977.

(4) Cubs fans have been faithful despite the team's lack of success. They have not demanded a winner by staying away from the ballpark.

In the preceding pages, 33 players, a coach and a manager reflect on their careers with the Cubs and their experiences with other teams — and offer insights into possible reasons the Cubs have not succeeded like other teams have over the years.

They talk about the pros and cons of playing in Wrigley Field, the lack of an adequate farm system, the reluctance of the front office to make trades, the disinterest of Wrigley, the experiments that failed such as the rotating coaching system and the loyalty of Cubs fans regardless of the team's performance.

The following statistics relate directly or indirectly to the comments of the players and to the four main factors that distinguish the Cubs from other teams.

As a point of reference, the first chart shows the Cubs' won-loss records, their position in the National League standings, how far out of first place they finished and who managed them for each year from 1946, the year after they won their last pennant, through 1999.

Cubs Season Records, 1945–1999

Year	W-L	Pct.	Finished	Games Out	Manager
1945	98-56	.636	1st	—	Grimm
1946	82-71	.536	3rd	14.5	Grimm
1947	69-85	.448	6th	25	Grimm
1948	64-90	.416	8th	27.5	Grimm
1949	61-93	.396	8th	36	Grimm/Frisch
1950	64-89	.418	7th	26.5	Frisch
1951	62-92	.403	8th	34.5	Frisch/Cavarretta
1952	77-77	.500	5th	19.5	Cavarretta
1953	65-89	.442	7th	40	Cavarretta
1954	64-90	.416	7th	33	Hack
1955	72-81	.471	6th	26	Hack
1956	60-94	.390	8th	33	Hack
1957	62-92	.403	7th (tie)	33	Scheffing
1958	72-82	.468	5th (tie)	20	Scheffing
1959	74-80	.481	5th (tie)	13	Scheffing
1960	60-94	.390	7th	35	Grimm/Boudreau

Year	W–L	Pct.	Finished	Games Out	Manager
1961	64–90*	.416	7th	29	Himsl/Craft/Klein/Tappe
1962	59–103*	.364	9th	42.5	Tappe/Metro/Klein
1963	82–80	.506	7th	17	Kennedy
1964	76–86	.469	8th	17	Kennedy
1965	72–90	.444	8th	25	Kennedy/Klein
1966	59–103	.364	10th	36	Durocher
1967	87–74	.540	3rd	14	Durocher
1968	84–78	.519	3rd	13	Durocher
1969	92–70	.568	2nd	8	Durocher
1970	84–78	.519	2nd	5	Durocher
1971	83–79	.512	3rd (tie)	14	Durocher
1972	85–70(s)	.548	2nd	11	Durocher/Lockman
1973	77–84	.478	5th	5	Lockman
1974	66–96	.407	6th	22	Lockman/Marshall
1975	75–87	.463	5th (tie)	17.5	Marshall
1976	75–87	.463	4th	26	Marshall
1977	81–81	.500	4th	20	Franks
1978	79–83	.488	3rd	11	Franks
1979	80–82	.494	5th	18	Franks/Amalfitano
1980	64–98	.395	6th	27	Gomez/Amalfitano
1981	38–85(s)	.369	6th	21.5	Amalfitano
1982	73–89	.451	5th	19	Elia
1983	71–91	.438	5th	19	Elia/Fox
1984	96–65	.596	1st	—	Frey
1985	77–84	.478	4th	23.5	Frey
1986	70–90	.438	5th	37	Frey/Vukovich/Michael
1987	76–85	.472	6th	18.5	Michael/Lucchesi
1988	77–85	.475	4th	24	Zimmer
1989	93–69	.574	1st	—	Zimmer
1990	77–85	.475	4th	18	Zimmer
1991	77–83	.481	4th	20	Zimmer/Altobelli/Essian
1992	78–84	.481	4th	18	Lefebvre
1993	84–78	.519	4th	13	Lefebvre
1994	49–64(s)	.434	5th	16.5	Trebelhorn
1995	73–71(s)	.507	3rd	12	Riggleman
1996	76–86	.469	4th	12	Riggleman
1997	68–94	.420	5th	16	Riggleman
1998	93–70(w)	.570	2nd (tie)	7	Riggleman
1999	67–95	.414	6th	30	Riggleman

*no manager; rotating coaches were in charge

(s) strike-shortened season

(w) wild card playoff team; Cubs finished tied with Giants for playoff spot at end of season and won one-game playoff

Cubs Managerial Records, 1945–1999

The Cubs, often accused of shuffling the deck too often, have had 30 managers since 1946, including three interims and five who served as "head coaches" in 1961 and 1962 — the most managerial switches in the National League. By comparison, the Brooklyn/Los Angeles Dodgers have had nine, including two interims. Of the 30 for the Cubs, only three had winning records overall — Leo Durocher, Don Zimmer and Jim Frey.

	W-L	Pct.
Charlie Grimm 1945–1949; 1960	240-288*	.454
Frankie Frisch 1949–1951	141-196	.418
Phil Cavarretta 1951–1953	169-213	.442
Stan Hack 1954–1956	199-272	.423
Bob Scheffing 1957–1959	208-254	.450
Lou Boudreau 1960	54-83	.394
Vedie Himsl 1961	10-21	.323
Harry Craft 1961	7-9	.437
Lou Klein 1961, 1962, 1965	65-83	.439
Elvin Tappe 1961, 1962	46-69	.400
Charlie Metro 1962	43-69	.384
Bob Kennedy 1963–1965	182-198	.479
Leo Durocher 1966–1972	535-526	.504
Whitey Lockman 1972–1974	157-162	.492
Jim Marshall 1974–1976	175-218	.445
Herman Franks 1977–1979	238-241	.495
Joe Amalfitano 1979–1981	66-116	.363
Preston Gomez 1980	38-52	.422
Lee Elia 1982–1983	127-158	.446
Charlie Fox 1983	17-22	.436
Jim Frey 1984–1986	196-182	.519
Pete Vukovich 1986	1-1	.500
Gene Michael 1986–1987	114-124	.479
Frank Lucchesi 1987	8-17	.320
Don Zimmer 1988–1991	265-258	.507
Joe Altobelli 1991	0-1	.000
Jim Essian 1991	59-63	.483
Jim Lefebvre 1992–1993	162-162	.500
Tom Trebelhorn 1994	49-64	.434
Jim Riggleman 1995–1999	377-396	.487

*Grimm served as manager of the Cubs for nine years prior to 1946

Managers with Most Wins Since 1945

1.	Leo Durocher	535
2.	Jim Riggleman	377
3.	Don Zimmer	265
4.	Charlie Grimm	240*
5.	Herman Franks	238
6.	Bob Scheffing	208
7.	Stan Hack	199
8.	Jim Frey	196
9.	Bob Kennedy	182
10.	Jim Marshall	175
11.	Phil Cavarretta	169
12.	Jim Lefebvre	162
13.	Whitey Lockman	157
14.	Frankie Frisch	141
15.	Lee Elia	127
16.	Gene Michael	114
17.	Joe Amalfitano	66
18.	Lou Klein	65
19.	Jim Essian	59
20.	Lou Boudreau	54
21.	Tom Trebelhorn	49
22.	Elvin Tappe	46
23.	Charlie Metro	43
24.	Preston Gomez	38
25.	Charlie Fox	17
26.	Vedie Himsl	10
27.	Frank Lucchesi	8
28.	Harry Craft	7
29.	John Vukovich	1
30.	Joe Altobelli	0

Does not include Grimm's wins as Cubs manager prior to 1946

THE WRIGLEY FIELD FACTOR

One valid way to assess a "Wrigley Field factor"—whether it has helped or hurt the Cubs to play all of their home games there—is to look at how their home record compares with their road record year after year, and compare that with the same figures of all other National League teams.

The following study covers 50 years of Cubs baseball, from 1946 through 1995. The study does not simply look at total number of wins at home — for it is assumed that all clubs win more games in good years than in bad years. But if there is such a thing as a "home field advantage," clubs should do much better at home than they do on the road in both the good and bad years.

The results show that statistically, the Cubs had a bigger home field advantage than any other team in the National League except the Houston Astros until 1989. They dropped to fifth overall in home field advantage in the span of just seven years, 1989 to 1995.

What caused the sudden drop? Significantly, the skid started in the first full season with lights in Wrigley Field.

The Cubs would appear to have enjoyed a "home field advantage" over the years — a bigger one than most other National League teams — based on how many more games they won at home than on the road. That conclusion is clouded by the fact that in many seasons the Cubs played so poorly on the road that their home record glistened in comparison. In 16 of the 50 years studied, the Cubs failed to win 30 games on the road.

Here is how the Cubs' home and road record since 1946 compares with that of other National League teams.

1946	Home	Road	+/– at home
St. Louis	49-29	49-29	—
Brooklyn	56-22	40-38	+ 16
Chicago	44-33	38-38	+ 6
Boston	45-31	36-41	+ 9
Philadelphia	41-36	28-49	+ 13
Cincinnati	35-42	32-45	+ 3
Pittsburgh	37-40	26-51	+ 11
New York	38-39	23-54	+ 15

1947	Home	Road	+/– at home
Brooklyn	52-25	42-35	+ 10
St. Louis	46-31	43-34	+ 3
Boston	50-27	36-41	+ 14
New York	45-31	36-42	+ 9
Cincinnati	42-35	31-46	+ 11
Chicago	36-43	33-42	+ 3
Philadelphia	38-38	24-54	+ 14
Pittsburgh	32-45	30-47	+ 2

1948	Home	Road	+/– at home
Boston	45-31	46-31	− 1
St. Louis	44-33	41-36	+ 3
Brooklyn	36-41	48-29	− 12
Pittsburgh	47-31	36-40	+ 11
New York	37-40	41-36	− 4
Philadelphia	32-44	34-44	− 2
Cincinnati	32-45	32-44	—
Chicago	35-42	29-48	+ 6

1949	Home	Road	+/– at home
Brooklyn	48-29	49-28	− 1
St. Louis	51-26	45-32	+ 6
Philadelphia	40-37	41-36	− 1
Boston	43-34	32-45	+ 11
New York	43-34	30-47	+ 13
Pittsburgh	36-41	35-42	+ 1
Cincinnati	35-42	27-50	+ 8
Chicago	33-44	28-49	+ 5

1950	Home	Road	+/– at home
Philadelphia	47-30	44-33	+ 3
Brooklyn	48-30	41-35	+ 7
New York	44-32	42-36	+ 2
Boston	46-31	37-40	+ 9
St. Louis	47-29	31-46	+ 16
Cincinnati	38-38	28-49	+ 10
Chicago	35-42	29-47	+ 6
Pittsburgh	33-44	24-52	+ 9

1951	Home	Road	+/– at home
New York	50-28	48-31	+ 2
Brooklyn	49-29	48-31	+ 1
St. Louis	44-34	37-39	+ 7
Boston	42-35	34-43	+ 8
Philadelphia	38-39	35-42	+ 3
Cincinnati	35-42	33-44	+ 2
Pittsburgh	32-45	32-45	—
Chicago	32-45	30-47	+ 2

1952	Home	Road	+/– at home
Brooklyn	45-33	51-24	+ 6
New York	50-27	42-35	+ 8

St. Louis	48-29	40-37	+ 8
Philadelphia	47-29	40-38	+ 7
Chicago	42-35	35-42	+ 7
Cincinnati	38-39	31-46	+ 7
Boston	31-45	33-44	− 2
Pittsburgh	23-54	19-58	+ 4

1953	*Home*	*Road*	*+/– at home*
Brooklyn	60-17	45-32	+ 17
Milwaukee	45-31	47-31	− 2
Philadelphia	48-29	35-42	+ 13
St. Louis	48-30	35-41	+ 13
New York	38-39	32-45	+ 6
Cincinnati	38-39	30-47	+ 8
Chicago	43-34	22-55	+ 21
Pittsburgh	26-51	24-53	+ 2

1954	*Home*	*Road*	*+/– at home*
New York	53-23	44-34	+ 9
Brooklyn	45-32	47-30	− 2
Milwaukee	43-34	46-31	− 3
Philadelphia	39-39	36-40	+ 3
Cincinnati	41-36	33-44	+ 8
St. Louis	33-44	39-38	− 6
Chicago	40-37	24-53	+ 16
Pittsburgh	31-46	22-55	+ 9

1955	*Home*	*Road*	*+/– at home*
Brooklyn	56-21	42-34	+ 14
Milwaukee	46-31	39-38	+ 7
New York	44-35	36-39	+ 8
Philadelphia	46-31	31-46	+ 15
Cincinnati	46-31	29-48	+ 17
Chicago	43-33	29-48	+ 14
St. Louis	41-36	27-50	+ 14
Pittsburgh	36-39	24-55	+ 12

1956	*Home*	*Road*	*+/– at home*
Brooklyn	52-25	41-36	+ 11
Milwaukee	47-29	45-33	+ 2
Cincinnati	51-26	40-37	+ 11

St. Louis	43-34	33-44	+ 10
Philadelphia	40-37	31-46	+ 9
New York	37-40	30-47	+ 7
Pittsburgh	35-43	31-45	+ 4
Chicago	39-38	21-56	+ 18

1957	Home	Road	+/– at home
Milwaukee	45-32	50-27	− 5
St. Louis	42-35	45-32	− 3
Brooklyn	43-34	41-36	+ 2
Cincinnati	45-32	35-42	+ 10
Philadelphia	38-39	39-38	− 1
New York	37-40	32-45	+ 5
Chicago	31-46	31-46	—
Pittsburgh	36-41	26-51	+ 10

1958	Home	Road	+/– at home
Milwaukee	48-29	44-33	+ 4
Pittsburgh	49-28	35-42	+ 14
San Francisco	44-33	36-41	+ 8
Cincinnati	40-37	36-41	+ 4
Chicago	35-42	37-40	− 2
St. Louis	39-38	33-44	+ 6
Los Angeles	39-38	32-45	+ 7
Philadelphia	35-42	34-43	+ 1

1959	Home	Road	+/– at home
Los Angeles	46-32	42-36	+ 4
Milwaukee	49-29	37-41	+ 12
San Francisco	42-35	41-36	+ 1
Pittsburgh	47-30	31-46	+ 16
Chicago	38-39	36-41	+ 2
Cincinnati	43-34	31-46	+ 12
St. Louis	42-35	29-48	+ 13
Philadelphia	37-40	27-50	+ 10

1960	Home	Road	+/– at home
Pittsburgh	52-25	43-34	+ 9
Milwaukee	51-26	37-40	+ 14
St. Louis	51-26	35-42	+ 16
Los Angeles	42-35	40-37	+ 2

San Francisco	45-32	34-43	+ 11
Cincinnati	37-40	30-47	+ 7
Chicago	33-44	27-50	+ 6
Philadelphia	31-46	28-49	+ 3

1961	*Home*	*Road*	*+/– at home*
Cincinnati	47-30	46-31	+ 1
Los Angeles	45-32	44-33	+ 1
San Francisco	45-32	40-37	+ 5
Milwaukee	45-32	38-39	+ 7
St. Louis	48-29	32-45	+ 16
Pittsburgh	38-39	37-40	+ 1
Chicago	40-37	24-53	+ 16
Philadelphia	22-55	25-52	– 3

1962	*Home*	*Road*	*+/– at home*
San Francisco	61-21	42-41	+ 19
Los Angeles	54-29	48-34	+ 6
Cincinnati	58-23	40-41	+ 18
Pittsburgh	51-30	42-38	+ 9
Milwaukee	49-32	37-44	+ 12
St. Louis	44-37	40-41	+ 4
Philadelphia	46-34	35-46	+ 11
Houston	32-48	32-48	—
Chicago	32-49	27-54	+ 5
New York	22-58	18-62	+ 4

1963	*Home*	*Road*	*+/– at home*
Los Angeles	53-28	46-35	+ 11
St. Louis	53-28	40-41	+ 13
San Francisco	50-31	38-43	+ 12
Philadelphia	45-36	42-39	+ 3
Cincinnati	46-35	40-41	+ 6
Milwaukee	45-36	39-42	+ 6
Chicago	43-38	39-42	+ 4
Pittsburgh	42-39	32-49	+ 10
Houston	44-37	22-59	+ 22
New York	34-47	17-64	+ 17

1964	*Home*	*Road*	*+/– at home*
St. Louis	48-33	45-35	+ 3
Cincinnati	47-34	45-36	+ 2

Philadelphia	46-35	46-35	—
San Francisco	44-37	46-35	− 2
Milwaukee	45-36	43-38	+ 2
Los Angeles	41-40	39-42	+ 2
Pittsburgh	42-39	38-43	+ 4
Chicago	40-41	36-45	+ 4
Houston	41-40	25-56	+ 16
New York	33-48	20-61	+ 13

1965	*Home*	*Road*	*+/– at home*
Los Angeles	50-31	47-34	+ 3
San Francisco	51-30	44-37	+ 7
Pittsburgh	49-32	41-40	+ 8
Cincinnati	49-32	40-41	+ 9
Milwaukee	44-37	42-39	+ 2
Philadelphia	45-35	40-41	+ 5
St. Louis	42-39	38-42	+ 4
Chicago	40-41	32-49	+ 8
Houston	36-45	29-52	+ 7
New York	29-52	21-60	+ 8

1966	*Home*	*Road*	*+/– at home*
Los Angeles	53-28	42-39	+ 11
San Francisco	47-34	46-34	+ 1
Pittsburgh	46-35	46-35	—
Philadelphia	48-33	39-42	+ 9
Atlanta	43-38	42-39	+ 1
St. Louis	43-38	40-41	+ 3
Cincinnati	46-33	30-51	+ 16
Houston	45-36	27-54	+ 18
New York	32-49	34-46	− 2
Chicago	32-49	27-54	+ 5

1967	*Home*	*Road*	*+/– at home*
St. Louis	49-32	52-28	− 3
San Francisco	51-31	40-40	+ 11
Chicago	49-34	38-40	+ 11
Cincinnati	49-32	38-43	+ 11
Philadelphia	45-35	37-35	+ 8
Pittsburgh	49-32	32-49	+ 17
Atlanta	48-33	29-52	+ 19

Los Angeles	42-31	31-50	+ 11
Houston	46-35	23-58	+ 23
New York	36-42	25-59	+ 11

1968	Home	Road	+/– at home
St. Louis	47-34	50-31	− 3
San Francisco	42-39	46-35	− 4
Chicago	47-34	37-44	+ 10
Cincinnati	40-41	43-38	− 3
Atlanta	41-40	40-41	+ 1
Pittsburgh	40-41	40-41	—
Los Angeles	41-40	35-46	+ 6
Philadelphia	38-43	38-43	—
New York	32-49	41-40	− 9
Houston	42-39	30-51	+ 12

1969	Home	Road	+/– at home
New York	52-30	48-32	+ 4
Chicago	49-32	43-38	+ 6
Pittsburgh	47-34	41-40	+ 6
St. Louis	42-38	45-37	− 3
Philadelphia	30-51	33-48	− 3
Montreal	24-57	28-53	− 4
Atlanta	50-31	43-38	+ 7
San Francisco	52-29	38-43	+ 14
Cincinnati	50-31	39-42	+ 11
Los Angeles	50-31	35-46	+ 15
Houston	52-29	29-52	+ 23
San Diego	28-53	24-57	+ 4

1970	Home	Road	+/– at home
Pittsburgh	50-32	39-41	+ 11
Chicago	46-34	38-44	+ 8
New York	44-38	39-41	+ 5
St. Louis	34-47	42-39	− 8
Philadelphia	40-40	33-48	+ 7
Montreal	39-41	34-48	+ 5
Cincinnati	57-24	45-36	+ 12
Los Angeles	39-42	48-32	− 9
San Francisco	48-33	38-43	+ 10
Houston	44-37	35-46	+ 9

Atlanta	42-39	34-47	+ 8
San Diego	31-50	32-49	− 1

1971	Home	Road	+/− at home
Pittsburgh	52-28	45-37	+ 7
St. Louis	45-36	45-36	—
Chicago	44-37	39-42	+ 5
New York	44-37	39-42	+ 5
Montreal	36-44	35-46	+ 1
Philadelphia	34-47	33-48	+ 1
San Francisco	51-30	39-42	+ 12
Los Angeles	42-39	47-34	− 5
Atlanta	43-39	39-41	+ 4
Cincinnati	46-35	33-48	+ 13
Houston	39-42	40-41	− 1
San Diego	33-48	28-52	+ 5

1972	Home	Road	+/− at home
Pittsburgh	49-29	47-30	+ 2
Chicago	46-31	39-39	+ 7
New York	41-37	42-36	− 1
St. Louis	40-37	35-44	+ 3
Montreal	35-43	35-43	—
Philadelphia	28-51	31-46	− 3
Cincinnati	42-34	53-25	− 11
Houston	41-36	43-33	− 2
Los Angeles	41-34	44-36	− 3
Atlanta	36-41	34-43	+ 2
San Francisco	34-43	35-43	− 1
San Diego	26-54	32-41	− 6

1973	Home	Road	+/− at home
New York	43-38	39-41	+ 4
St. Louis	43-38	38-43	+ 5
Pittsburgh	41-40	39-42	+ 2
Montreal	43-38	36-45	+ 7
Chicago	41-39	36-45	+ 5
Philadelphia	38-43	33-48	+ 5
Cincinnati	50-31	49-32	+ 1
Los Angeles	50-31	45-35	+ 5
San Francisco	47-34	41-40	+ 6

Houston	41-40	41-40	—
Atlanta	40-40	36-45	+ 4
San Diego	31-50	29-52	+ 2

1974	Home	Road	+/– at home
Pittsburgh	52-29	36-45	+ 16
St. Louis	44-37	42-38	+ 2
Philadelphia	46-35	34-47	+ 12
Montreal	42-38	37-44	+ 5
New York	36-45	35-46	+ 1
Chicago	32-49	34-47	– 2
Los Angeles	52-29	50-31	+ 2
Cincinnati	50-31	48-33	+ 2
Atlanta	46-35	42-39	+ 4
Houston	46-35	35-46	+ 11
San Francisco	37-44	35-46	+ 2
San Diego	36-45	24-57	+ 12

1975	Home	Road	+/– at home
Pittsburgh	52-28	40-41	+ 12
Philadelphia	51-30	35-46	+ 16
New York	42-39	40-41	+ 2
St. Louis	45-36	37-44	+ 8
Chicago	42-39	33-48	+ 9
Montreal	39-42	36-45	+ 3
Cincinnati	64-17	44-37	+ 20
Los Angeles	49-32	39-42	+ 10
San Francisco	46-35	34-46	+ 12
San Diego	38-43	33-48	+ 5
Atlanta	37-43	30-51	+ 7
Houston	37-44	27-53	+ 10

1976	Home	Road	+/– at home
Philadelphia	53-28	48-33	+ 5
Pittsburgh	47-34	45-36	+ 2
New York	45-37	41-39	+ 4
Chicago	42-39	33-48	+ 9
St. Louis	37-44	35-46	+ 2
Montreal	27-53	28-54	– 1
Cincinnati	49-32	53-28	– 4
Los Angeles	49-32	43-38	+ 6

Houston	46-36	34-46	+ 12
San Francisco	40-41	34-47	+ 6
San Diego	42-38	31-51	+ 11
Atlanta	34-47	36-45	− 2

1977	*Home*	*Road*	*+/− at home*
Philadelphia	60-21	41-40	+ 19
Pittsburgh	58-23	38-43	+ 20
St. Louis	52-31	31-48	+ 21
Chicago	46-35	35-46	+ 11
Montreal	38-43	37-44	+ 1
New York	35-44	29-52	+ 6
Los Angeles	51-30	47-34	+ 4
Cincinnati	48-33	40-41	+ 8
Houston	46-35	35-46	+ 11
San Francisco	38-43	37-44	+ 1
San Diego	35-46	34-47	+ 1
Atlanta	40-41	21-60	+ 19

1978	*Home*	*Road*	*+/− at home*
Philadelphia	54-28	36-44	+ 18
Pittsburgh	55-26	33-47	+ 22
Chicago	44-38	35-46	+ 9
Montreal	41-39	35-47	+ 6
St. Louis	37-44	32-49	+ 5
New York	33-47	33-49	—
Los Angeles	54-27	41-40	+ 13
Cincinnati	49-31	43-38	+ 6
San Francisco	50-31	39-42	+ 11
San Diego	50-31	34-47	+ 16
Houston	50-31	24-57	+ 26
Atlanta	39-42	30-51	+ 9

1979	*Home*	*Road*	*+/− at home*
Pittsburgh	48-33	50-31	− 2
Montreal	56-25	39-40	+ 17
St. Louis	42-39	44-37	− 2
Philadelphia	43-38	41-40	+ 2
Chicago	45-36	35-46	+ 10
New York	28-53	35-46	− 7
Cincinnati	48-32	42-39	+ 6

Houston	52-29	37-44	+ 15
Los Angeles	46-35	33-48	+ 13
San Francisco	38-43	33-48	+ 5
San Diego	39-42	29-51	+ 10
Atlanta	34-45	32-49	+ 2

1980	*Home*	*Road*	*+/– at home*
Philadelphia	49-32	42-39	+ 7
Montreal	51-29	39-43	+ 12
Pittsburgh	47-34	36-45	+ 11
St. Louis	41-40	33-48	+ 8
New York	38-44	29-51	+ 9
Chicago	37-44	27-54	+ 10
Houston	55-26	38-44	+ 17
Los Angeles	55-27	37-44	+ 18
Cincinnati	44-37	45-36	– 1
Atlanta	50-30	31-50	+ 19
San Francisco	44-37	31-49	+ 13
San Diego	45-36	28-53	+ 17

1981	*Home*	*Road*	*+/– at home*
St. Louis	32-21	27-22	+ 5
Montreal	38-18	22-30	+ 16
Philadelphia	36-19	23-29	+ 13
Pittsburgh	22-28	24-28	– 2
New York	24-27	17-35	+ 7
Chicago	27-30	11-35	+ 16
Cincinnati	32-22	34-20	– 2
Los Angeles	33-23	30-24	+ 3
Houston	31-20	30-29	+ 1
San Francisco	29-24	27-31	+ 2
Atlanta	22-27	28-29	– 6
San Diego	20-35	21-34	– 1

1982	*Home*	*Road*	*+/– at home*
St. Louis	46-35	27-48	+ 19
Philadelphia	51-30	38-43	+ 13
Montreal	40-41	46-35	– 6
Pittsburgh	42-39	42-39	—
Chicago	38-43	35-46	+ 3
New York	33-48	32-49	+ 1

Atlanta	42-39	47-34	−	5
Los Angeles	43-38	45-36	−	2
San Francisco	45-36	42-39	+	3
San Diego	43-38	38-43	+	5
Houston	43-38	34-47	+	9
Cincinnati	33-48	28-53	+	5

1983	*Home*	*Road*	*+/− at home*
Philadelphia	50-31	40-41	+ 10
Pittsburgh	41-40	43-38	− 2
Montreal	46-35	36-45	+ 10
St. Louis	44-37	35-46	+ 9
Chicago	43-38	28-53	+ 15
New York	41-41	27-53	+ 14
Los Angeles	48-32	43-39	+ 5
Atlanta	46-34	42-40	+ 4
Houston	46-36	39-42	+ 7
San Diego	47-34	34-47	+ 13
San Francisco	43-38	36-45	+ 7
Cincinnati	36-45	38-43	− 2

1984	*Home*	*Road*	*+/− at home*
Chicago	51-29	45-36	+ 6
New York	48-33	42-39	+ 6
St. Louis	44-37	40-41	+ 4
Philadelphia	39-42	42-39	+ 3
Montreal	39-42	39-41	—
Pittsburgh	41-40	34-47	+ 7
San Diego	48-33	44-37	+ 4
Atlanta	38-43	42-39	− 4
Houston	43-38	37-44	+ 6
Los Angeles	40-41	39-42	+ 1
Cincinnati	39-42	31-50	+ 8
San Francisco	35-46	31-50	+ 4

1985	*Home*	*Road*	*+/− at home*
St. Louis	54-27	47-34	+ 7
New York	51-30	47-34	+ 4
Montreal	44-37	40-40	+ 4
Chicago	41-39	36-45	+ 5
Philadelphia	41-40	34-47	+ 7

Pittsburgh	35-45	22-59	+ 13
Los Angeles	48-33	47-34	+ 1
Cincinnati	47-34	42-38	+ 5
Houston	44-37	39-42	+ 5
San Diego	44-37	39-42	+ 5
Atlanta	32-49	34-47	− 2
San Francisco	38-43	24-57	+ 14

1986	Home	Road	+/– at home
New York	55-26	53-28	+ 2
Philadelphia	49-31	37-44	+ 12
St. Louis	42-39	37-43	+ 5
Montreal	36-44	42-39	− 6
Chicago	42-38	28-52	+ 14
Pittsburgh	31-50	33-48	− 2
Houston	52-29	44-37	+ 8
Cincinnati	43-38	43-38	—
San Francisco	46-35	37-44	+ 9
San Diego	43-38	31-50	+ 12
Los Angeles	46-35	27-54	+ 19
Atlanta	41-40	31-49	+ 10

1987	Home	Road	+/– in home
St. Louis	49-32	46-35	+ 3
New York	49-32	43-38	+ 6
Montreal	48-33	43-38	+ 5
Philadelphia	43-38	37-44	+ 6
Pittsburgh	47-34	33-48	+ 14
Chicago	40-40	36-45	+ 4
San Francisco	46-35	44-37	+ 2
Cincinnati	42-39	42-39	—
Houston	47-34	29-52	+ 18
Los Angeles	40-41	33-48	+ 7
Atlanta	42-39	27-53	+ 15
San Diego	37-44	28-53	+ 9

1988	Home	Road	+/– at home
New York	56-24	44-36	+ 12
Pittsburgh	43-38	42-37	+ 1
Montreal	43-38	38-43	+ 5
Chicago	39-42	38-43	+ 1

St. Louis	41-40	35-46	+ 6
Philadelphia	38-42	27-54	+ 11
Los Angeles	45-36	49-31	− 4
Cincinnati	45-35	42-39	+ 3
San Diego	47-34	36-44	+ 11
San Francisco	45-36	38-43	+ 7
Houston	44-37	38-43	+ 6
Atlanta	28-51	26-55	+ 2

1989	Home	Road	+/- at home
Chicago	48-33	45-36	+ 3
New York	51-30	36-45	+ 15
St. Louis	46-35	40-41	+ 6
Montreal	44-37	37-44	+ 7
Pittsburgh	39-42	35-46	+ 4
Philadelphia	38-42	29-53	+ 9
San Francisco	53-28	39-42	+ 14
San Diego	46-35	43-38	+ 3
Houston	47-35	39-41	+ 8
Los Angeles	44-37	33-46	+ 11
Cincinnati	38-43	37-44	+ 1
Atlanta	33-46	30-51	+ 3

1990	Home	Road	+/- at home
Pittsburgh	49-32	46-35	+ 3
New York	52-29	39-42	+ 13
Montreal	47-34	38-43	+ 9
Chicago	39-42	38-43	+ 1
Philadelphia	41-40	36-45	+ 5
St. Louis	34-47	36-45	− 2
Cincinnati	46-35	45-36	+ 1
Los Angeles	47-34	39-42	+ 8
San Francisco	49-32	36-45	+ 13
Houston	49-32	26-55	+ 23
San Diego	37-44	38-43	− 1
Atlanta	37-44	28-53	+ 1

1991	Home	Road	+/- at home
Pittsburgh	52-32	46-32	+ 6
St. Louis	52-32	32-46	+ 20
Philadelphia	47-36	37-48	+ 10

	Home	Road	+/−
Chicago	46-37	31-46	+ 15
New York	40-42	37-42	+ 3
Montreal	33-45	38-55	− 5
Atlanta	48-31	46-35	+ 2
Los Angeles	54-27	39-42	+ 15
San Diego	42-39	42-39	—
San Francisco	43-38	32-49	+ 11
Cincinnati	39-42	35-46	+ 4
Houston	37-44	28-53	+ 9

1992	Home	Road	+/− home and road
Pittsburgh	53-28	43-38	+ 10
Montreal	43-38	44-37	− 1
St. Louis	45-36	38-43	+ 7
Chicago	43-38	35-46	+ 8
New York	41-40	31-50	+ 10
Philadelphia	41-40	29-52	+ 12
Atlanta	51-30	47-34	+ 4
Cincinnati	53-28	37-44	+ 16
San Diego	45-36	37-44	+ 8
Houston	47-34	34-47	+ 13
San Francisco	42-39	30-51	+ 12
Los Angeles	37-44	26-55	+ 11

1993	Home	Road	+/− at home
Philadelphia	52-29	45-36	+ 7
Montreal	55-26	39-42	+ 16
St. Louis	49-32	38-42	+ 11
Chicago	43-38	41-40	+ 2
Pittsburgh	40-41	35-46	+ 5
Florida	35-46	29-52	+ 6
New York	28-53	31-50	− 3
Atlanta	51-30	53-28	− 2
San Francisco	50-31	53-28	− 3
Houston	44-37	41-40	+ 3
Los Angeles	41-40	40-41	+ 1
Cincinnati	41-40	32-49	+ 9
Colorado	39-42	28-53	+ 11
San Diego	34-47	27-54	+ 7

1994	Home	Road	+/− at home
Montreal	32-20	42-20	− 10
Atlanta	31-24	37-22	− 6

New York	23-30	32-28	− 9
Philadelphia	34-26	20-35	+ 14
Florida	25-34	26-30	− 1
Cincinnati	37-22	29-26	+ 8
Houston	37-22	29-27	+ 8
Pittsburgh	32-29	21-32	+ 11
St. Louis	23-33	30-28	− 7
Chicago	20-39	29-25	− 9
Los Angeles	33-22	25-34	+ 8
San Francisco	29-31	26-29	+ 3
Colorado	25-32	28-32	− 3
San Diego	26-31	21-39	+ 5

1995	*Home*	*Road*	*+/− in home*
Atlanta	44-28	46-26	− 2
New York	40-32	29-43	+ 11
Philadelphia	35-37	34-38	+ 1
Florida	37-44	30-42	+ 7
Montreal	31-41	35-37	− 4
Cincinnati	44-28	41-31	+ 3
Houston	36-36	40-32	− 4
Chicago	34-38	39-33	− 5
St. Louis	39-33	27-45	+ 12
Pittsburgh	31-41	27-45	+ 4
Los Angeles	39-33	39-33	—
Colorado	44-28	33-39	+ 11
San Diego	40-32	30-42	+ 10
San Francisco	37-35	30-42	+ 7

Total Difference, Home Wins Versus Road Wins, 1946–1995

Team	*+/− wins at home*	*no. of years*	*ave. +/− wins at home*
Houston	+ 349	34	+ 10.2
NY/San Francisco	+ 345	50	+ 6.9
Pittsburgh	+ 344	50	+ 6.9
Philadelphia	+ 342	50	+ 6.8
Chicago	**+ 339**	**50**	**+ 6.7**
Cincinnati	+ 299	50	+ 6.0
St. Louis	+ 289	50	+ 5.8

Team	+/– wins at home	no. of years	ave. +/– wins at home
Brooklyn/LA	+ 276	50	+ 5.5
Bos/Mil/Atlanta	+ 234	50	+ 4.6
New York	+ 162	34	+ 4.7
San Diego	+ 176	27	+ 6.5
Montreal	+ 92	27	+ 3.1
Florida	+ 14	3	+ 4.6
Colorado	+ 13	3	+ 4.3

THE WRIGLEY FIELD LIGHTS FACTOR

Between 1946 and 1988, the Chicago Cubs were second only to the Houston Astros in home field advantage — the difference between the number of games they won at home and the number of games they won on the road every year.

In the seven-year span from 1989 to 1995, the Cubs' home field advantage shrunk so that the final totals show them as fifth best in home field advantage. (See chart on previous page.) The span of 1989 to 1995 is the first seven years the Cubs played night games in Wrigley Field.

Statistically, when the Cubs started playing night games at home, they lost the dominant home field advantage they had over most teams.

Home Wins Versus Road Wins, 1946–1988 (Before Lights in Wrigley Field)

Team	+/– wins at home	no. of years	ave. +/– wins at home
Houston	+ 289	27	+ 10.7
Chicago	**+ 324**	**43**	+ 7.5
San Diego	+ 144	20	+ 7.2
Pittsburgh	+ 301	43	+ 7.0
NY/San Francisco	+ 288	43	+ 6.7
Philadelphia	+ 284	43	+ 6.6
Cincinnati	+ 257	43	+ 6.0
St. Louis	+ 242	43	+ 5.6
Bos/Mil/Atlanta	+ 226	43	+ 5.2

Team	+/− wins at home	no. of years	ave. +/− wins at home
Brooklyn/LA	+ 222	43	+ 5.2
New York	+ 122	27	+ 4.5
Montreal	+ 80	20	+ 4.0

Home Wins Versus Road Wins, 1989–1995 (After Lights in Wrigley Field)

Houston	+ 60	7	+ 8.6
Philadelphia	+ 58	7	+ 8.1
NY/San Francisco	+ 57	7	+ 8.1
Brooklyn/LA	+ 54	7	+ 7.7
St. Louis	+ 47	7	+ 6.7
Pittsburgh	+ 43	7	+ 6.1
Colorado	+ 19	3	+ 6.1
Cincinnati	+ 42	7	+ 6.0
New York	+ 40	7	+ 5.7
San Diego	+ 32	7	+ 4.6
Florida	+ 12	3	+ 4.0
Chicago	+ 15	7	+ 2.1
Montreal	+ 12	7	+ 1.7
Bos/Mil/Atlanta	+ 8	7	+ 1.0
Montreal	+ 12	7	+ 1.7

THE PHILIP K. WRIGLEY FACTOR

Many who played for the Cubs under the ownership of Philip K. Wrigley criticized his apparent disinterest in the ballclub. He seldom attended games.

He owned the Cubs from 1932, when he inherited the club from his father, William Wrigley, until his death in 1977. The Wrigley family retained ownership of the Cubs until Philip Wrigley's heirs sold the team to the Chicago Tribune Corporation in 1981.

The Cubs won pennants in 1929, 1932, 1935 and 1938 with players Phil Wrigley's father developed, recruited or got in trades with other teams. In 1945, the Cubs won the pennant with a collection of players too old to serve in World War II or who couldn't pass the physical examination required by the armed services. The Cardinals were National League champions in 1943, 1944, 1946 and 1947. The Cubs championship proved to be just a hiccup.

Don Johnson, who played for the Cubs from 1942 to 1947 and was the starting second baseman on the 1945 championship team, thinks Philip Wrigley was too interested in the company that made the family fortune — Wrigley chewing gum — than he was in the baseball team. "You don't put a plumber in charge of the airline," he says wryly.

Third baseman Alvin Dark, who played for Wrigley in the 1950s, says the owner's biggest mistake was not having sharp baseball people in his front office. "You can't run the ballclub from downtown," says Dark.

Dick Ellsworth, one of the best Cubs pitchers of the early 1960s, says there were never high expectations for the Cubs, therefore no pressure to win, therefore no winning tradition that anyone felt compelled to uphold. "A winning attitude has to start at the top, and it just didn't with the Cubs back in those days," says Ellsworth.

When Wrigley did get involved with the ballclub, he did some strange things — and the results were sometimes disastrous and often long lasting.

He often hired old Cubs ballplayers — players he liked — to be his managers. The list is long — Charlie Grimm (three different stints), Gabby Hartnett, Phil Cavarretta, Stan Hack, Bob Scheffing, Jim Marshall. The Wrigley family hired former Cubs infielder Joe Amalfitano to manage the club for a short time after Phil Wrigley died.

Cavarretta, Hack and Scheffing were in succession, from 1951 to 1959. In 1960, Grimm returned for his third stint as manager and lasted 17 games before switching places with Cubs radio announcer Lou Boudreau, a cute move that got its fair share of publicity but was not destined to last long. Boudreau, who had previous managerial experience and won a World Series with the Indians in 1948, remained the Cubs manager only for the rest of the 1960 season.

In 1961, Wrigley instituted the ill-fated rotating coaching system in which the Cubs went without a manager for two years while several men rotated as "head coach." The Cubs finished seventh in an eight-team league in 1961 and ninth in a ten-team league in 1962. The experiment was dropped at the end of the 1962 season.

Wrigley redeemed some of his management follies when he hired Leo Durocher to manage the club in 1966. Three years later, the Cubs made their strongest run for a pennant in 24 years, leading most of the way until being overtaken by the Mets. The Cubs were strong contenders the next two years too, but Durocher was wearing out his welcome with Cubs players. There were numerous reports of dissension on the field and arguments in the clubhouse.

Wrigley responded to the unrest with another strange move. On August 3, 1971, he placed a full page ad in the *Chicago Tribune* that was an open letter to Chicago Cubs fans. In it, he told of the frustrations of trying to build a winning team in Chicago and that the commitment to winning was demonstrated with the hiring of Durocher in 1966. He further noted the recent player dissension over Durocher's management style and assured fans that Durocher would be staying on as manager. He said in the letter that if players were not happy with that decision, efforts would be made to move them to other teams.

Wrigley added a curious postscript to the already bizarre letter. It said, "It's too bad we don't have more team players like Ernie Banks"—a line that poured gasoline on a fire Wrigley should have been trying to put out.

Durocher was gone after 90 games of the next season.

It was during Wrigley's regime that the Cubs made some infamous trades — sending veteran slugger Hank Sauer to the Cardinals for an unknown named Pete Whisenant; trading future Hall of Famer Lou Brock to the Cardinals for Ernie Broglio, a pitcher who was out of baseball with a sore arm three years later; sending young pitcher Joe Niekro to San Diego for Dick Selma, who lasted one year with the Cubs while Niekro won close to 200 games over the next 19 years; and trading promising left-hander Larry Gura to Texas for pitcher Mike Paul, who didn't win a game for the Cubs in parts of two years while Gura later became the all-time winning percentage leader for the Kansas City Royals.

All of these observations are subjective. A more fair appraisal of the Wrigley leadership would be to compare how his ballclub did from 1946 on, during his tenure, with how well it has done since the Wrigleys relinquished ownership.

Between 1946 (the first season after their championship year) and 1981, when the Wrigleys sold the team, the Cubs won no championships, finished second three times and finished with a record under .500 in 25 of those 36 years.

Since 1981, the Cubs still have not won the National League championship, but have been the league's division champion twice and a wild card winner once, placing them in the National League playoffs three times in 19 years. Only four other National League teams, the Braves, the Dodgers the Cardinals and the Astros, have been in the playoffs more often.

National League Playoff Teams Since 1981

(Two division winners made the playoffs until 1994.)

Division winners:

1981	Los Angeles, Montreal
1982	St. Louis, Atlanta
1983	Philadelphia, Los Angeles
1984	Chicago, San Diego
1985	St. Louis, Los Angeles
1986	New York, Houston
1987	St. Louis, San Francisco
1988	New York, Los Angeles
1989	Chicago, San Francisco
1990	Pittsburgh, Cincinnati
1991	Pittsburgh, Atlanta
1992	Pittsburgh, Atlanta
1993	Philadelphia, Atlanta
1994	STRIKE

(Starting in 1995, the playoffs consisted of
three division winners and a wild card team.)

Playoff teams:

1995	Atlanta, Cincinnati, Los Angeles, Colorado
1996	Atlanta, St. Louis, San Diego, Los Angeles
1997	Florida, Atlanta, San Francisco, Houston
1998	Chicago, Atlanta, Houston, San Diego
1999	Arizona, New York, Atlanta, Houston

Total playoff appearances by National League teams since 1981:

Atlanta	9	New York	3
Los Angeles	6	Cincinnati	2
St. Louis	4	Philadelphia	2
Houston	4	Florida	1
Chicago	3	Colorado	1
Pittsburgh	3	Montreal	1
San Francisco	3	Arizona	1
San Diego	3		

THE FAN FACTOR

Paid attendance figures at Wrigley Field since 1946 give a clear indication of the loyalty of Cubs fans, particularly since the Leo Durocher era, 1966–1972. Under Durocher, the Cubs became a contender — and the fans responded.

Since that time, the club has had its ups and downs (more downs than ups) and yet Cubs fans have not demanded a winner.

Baseball fans in major league cities all over the country vote with their feet and with their wallets. When they lose interest and stop coming to the ballpark, management usually exercises one of two options: they either aggressively go after ballplayers who will help the ballclub move up in the standings or bring people back to the ballpark to see them play, or they move the franchise to another city.

The White Sox, who play their home games on the other side of Chicago, considered moving out of Chicago in the late 1970s before Bill Veeck bought the team (his second stint as a White Sox owner). In recent years, the White Sox have consistently spent millions of dollars on free agents, most recently Albert Belle, a slugger who did not help produce a winner in Chicago and whose presence did not bolster White Sox attendance. Cubs management has not been forced to spend millions on free agents to bolster attendance or think about moving — because the fans keep coming to Wrigley Field.

Part of the success with attendance is that Wrigley Field is a tourist attraction. The Wrigley family wanted it that way — and on that point, they turned out to be right. The green ivy vines, the old, manually operated scoreboard in center field, the distinctive bleachers in left field and right field, the close proximity of the box seats to the field — all are a part of the charm of the place.

Adding to all of this is the Cubs television outlet, WGN, the "superstation" which broadcasts Cubs games to cable subscribers throughout the country. Those who have watched the Cubs on TV have seen the old scoreboard, the bleachers, the ivy-covered walls for many years. When they come to Chicago on vacation or on business, Wrigley Field is one of the places they want to see — and it doesn't matter whether the Cubs are winning or losing.

The players appreciate the fan support but some acknowledge that neither Cubs management nor the fans created a mandate for them to win.

Dick Ellsworth, a mainstay on the Cubs pitching staff in the 1960s, said there was never any burning desire to win, no motivation to maintain a tradition, no pride like players experienced wearing Yankee pinstripes or Dodger blue.

"We didn't have a winning attitude. There was no sense of Cubs pride to inspire you," he said.

Thirty years later, catcher Rick Wrona said Cubs fans thought of a day at the ballpark like a day at the county fair. Win or lose, they went home happy. They had a good time at the ballpark. So, for the players, there was never any real pressure to win from that standpoint.

In fact, said some players, fans have almost come to expect the Cubs to lose. Both Dave LaRoche, who later played on a championship team with the Yankees, and Larry Gura, who later played on a championship team with the Kansas City Royals, said they were shocked by the "here they go again" reaction of fans when the Cubs lost a few games in August in the early 1970s.

A few years later, a fan brought a banner to the ballpark that said "Wait Til Next Year" on Opening Day.

But year after year, the fans keep coming, because they have learned that, as the late Harry Caray used to say on his broadcasts, "there's nothing like fun at the old ballpark"— particularly if that ballpark is "the friendly confines" of Wrigley Field.

Cubs Season Records, 1946–1999

Year	W-L	Pct.	Finished	Attendance
1946	82-71	.536	3rd	1,342,870
1947	69-85	.448	6th	1,364,039
1948	64-90	.416	8th	1,237,792
1949	61-93	.396	8th	1,143,139
1950	64-89	.418	7th	1,165,944
1951	62-92	.403	8th	894,415
1952	77-77	.500	5th	1,024,826
1953	65-89	.442	7th	763,653
1954	64-90	.416	7th	748,183
1955	72-81	.471	6th	875,800
1956	60-94	.390	8th	720,118
1957	62-92	.403	7th (tie)	670,629
1958	72-82	.468	5th (tie)	979,904
1959	74-80	.481	5th (tie)	858,255

Year	W-L	Pct.	Finished	Attendance
1960	60-94	.390	7th	809,770
1961	64-90*	.416	7th	673,057
1962	59-103*	.364	9th	609,802
1963	82-80	.506	7th	979,551
1964	76-86	.469	8th	751,647
1965	72-90	.444	8th	641,361
1966	59-103	.364	10th	635,891
1967	87-74	.540	3rd	977,226
1968	84-78	.519	3rd	1,043,409
1969	92-70	.568	2nd	1,674,993
1970	84-78	.519	2nd	1,642,705
1971	83-79	.512	3rd (tie)	1,653,007
1972	85-70 (s)	.548	2nd	1,229,163
1973	77-84	.478	5th	1,351,705
1974	66-96	.407	6th	1,015,378
1975	75-87	.463	5th (tie)	1,034,819
1976	75-87	.463	4th	1,026,217
1977	81-81	.500	4th	1,439,834
1978	79-83	.488	3rd	1,525,311
1979	80-82	.494	5th	1,648,587
1980	64-98	.395	6th	1,206,776
1981	38-85(s)	.369	6th	556,637*
1982	73-89	.451	5th	1,249,278
1983	71-91	.438	5th	1,479,717
1984	96-65	.596	1st	2,107,655
1985	77-84	.478	4th	2,161,534
1986	70-90	.438	5th	1,859,102
1987	76-85	.472	6th	2,035,130
1988	77-85	.475	4th	2,089,034
1989	93-69	.574	1st	2,491,942
1990	77-85	.475	4th	2,243,791
1991	77-83	.481	4th	2,314,250
1992	78-84	.481	4th	2,216,720
1993	84-78	.519	4th	2,653,763
1994	49-64 (s)	.434	5th	1,845,208*
1995	73-71 (s)	.507	3rd	1,918,265*
1996	76-86	.469	4th	2,219,110
1997	68-94	.420	5th	2,190,308
1998	93-70 (w)	.570	2nd (tie)	2,623,194
1999	67-95	.414	6th	2,813,854

*strike-shortened season

Part VI. The Last Hurrah

THE 1945 WORLD SERIES

The Chicago Cubs and Detroit Tigers matched up in the 1945 World Series, a Series that is remembered for its many quirks. It matched the Cubs, who had lost seven of their last nine World Series appearances, with the Tigers, who had lost five of their last six.

And it featured a Tiger team whose roster during the year was far different than normal because so many regular players were in the armed services. The Cubs, on the other hand, were a team with most of its players too old for the military. Veteran Chicago sportswriter Warren Brown of the *Chicago American* wrote before the Series started: "I've seen them both play. I don't think either team can win."

The Cubs had great opportunities to win it. Because of railroad travel restrictions, imposed to give preferential treatment to servicemen returning home from the war, only one road trip was scheduled. Instead of the usual 2-3-2, home-road-home schedule, it was decided that the first three games would be played in Detroit with the final four being played in Chicago. When the Cubs won two out of three at Detroit, they were a heavy favorite to come home and win the championship. But it didn't work out that way. Detroit took three out of four at Wrigley Field to win it. Some of the Series oddities:

- When the Cubs lost the Series, four games to three, it marked the eighth time they had lost in their last 10 World Series appearances —

and seventh in a row. The two times they won the World Series —
in 1907 and 1908, they beat the Tigers.

- The Tigers had won only one other World Series, in 1935 — when
  they beat the Cubs.
- Detroit was shut out in the first and third games and for the first
  four innings of the fourth game. In the second game, they scored
  all four of their runs in one inning and did the same thing in the
  fourth game. So they were blanked in 33 of the first 35 innings of
  the Series — all but two innings of the first four games — and still
  won two of those games and went on to win the Series.
- Claude Passeau's one-hitter in Game 3 was, at that time, the greatest World Series pitching feat of all time.
- Passeau was winning Game 6, 5–1, in the seventh inning, when a
  line drive bent back the index finger on his pitching hand. He was
  forced to leave the game, and the Cubs used three other starters in
  relief roles to salvage a 12-inning win to force a seventh game.
- Detroit would have won the sixth game in nine innings if Charlie
  Hostetler hadn't tripped and fallen coming from third to home,
  prompting him to be tagged out easily in the seventh inning.
- The winning run in Game 6 scored when a base hit by the Cubs' Stan
  Hack hit a sprinkler head imbedded in the ground in left field, caus-
  ing the ball to bounce up and over left fielder Hank Greenberg's head.
- Chicago pitcher Hank Borowy had four decisions in the Series —
  two wins and two losses.
- Bill Sianis, a Chicago tavern owner, tried to bring his pet goat into
  one of the Series games at Wrigley Field and was turned away. Leg-
  end has it that Sianis put a curse on Wrigley Field that has kept the
  Cubs out of the World Series ever since.

Game 1: Oct. 3, 1945, at Detroit

Cubs first baseman and National League Most Valuable Player Phil
Cavarretta homered and the Cubs rocked Detroit ace Hal Newhouser for
seven runs and eight hits in the first three innings. Hank Borowy worked
out of some jams to preserve his shutout, and the Cubs won easily, 9–0.

Chicago	AB	R	H	Detroit	AB	R	H
Hack, 3b	5	0	1	Webb, ss	4	0	1
Johnson, 2b	5	2	2	McHale (d)	1	0	0
Lowrey, lf	4	0	0	Mayo, 2b	4	0	2

Chicago	AB	R	H		Detroit	AB	R	H
Cavarretta, 1b	4	3	3		Cramer, cf	3	0	0
Pafko, cf	4	3	3		Greenberg, lf	2	0	1
Nicholson, rf	4	1	2		Cullenbine, rf	3	0	0
Livingston, c	4	0	2		York, 1b	3	0	1
Hughes, ss	3	0	0		Outlaw, 3b	4	0	1
Borowy, p	3	0	0		Richards, c	2	0	0
Totals	36	9	13		Hostetler (b)	1	0	0
					Newhouser, p	1	0	0
					Benton, p	0	0	0
					Eaton (a)	1	0	0
					Tobin, p	1	0	0
					Mueller, p	0	0	0
					Borom (c)	1	0	0
					Totals	31	0	6

Chicago   4 0 3   0 0 0   2 0 0   -   9   13   0
Detroit   0 0 0   0 0 0   0 0 0   -   0   6   0

(a) struck out for Benton in fourth; (b) grounded out for Richards in ninth; (c) grounded out for Mueller in ninth; (d) flied out for Webb in ninth
Doubles — Johnson, Pafko. Triple — Nicholson. Home run — Cavarretta. Sacrifices — Lowrey, Borowy. Runs batted in — Nicholson 3, Livingston, Pafko, Cavarretta 2. Stolen bases — Johnson, Pafko. Double plays — Hughes, Johnson and Cavarretta; Johnson, Hughes and Cavarretta

	IP	H	R	BB	SO
Borowy	9	6	0	5	4 (winner, 1-0)
Newhouser	2.2	8	7	1	3 (loser, 0-1)
Tobin	3	4	2	1	1
Mueller	2	0	0	1	1
Benton	1.1	1	0	0	1

Hit by pitcher — By Borowy, 1 (Greenberg). Passed balls — Richards, 2. Left on base — Detroit, 10; Chicago, 5. Umpires — Bill Summers (AL), Lou Jorda (NL), Art Passerella (AL), Jocko Conlan (NL). Time — 2:10. Attendance — 54,637

Game 2: Oct. 4, 1945, at Detroit

Hank Greenberg, who started the season in the military, returned home in time to hit a grand slam home run against the St. Louis Browns on the last day of the season to clinch the pennant for the Tigers. In this game, he hit a three-run homer off of Chicago's 22-game winner Hank Wyse as Detroit ace Virgil Trucks, another returning war veteran, got the win, 4–1.

Chicago	AB	R	H	Detroit	AB	R	H
Hack, 3b	3	0	3	Webb, ss	4	1	2
Johnson, 2b	3	0	0	Mayo, 2b	3	1	0
Lowrey, lf	4	0	2	Cramer, cf	4	1	3
Cavarretta, 1b	4	1	1	Greenberg, lf	3	1	1
Pafko, cf	4	0	0	Cullenbine, rf	2	0	0
Nicholson, rf	3	0	1	York, 1b	4	0	0
Gillespie, c	4	0	0	Outlaw, 3b	4	0	1
Hughes, ss	3	0	0	Richards, c	4	0	0
Wyse, p	3	0	0	Trucks, p	3	0	0
Secory (a)	1	0	0	**Totals**	**31**	**4**	**7**
Erickson, p	0	0	0				
Becker (b)	1	0	0				
Totals	**32**	**1**	**7**				

```
Chicago    000 100 000 - 1 7 0
Detroit    000 040 000 - 4 7 0
```

(a) flied out for Wyse in seventh; (b) struck out for Erickson in ninth Doubles — Cavarretta, Hack. Home run — Greenberg. Sacrifice — Johnson. Runs batted in — Nicholson, Cramer, Greenberg 3.

	IP	H	R	BB	SO
Wyse	6	5	4	3	1 (loser, 0-1)
Erickson	2	2	0	1	1
Trucks	9	7	1	3	4 (winner, 1-0)

Left on base — Chicago 8, Detroit 7. Time —1:48. Attendance — 53,636.

Game 3: Oct. 4, 1945, at Detroit

Chicago's Claude Passeau threw a one-hitter, giving up only a single by Rudy York in the third inning as the Cubs won, 3–0. It was the greatest pitching performance in World Series history at that time. The only other Tiger baserunner was Bob Swift who reached on a walk but was thrown out trying to steal.

Chicago	AB	R	H	Detroit	AB	R	H
Hack, 3b	5	0	2	Webb, ss	3	0	0
Johnson, 2b	5	0	0	McHale (d)	1	0	0
Lowrey, lf	4	1	2	Mayo, 2b	3	0	0
Cavarretta, 1b	2	0	1	Cramer, cf	3	0	0
Pafko, cf	2	1	0	Greenberg, lf	3	0	0
Nicholson, rf	4	0	1	Cullenbine, rf	3	0	0
Livingston, c	4	1	1	York, 1b	3	0	1
Hughes, ss	3	0	1	Outlaw, 3b	3	0	0
Passeau, p	4	0	0	Swift, c	1	0	0
Totals	33	3	8	Borom (a)	1	0	0
				Richards, c	1	0	0
				Overmire, p	1	0	0
				Walker (b)	1	0	0
				Benton, p	0	0	0
				Hostetler (c)	1	0	0
				Totals	28	1	0

```
Chicago    0 0 0  2 0 0  1 0 0 - 3 8 0
Detroit    0 0 0  0 0 0  0 0 0 - 0 1 0
```

(a) ran for Swift in sixth; (b) grounded into double play for Overmire in sixth; (c) grounded out for Benton in ninth; (d) fouled out for Webb in ninth Errors — Webb, Mayo. Doubles — Lowrey, Livingston, Hack. Sacrifices — Cavarretta, Hughes, Pafko. Runs batted in — Nicholson, Hughes, Passeau. Double play — Johnson and Cavarretta.

	IP	H	R	BB	SO
Passeau	9	1	0	1	1 (winner, 1-0)
Overmire	6	4	2	2	2 (loser, 0-1)
Benton	3	4	1	0	3

Left on base — Chicago 8, Detroit 1. Time: 1:55. Attendance — 55,500

Game 4: Oct. 6, 1945, at Chicago

Following Claude Passeau's one-hitter, Chicago's Ray Prim retired the first 10 Detroit batters, but got knocked out in the Tigers' four-run fifth inning. It was the only inning in which the Tigers scored but it was good enough as Dizzy Trout held off the Cubs in a 4–1 Detroit victory.

Detroit	AB	R	H	Chicago	AB	R	H
Webb, ss	5	0	0	Hack, 3b	4	0	0
Mayo, 2b	3	1	0	Johnson, 2b	4	1	2
Cramer, cf	4	1	2	Lowrey, lf	4	0	1
Greenberg, lf	3	1	1	Cavarretta, 1b	4	0	0
Cullenbine, rf	3	1	1	Pafko, cf	4	0	0
York, 1b	3	0	0	Nicholson, rf	4	0	0
Outlaw, 3b	4	0	1	Livingston, c	3	0	1
Richards, c	4	0	1	Hughes, ss	1	0	0
Trout, p	4	0	1	Becker (b)	1	0	1
Totals	33	4	7	Merullo (c), ss	0	0	0
				Prim, p	0	0	0
				Derringer, p	0	0	0
				Secory (a)	1	0	0
				Vandenberg, p	0	0	0
				Gillespie (d)	1	0	0
				Erickson, p	0	0	0
				Totals	31	1	5

Detroit   000 040 100 – 4 7 0
Chicago   000 000 000 – 1 5 0

(a) struck out for Derringer in fifth; (b) singled for Hughes in seventh; (c) ran for Becker in seventh; (d) grounded out for Vandenberg in seventh Errors — York, Nicholson. Double — Cullenbine. Triple — Johnson. Sacrifice — Prim. Runs batted in — Greenberg, Cullenbine, Outlaw, Richards.

	IP	H	R	BB	SO
Trout	9	4	1	1	6 (winner, 1-0)
Prim	3.1	3	4	1	1 (loser, 0-1)
Derringer	1.2	2	0	2	1
Vandenberg	2	0	0	0	0
Erickson	2	2	0	1	2

Passed ball — Livingston. Left on base — Detroit 6, Chicago 5. Time — 2:00. Attendance — 42,923

Game 5: Oct. 7, 1945, at Chicago

The pitching matchup was the same as in Game 1 — Borowy versus Newhouser — only this time Newhouser prevailed for an 8–4 victory. Greenberg sparked the Tigers with three doubles as Detroit won its second straight game in Chicago to take a 3-2 series lead.

Detroit	AB	R	H		Chicago	AB	R	H
Webb, ss	4	1	1		Hack, 3b	3	0	1
Mayo, 2b	4	0	2		Johnson, 2b	3	0	0
Cramer, cf	4	2	1		Lowrey, lf	4	1	1
Greenberg, lf	5	3	3		Cavarretta, 1b	3	1	1
Cullenbine, rf	4	1	2		Pafko, cf	4	1	0
York, 1b	5	1	1		Nicholson, rf	4	0	1
Outlaw, 3b	4	0	0		Livingston, c	4	0	1
Richards, c	4	0	1		Merullo, ss	2	0	0
Newhouser, p	3	0	0		Williams (b)	1	0	0
Totals	**37**	**8**	**11**		Schuster, ss	1	0	0
					Borowy, p	1	1	1
					Sauer (a)	1	0	0
					Vandenberg, p	0	0	0
					Chipman, p	0	0	0
					Derringer, p	0	0	0
					Secory (c)	1	0	1
					Erickson, p	0	0	0
					Totals	**32**	**4**	**7**

```
Detroit    0 0 1  0 0 4  1 0 2 - 8  11  0
Chicago    0 0 1  0 0 0  2 0 1 - 4   7  2
```

(a) struck out for Chipman in sixth; (b) struck out for Merullo in seventh;
(c) singled for Derringer in eighth

Errors — Hack, Pafko. Doubles — Borowy, Greenberg 3, Cullenbine, Livingston, Cavarretta. Sacrifices — Outlaw, Cullenbine, Johnson. Runs batted in — Cramer, Hack, Greenberg, York, Newhouser, Webb, Outlaw, Nicholson 2, Livingston, Cullenbine 2. Double plays — Mayo, York, Webb and Mayo; Johnson, Merullo and Cavarretta.

	IP	H	R	BB	SO
Newhouser	9	7	4	2	9 (winner, 1-1)
Borowy	5	8	5	1	4 (loser, 1-1)
Vandenberg	0.2	0	0	2	0
Chipman	0.1	0	0	1	0
Derringer	2	1	1	0	0
Erickson	1	2	2	0	0

Hit by pitch — By Erickson (Cramer); Left on base — Detroit 9, Chicago 4. Time — 2:18. Attendance — 43,463

Game 6: Oct. 8, 1945, at Chicago

Claude Passeau sailed into the seventh inning with a 5–1 lead, gunning for his second World Series victory, but had to leave the game when a line drive off the bat of Jimmy Outlaw struck him in his pitching hand. The Tigers rallied to tie the game on Hank Greenberg's homer in the eighth inning. In the ninth inning, Hank Borowy came on in relief — the fourth Cubs starter to appear in the game. Borowy tossed four shutout innings and Stan Hack doubled home the winning run for the Cubs — a ball that appeared to be a routine single to left when it hit a sprinkler head embedded in the outfield grass and bounded over Greenberg's head. The Cubs won this wild one, 8–7, to force a seventh and deciding game.

Chicago	AB	R	H	Detroit	AB	R	H
Hack, 3b	5	1	4	Webb, ss	3	0	0
Johnson, 2b	4	0	0	Mayo, 2b	6	0	1
Lowrey, lf	5	1	1	Cramer, cf	6	1	2
Cavarretta, 1b	5	1	2	Greenberg, lf	5	2	1
Pafko, cf	6	0	2	Cullenbine, rf	5	1	2
Nicholson, rf	5	0	0	York, 1b	6	0	2
Livingston, c	3	2	2	Outlaw, 3b	5	0	1
Gillespie (e)	1	0	0	Richards, c	0	0	0
Hughes, ss	4	1	3	Maier (a)	1	0	1
Becker (f)	0	0	0	Swift, c	2	1	1
Secory (h)	1	0	1	Trucks, p	1	0	0
Block (g)	0	0	0	Caster, p	1	0	0
Merullo ss	0	0	0	McHale (b)	1	0	0
Schuster (i)	0	1	0	Bridges, p	0	0	0
Passeau, p	3	1	0	Benton, p	0	0	0
Wyse, p	1	0	0	Walker (d)	1	1	1
Prim, p	0	0	0	Trout, p	2	0	0
Borowy, p	2	0	0	Hostetler (c)	1	0	0
				Hoover, ss	3	1	1
Totals	46	8	15	Totals	48	7	13

Chicago   0 0 0 0 4 1 2 0 0 0 0 1 - 8 15 3
Detroit   0 1 0 0 0 0 2 4 0 0 0 0 - 7 13 1

(a) singled for Richards in sixth; (b) struck out for Caster in sixth; (c) reached on error for Webb in seventh; (d) doubled for Benton in eighth; (e) grounded out for Livingston in ninth; (f) walked for Hughes in ninth; (g) hit into force play for Becker in ninth; (h) singled for Merullo in 12th; (i) pinch ran for Secory in 12th

Errors — Richards, Hack 2, Johnson 1. Doubles — York, Livingston, Hughes, Walker, Pafko, Hack. Home run — Greenberg. Sacrifices — Johnson 2. Runs batted in — Richards, Hack 3, Cavarretta 2, Hughes 2, York, Livingston, Cullenbine, Hoover, Greenberg, Mayo, Cramer. Stolen base — Cullenbine. Double plays — Mayo, Webb, Richards and Webb; Merullo, Johnson and Cavarretta; Mayo, Hoover and York.

	IP	H	R	BB	SO
Passeau	6.2	5	3	6	2
Wyse	.2	3	3	1	0
Prim	.2	1	1	0	0
Borowy	4	4	0	0	0 (winner, 2-1)
Trucks	4.1	7	4	2	3
Caster	.2	0	0	0	1
Bridges	1.2	3	3	3	1
Benton	.1	1	0	0	1
Trout	4.2	4	1	2	3 (loser, 1-1)

Left on base — Detroit 12, Chicago 12. Time — 3:28. Attendance — 41,708

```
Detroit    0 1 0  0 0 0  2 4 0  0 0 0  -  7  13  1
Chicago    0 0 0  0 4 1  2 0 0  0 0 1  -  8  15  3
```

Game 7: Oct. 10, 1945, at Chicago

Cubs manager Charlie Grimm used four starting pitchers to salvage Game 6. In Game 7, he gambled and went with his veteran, Hank Borowy, though Borowy had gone five innings in a start in Game 5 and four innings in relief in Game 6.

With one day's rest, Borowy took the mound but didn't last long. He gave up three straight singles in the first inning and was knocked out. The Tigers went on to score five in the first and coasted to a 9–3 win in the third matchup of Borowy and Hal Newhouser.

Detroit	AB	R	H	*Chicago*	AB	R	H
Webb, ss	4	2	1	Hack, 3b	5	0	0
Mayo, 2b	5	2	2	Johnson, 2b	5	1	1
Cramer, cf	5	2	3	Lowrey, lf	4	1	2
Greenberg, lf	2	0	0	Cavarretta, 1b	4	1	3
Cullenbine, rf	2	2	0	Pafko, cf	4	0	1
York, 1b	4	0	0	Nicholson, rf	4	0	1

Detroit	AB	R	H
Outlaw, 3b	4	1	1
Richards, c	4	0	2
Swift, c	1	0	0
Newhouser, p	4	0	0
Mierkowicz	0	0	0
Totals	**35**	**9**	**9**

Chicago	AB	R	H
Livingston, c	4	0	1
Hughes, ss	3	0	1
Borowy, p	0	0	0
Derringer, p	0	0	0
Vandenberg, p	1	0	0
Sauer (a)	1	0	0
Erickson, p	0	0	0
Secory (b)	1	0	0
Passeau, p	0	0	0
Wyse, p	0	0	0
McCullough (c)	1	0	0
Totals	**37**	**3**	**10**

Detroit　　5 1 0 0 0 0 1 2 0 - 9　9 1

Chicago　　1 0 0 1 0 0 0 1 0 - 3 10 0

(a) struck out for Vandenberg in fifth; (b) struck out for Erickson in seventh; (c) struck out for Wyse in ninth

Error — Newhouser. Doubles — Richards 2, Mayo, Nicholson, Johnson. Triple — Pafko. Sacrifice — Greenberg. Runs batted in — Cramer, Outlaw, Richards 4, Cavarretta, York, Pafko, Mayo, Greenberg, Nicholson. Stolen bases — Outlaw, Cramer. Double play — Webb, Mayo and York.

	IP	H	R	BB	SO
Newhouser	9	10	3	1	10 (winner, 2-1)
Borowy	0	3	3	0	0 (loser, 2-2)
Derringer	1.2	2	3	5	0
Vandenberg	3.1	1	0	1	3
Erickson	2	2	1	1	2
Passeau	1	1	2	1	0
Wyse	1	0	0	0	0

Wild pitch — Newhouser. Left on base — Detroit 8, Chicago 8. Time — 2:32. Attendance — 41,500

Bibliography

Chicago Tribune, Aug. 3, 1971.

Dark, Alvin, and John Underwood. *When in Doubt, Fire the Manager: My Life and Times in Baseball*. New York: E. P. Dutton, 1980.

Devaney, John, and Dave Goldblatt. *The World Series: A Complete Pictorial History*. Chicago: Rand McNally, 1981.

Dittmar, Joseph J. *Baseball's Benchmark Boxscores*. Jefferson, N.C.: McFarland, 1990.

Frisch, Frank, and J. Roy Stockton. *Frank Frisch: The Fordham Flash*. New York: Doubleday, 1962.

Fulk, David, and Dan Riley. *The Cubs Reader*. Boston: Houghton Mifflin, 1991.

Gallagher, Mark. *Day by Day in New York Yankees History*. New York: Leisure Press, 1983.

Gettelson, Leonard. *Official World Series Records*. St. Louis: The Sporting News, 1976.

Gifford, Barry. *The Neighborhood of Baseball: A Personal History of the Chicago Cubs*. New York: E. P. Dutton, 1981.

Leptich, John, and Dave Barenowski. *This Date in St. Louis Cardinal History*. New York: Stein & Day, 1983.

Marazzi, Rich, and Len Fiorito. *Aaron to Zuverink*. New York: Stein & Day, 1982.

Okrent, Daniel, and Harris, Lewine. *The Ultimate Baseball Book*. Boston: Houghton Mifflin, 1988.

Peary, Danny. *We Played the Game*. New York: Hyperion, 1994.

Reichler, Joseph. *The Baseball Encyclopedia*. New York: Macmillan, 1995.

Smith, Ron. *The Sporting News Chronicle of Baseball*. New York: BDD Illustrated Books, 1993.

Talley, Rick. *The Cubs of '69: Recollections of the Team That Should Have Been*. Chicago: Contemporary Books, 1989.

Thorn, John, and Pete Palmer. *Total Baseball*. New York: Warner Books, 1989.

Warfield, Don. *The Roaring Redhead, Larry MacPhail: Baseball's Greatest Innovator*. South Bend, Ind.: Diamond Communications, 1987.

Index